3ds Max Basics

for Modeling Video Game Assets

Volume One

Model a Complete Game Environment and
Export to Unity or Other Game Engines

3ds Max Basics
for Modeling Video Game Assets

Volume One

Model a Complete Game Environment and
Export to Unity or Other Game Engines

Bill Culbertson

CRC Press
Taylor & Francis Group
Boca Raton London New York

CRC Press is an imprint of the
Taylor & Francis Group, an **informa** business

CRC Press
Taylor & Francis Group
6000 Broken Sound Parkway NW, Suite 300
Boca Raton, FL 33487-2742

© 2019 by William Culbertson
CRC Press is an imprint of Taylor & Francis Group, an Informa business

No claim to original U.S. Government works

Printed on acid-free paper

International Standard Book Number-13: 978-1-138-34512-6 (Hardback)
International Standard Book Number-13: 978-1-138-34506-5 (Paperback)

Visit the Taylor & Francis Web site at
http://www.taylorandfrancis.com

and the CRC Press Web site at
http://www.crcpress.com

KV 04.17.2019 1302

Contents

Contents

Acknowledgments

During my career, I have had the privilege of working with extremely talented and creative people. Thanks to Jim Paulsen, my friend and mentor from my undergraduate days at Towson University, for his teaching of the concepts of sculpting form, starting my long path of adventure. Thanks to my instructors at Rhode Island School of Design for the integration of design into the mix. Thanks to Hasbro for the opportunity to put all that learning together to learn the industrial side of the field. Thanks to the art directors at Disney, Sesame Street, Henson and others for all the high-level design concepts they taught me over the years through critiques.

Thanks to those who helped me enter the digital 3D world back in the 1990s. Thanks to Autodesk for creating some amazing software. Thanks to New England Tech for the opportunity to teach and work with their students and the Video Game Department faculty.

Thanks to CRC Press/Taylor & Francis Group and Sean Connelly for this opportunity.

A special thanks to my amazing wife and family for putting up with and allowing me to go on a bizarre and wild career path, from sculpting toys to monumental public art, from designing theme park amusement rides to creating video games. Somehow it all fit together, a truly great adventure.

Author

Bill Culbertson, Creative Director/Owner Whooplah LLC, has traveled along several diverse paths that crisscrossed, overlapped and eventually merged together over his career: a fine artist, commercial artist, corporate director, freelancer, entertainment media producer and associate professor.

A graduate in fine art at Towson University in Maryland, Bill earned a Master of Arts in Art Education degree from The Rhode Island School of Design. Commercially, Bill began his career at Hasbro, Inc., as an Industrial Designer in the Research And Design department. Within a short time, he was the Director of the Sculpture Department, guiding the sculpting of the company's popular toy lines such as G.I. Joe and My Little Pony. Moving into the freelance community, Bill developed an international clientele including manufacturers, theme parks and cruise lines. Specializing in licensed characters, he worked extensively with the Walt Disney Company, Jim Henson Company, Sesame Street Workshop, Nickelodeon and others. As an inventor, Bill is responsible for a number of manufactured toy concepts. Additionally, Bill created and produced the award-winning puppet show "Li'l Rhody!" for Rhode Island PBS.

As a fine artist, Bill has been recognized nationally and internationally for his work through numerous large-scale public art works. He has been distinguished as a Copley Master by the Copley Society of Boston. As an Associate Professor at New England Institute of Technology, Bill is a member of the nationally ranked Video Game Development and Design Department. His main concentration is in 3D modeling, animation and game development.

As the founder of Whooplah LLC, Bill is committed to creating family-fun entertainment that helps parents meet and exceed their parenting goals. The company's first game released, "Pollywog Pond," is an early learner portal to reading, music, videos, games and more.

For more information, please visit: Whooplah.com and PollywogPond.com

Introduction

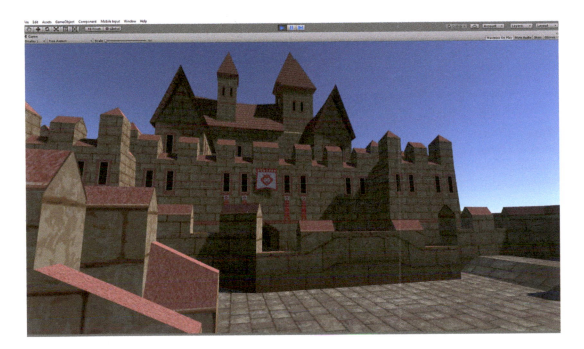

In this book, through a series of progressive chapter projects, you will be introduced to the basic workflow pipeline for modeling and be exposed to the basic tools in 3ds Max. Completing these projects in the order they are presented is recommended as the concepts and techniques are organized in a progressive order, building skills upon skills in a step-by-step lesson format. The projects will prepare you for developing, modeling, unwrapping and texturing objects for export to video game engines. During the process of creating these objects, you will repeatedly use tools and techniques to reinforce and gain mastery of them.

You will be modeling some basic environmental assets: creating modular pieces to create a complete game scene. The lessons will attempt to show you a variety of techniques and methods, so that you will be aware of different options available to you as you work. The purpose of this series of chapters is not to necessarily show you the most efficient way to model; rather, our goal is to introduce the various basic tools, so that they become part of your digital tool box. Knowing when and where to use the tools in creative ways will be key to your long-term success as a modeler.

The approach to learning 3D modeling can be done in a variety of ways. Modeling programs, like 3ds Max, are large programs with extensive features and capabilities. In all likelihood, you will only utilize a fraction of the tools and features. The principles and workflow of basic modeling are pretty much the same for most 3D modeling programs. Migrating from one program to another shouldn't be a big ordeal: the buttons, keys and interface may be different, but the workflows should be relatively the same. The step-by-step methodology used in this book is based on the experience of successfully teaching well over a thousand students the basics of 3D modeling.

While using 3ds Max, you will find that there are typically two or three different ways to perform the same or similar procedure all yielding the same result. Some procedures may be easier or more efficient to use than others. Personal preference can come into play. For example, some people prefer hotkeys, some people prefer floating menus, and some others like using the toolbar menus. 3ds Max is a flexible software in that almost everything in 3ds Max is customizable.

The main target audience for this book is the potential modeler for video game assets. With the current state of the hardware available, video game assets need to be on the low end of the polygon count spectrum to keep the game running with a minimum of lag. We will be striving to keep our model meshes low-poly: using as few polygons as necessary to create the assets. Although the projects here target a video game, the same principles of modeling will apply for other industries: simulation, film, animation, architecture and others.

Another goal of this book is to give the reader a taste of what it might be like to work in a game studio as a modeler. In the first chapter, you'll be introduced to the fictitious game studio we will be working at and the game project being undertaken. We will take on the responsibilities of creating the game assets for the environment from concept to exporting to a game engine, in this case, Unity 3D.

Please note, the companion files for this book, including the saved 3ds Max project iteration files from the chapters (noted after some image numbers (i.e. (Save 2-5)) and additional notes can be found at: www. whooplah.com/book/3dsMaxBasics

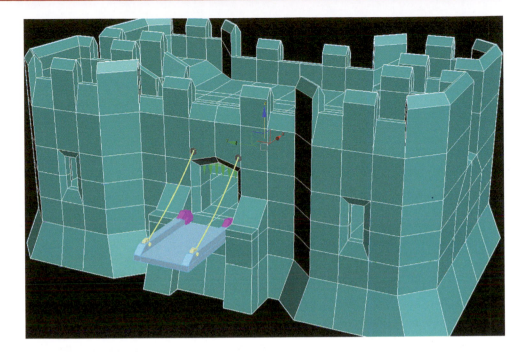

CHAPTER 1

Introduction to 3D Modeling

Topics in This Chapter

- UI Navigation
- Local Coordinate System
- World Coordinate System
- Geometric Primatives
- Standard Primitives
- Objects
  - Spline
  - Vertices
  - Segment
  - Polygon
  - Elements
- Object Properties
  - Vertex Sub-Object Level
  - Edge Sub-Object Level
  - Border Sub-Object Level
  - Element Sub-Object Level

- Command Panel
  - Create Panel
    - Geometry
    - Splines
  - Modify Tab
- Editable Poly
- Normals
  - Flipped Faces

UI Navigation

Navigating through a 3D modeling program's world might take a little adjusting to at first, but you should adapt quickly. After all, you live in a 3D world, and you've got lots of experience moving around in it. You are pretty good at it, and you can move through doorways, can handle and arrange objects, and can identify objects and shapes. You do this basically by orienting things relative to you. You are the center point for the orientation of things around you. As you move, your "center point" moves with you. You function in a local coordinate system. That's a complex and flexible navigation system that your brain handles. Let's shift to the digital world.

Instead of a movable center point, a digital 3D environment has a fixed center or origin point, located at 0, 0, 0 on an X, Y, Z coordinate system. Everything in the digital world exists relative to the origin point. Mathematically, the program keeps track of everything you create using the coordinates relative to 0, 0, 0. This is the world coordinate system, using 3D Cartesian coordinates. In the 3D world, you can switch to several different coordinate systems to facilitate your work flow. For instance, in 3ds Max, you can switch to the Local Coordinate System, changing the coordinate system center point to an object, away from the 0, 0, 0 origin point.

The first time you use a 3D modeling program, you discover the third dimension, the Z-axis. Within a short time, you realize that, as you work, you need to constantly change your viewpoint perspective to view an item from different angles to control modifications you are applying to it. For example, an object might look perfectly positioned in the X- and Z-axes, but it may be way off in the Y-axis.

To get started, there are some concepts you need to understand or be aware of about the 3D digital world. The following is a trimmed-down version of essential 3D modeling terms. Understanding these few terms and concepts will allow you to dive right into modeling.

3D Modeling Concepts

First, let's cover a few of the 3D modeling concepts, definitions and terms we will be using:

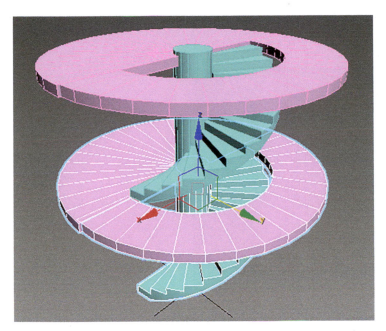

IMAGE 1.1

- Shape
- Vertex
- Segment
- Spline
- Plane
- Polygon
- Element
- Geometric Primitives
- Compound Objects
- Sub-object
- Normal
- Types of Basic Modeling
  - Box
  - Plane
  - Spline

Shape

A shape is a 2D or 3D object made from one or more curved or straight lines. Shapes in 3ds Max are typically made from splines but can also be made from nonuniform rational B-splines (NURBS) curves.

Vertex

A vertex is a single point in 3D space with its position typically defined by values for the X-, Y- and Z-axes. A vertex is the basic structure that forms geometric objects in 3ds Max (plural form: vertices). A vertex in the 3ds Max viewport will be represented by a cross on a spline or as a colored dot on a mesh or as a yellow or white box along a spline.

IMAGE 1.2

Vertices

Vertices are points in space, relative to the coordinates 0, 0, 0 in the X, Y and Z planes.

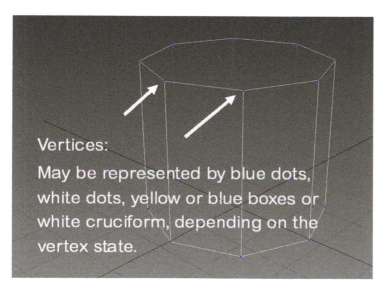

IMAGE 1.3

Splines

A spline is a type of curve created by the interpolation between two endpoints with two or more tangents that influence the direction of the curve. Basically, it is a line or curve between two endpoints.

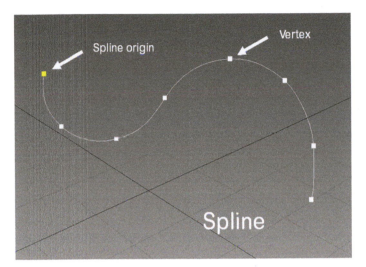

Segment or Edge

The line or part of a spline between two vertices is a segment.

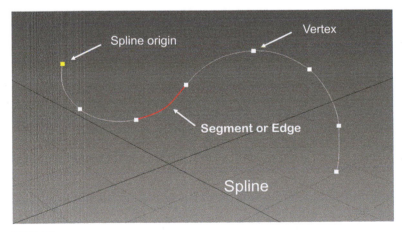

Polygon/Face

A polygon and a face are planar objects that fill in the space between the edges of a mesh. A face has three sides, while a polygon is made up of three or more sides. While modeling, polygons are treated as a single object. When rendered or in a 3D game engine, polygons are treated as two or more triangular faces, which in reality, they are.

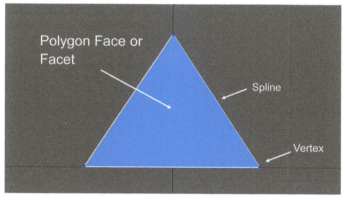

IMAGE 1.6

Element

When you group two or more meshes into a single object, the individual meshes are called elements. Modifying the object will affect all the elements; however, individual elements can be modified without affecting the other elements of the object.

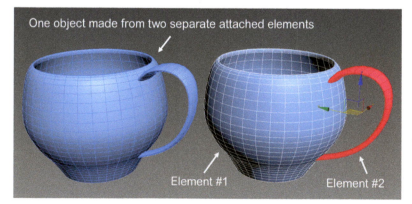

IMAGE 1.7

Object

An object is an item in the scene, such as a box or sphere. Objects can be primitive geometry or complex geometry. Geometric objects can be rendered as an image or animation. There are also non-renderable objects: lights, cameras, space warp icons, helpers and others. Every object has its own set of properties, found in the Object Properties window. The Object Properties window can be accessed by right-mouse clicking on an object and selecting "Object Properties" from the Quad Menu.

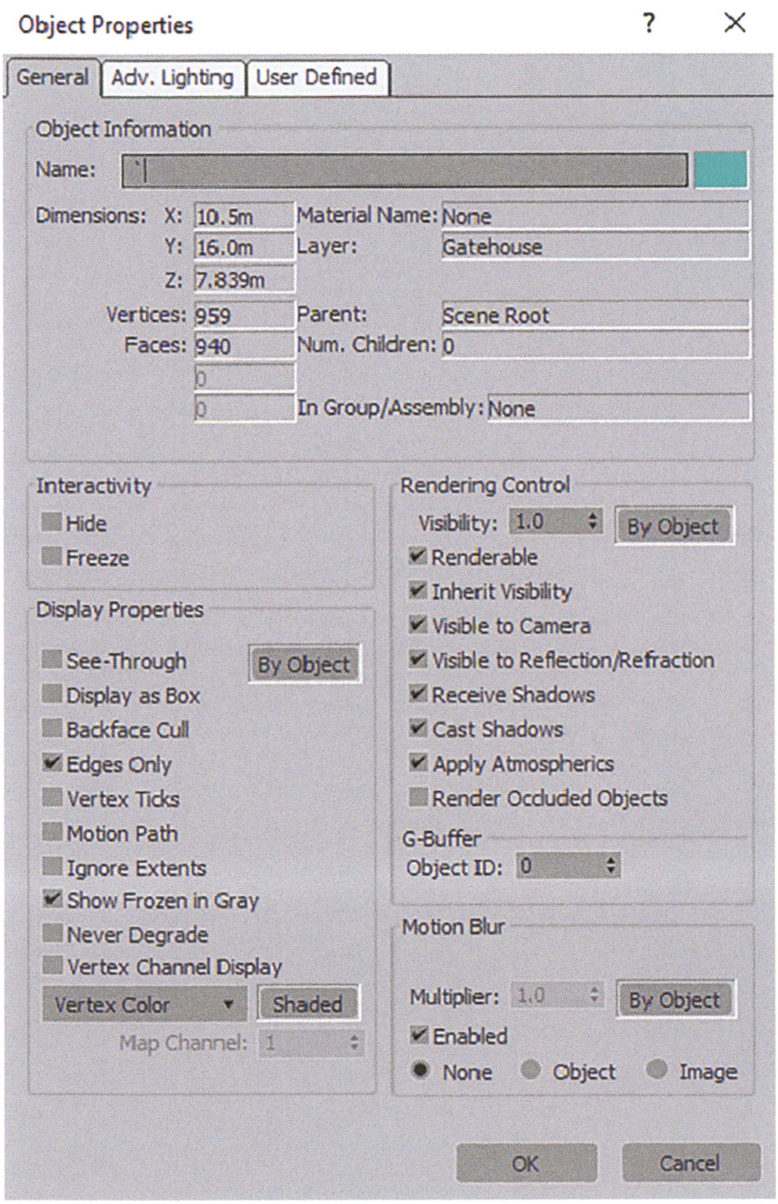

IMAGE 1.8

Geometric Primitives

Geometric primitives are basic parametric shapes that 3ds Max provides as pre-made objects (the parameters can be manipulated). Primitives are divided into two categories: Standard Primitives and Extended Primitives. You can combine both types of primitives to create more complex objects and further refine them with modifiers.

A parameter is a setting or value that you can change. Many objects in 3ds Max have parameters that you can change to alter the size or the shape of the object. This type of object can be described as "parametric."

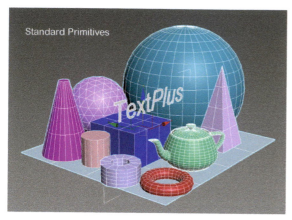

IMAGE 1.9

Sub-Object and Sub-Object Level

Some types of objects let you access a sub-object level to edit their component parts. A sub-object is an individual part or subset of an object's geometry, such as vertex, edge, polygon or element. To modify an object, typically you change its sub-object properties. By moving the vertices in the model shown here, we can change or modify its shape.

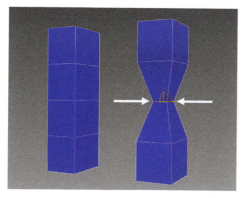

IMAGE 1.10

To access an object's sub-object properties, the object must first be converted to an editable object, usually an Editable Mesh or Editable Poly.

Individual sub-objects, such as vertices, edges and polygons, all have unique IDs that can be accessed in the Modify tab of the Command Panel when in sub-object level mode. While working in the sub-object state, you can only work with the selected object, and all other objects will be isolated.

In the Modify tab of the Command Panel, the sub-object parts of an object can be selected using the sub-object names or the icons (shown below). These sub-object parts are Vertex, Edge, Border, Face, Polygon and Element.

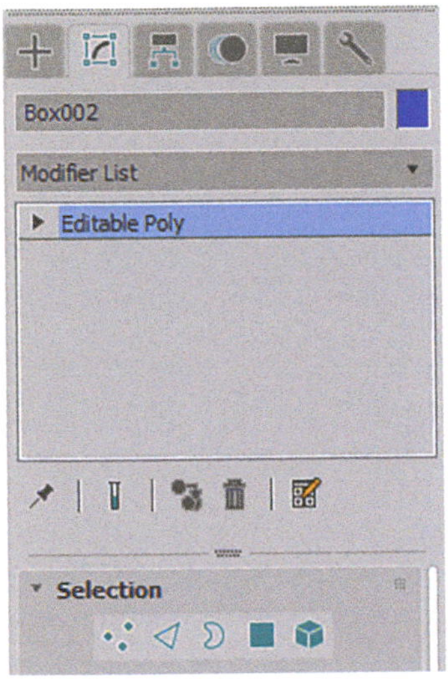

IMAGE 1.11

Sub-Object Level Modes

Vertex
This accesses the Vertex sub-object level, which lets you select individual or multiple vertices.

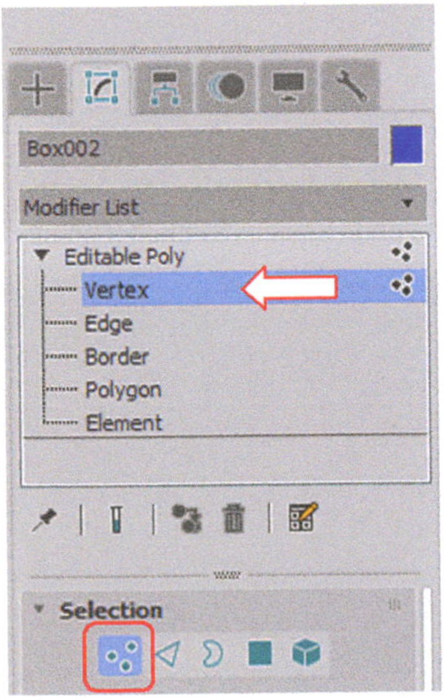

IMAGE 1.12

Edge

This accesses the Edge sub-object level, which lets you select a polygon edge. An edge is a straight or curved line that connects two vertices in a mesh object or spline. You can modify object shapes by transforming its edges.

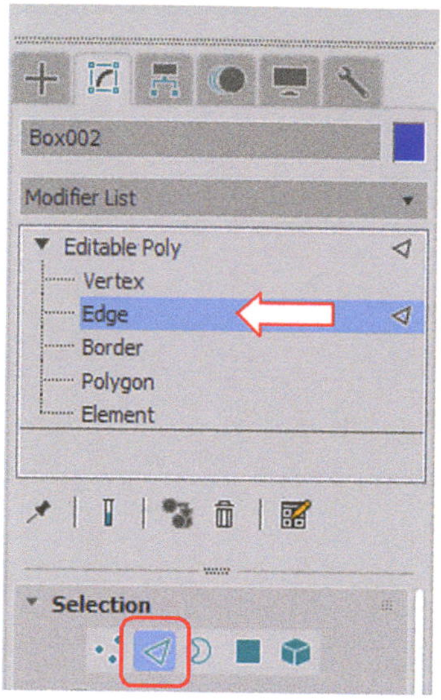

IMAGE 1.13

Border

This accesses the Border sub-object level, which lets you select a sequence of connected edges that border a hole in the mesh. A border comprises only connected edges with faces on only one side of them. A Border is always a complete loop. A Border can be capped to close an open space.

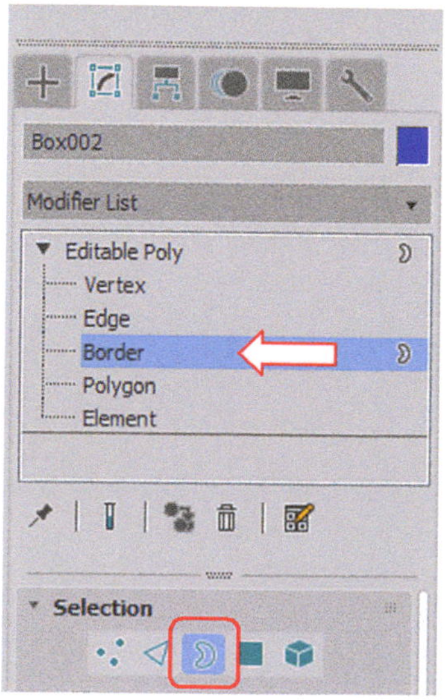

IMAGE 1.14

Polygon

This accesses the Polygon sub-object level, which lets you select individual or multiple polygons.

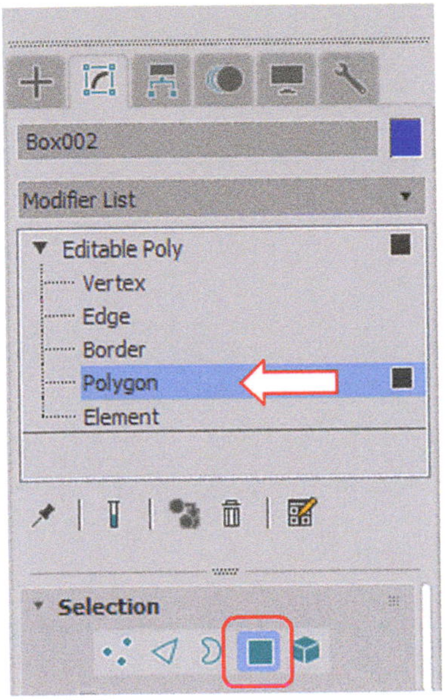

IMAGE 1.15

Element

This accesses the Element sub-object level, which lets you select an element's polygons that make up a mesh.

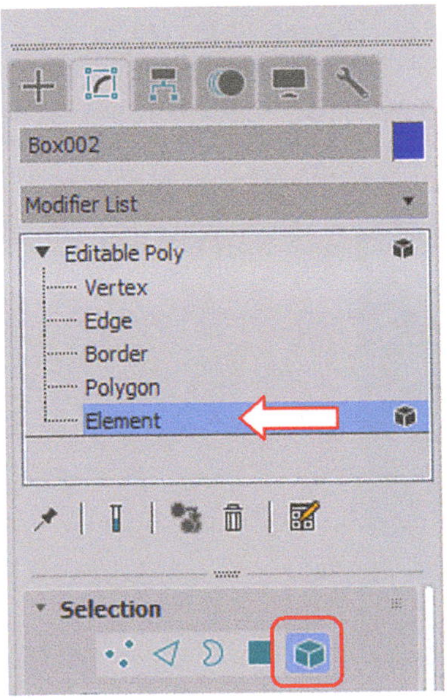

IMAGE 1.16

Normals

Vertices, faces and polygons have direction. A normal is a vector that defines which way a face or vertex is pointing. The direction of the normal projecting off the vertex, face or polygon indicates the front or outer surface.

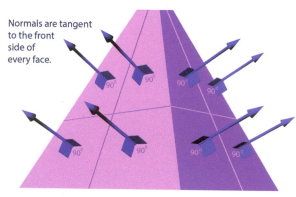

Normals are tangent to the front side of every face.

IMAGE 1.17

When you create an object, normals are generated automatically. Usually, objects render correctly utilizing the default normals. Sometimes, however, you need to adjust the normals. Normals allow an object to be "seen" when rendered.

Faces of an Object

"Normals" face outward and can be seen. A black face usually indicates you are looking at the back of a face. Back faces do not render.

Flipped faces, with their normals facing inward, will not appear when rendered! When flipped using the "Flip" button to turn the normal inward, a face will appear in the viewport, but it will not appear when rendered. In the image of a pyramid below, one face has been selected and "flipped." In the rendered image (an image outputted by the program as a .jpg, .png, .avi, etc.), the flipped image does not render. The polygons inside the pyramid are the backsides with normals facing outward, the insides do not render.

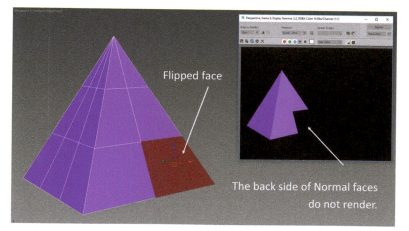

Flipped face

The back side of Normal faces do not render.

IMAGE 1.18

Inside faces will not render unless faces inside are flipped or when rendering with the "Force 2-sided" option selected in the Render Setup window before rendering.

Here's a clue to check if a face is flipped: Flipped faces usually appear a darker red than usual when selected or can be black in viewport depending on the lighting.

Different Types of Modeling in 3ds Max

Primitive
Box
Polygon
Spline
Patch (a patch is a type of deformable object)
NURBS (complex curves)
Loft (two-dimensional shapes extruded along a third axis)
Boolean (combines two objects)

In the upcoming projects that we will be modeling, we will utilize the first four types listed, sometimes combining two or more types to achieve the desired results.

CHAPTER 2

The Game Studio

Topics in This Chapter

- The Game Studio – Our Project
- The Workflow Pipeline
- Game Design Documents (GDDs)
- Art Design Documents (ADDs)
- Low Polygon Modeling
- Opening 3ds Max
- Changing the User Interface (UI)
- Saving Files – Auto Backup
- Units Setup

As a 3D modeler, your job functions might vary depending on the type of studio where you are employed. The larger the studio, the more specialized your position might be. In a small studio, you will likely need to be more of a generalist, having competency in many aspects of modeling, texturing, rigging and animating. As we progress through the projects in this book, we will proceed as though we are developers in a small video game studio. You and I are the primary modelers in the company. Many of the procedures and techniques we will use will make for good work habits often expected by studios. Keep in mind that in the studio, your files will be internally public, possibly being accessed by other designers and the programmers who will implement your models into the game. Complying with studio parameters is essential for keeping work flowing successfully through the pipeline.

To begin our imaginary modeling journey, our "Studio" has come up with a first-person shooter (FPS) game. The game designers and management have developed and refined a game design document (GDD) that will serve as the bible for the game. A living document, the GDD will be constantly updated with additions, subtractions and changes. It will be reviewed by potential investors, and most importantly, by everyone on the development team. The GDD contains descriptions of everything related to the game from gameplay to marketing. GDD content varies from company to company, but they all contain at a minimum the essentials for developing the game. GDDs are crucial for limiting "feature creep": adding nonessential game play, assets or features that will delay completing the game development. The GDD is management's tool for completing the game. As modelers, we are mainly interested in the parts that will pertain to our job functions. Sometimes the GDD is broken into sub-documents, like the art design document (ADD). That is the section we, as modelers, are after. It will have descriptions of all the game assets that are required for the game that we will be asked to develop. The descriptions of each object will include functionality requirements, style guidelines and other notes. There may be a range of visuals from rough visual reference, to help as a starting point for design development, to finished presentation art to guide the modeling development. We don't have room here to publish a full GDD or ADD, so I have created a brief, general synopsis below of the game project and assets that we can use as our guide.

Game Name: Castle Keep: Red vs. Blue

- **General Features:**   3D environment
               Multiplayer, FPS
               Medieval, Fantasy theme

- **Gameplay:**   "Capture the Flag"
               Two kingdoms, the Red and the Blue, battle
               for control of each other's castle

- **Game Engine/Editor:** Unity 3D

- **Player Characters:**   King, Queen, Knight, Footman, Dragon

- **Environment:**   Toon style, Hand-painted, Medieval fantasy

  - Main Environment Asset Modules (see requirement for each):
    – The Fixed Bridge
    – The Drawbridge
    – The Barbican

- – The Gate House
- – The Curtain Wall
- – The Turrets
- – The Keep
- – The Apartments

- • Minor Environment Assets (see requirement for each):
  - – Water Well
  - – Stables
  - – Catapult
  - – Battering Ram
  - – Ballista
  - – Bombard

From reading this summary of the ADD, we have learned we will be modeling a medieval castle environment in a hand-painted style. The various parts of the castle will be modular, allowing for variation in our castle construction allowing several different castles to be constructed using the same modules. Using modules, we can also limit the file size of our assets in the game, a good thing. It is more efficient game design to use modular construction to create our game environment and apply different textures to add variety. For example, we can create two different-looking "kingdoms" in our game by arranging the modules in different orientations and use two different color-based textures to differentiate them further. One kingdom will have blue color hues, and the other will have red color hues.

As we are in a small studio, we will be responsible for the full range of asset development. The typical workflow pipeline progression for modeling 3D assets in a studio would be as follows:

- • Preliminary research for reference, functionality and style.
- • Design development sketches.
- • Creating placeholder objects.
- • Modeling the final assets.
- • Unwrapping and texturing the assets.
- • Rigging the assets, if necessary.
- • Animation cycles, if necessary.
- • Exporting in a format suitable for the game engine.

Going hand in hand with the workflow pipeline is the project schedule. Every asset in the game would be listed in the project schedule and the above workflow items scheduled into the timeline. The schedule provides a tracking mechanism to insure the game's development moves toward completion.

Most companies rely on some type of project-tracking software such as Perforce, Git, and Azure. For our purposes, we can track our progress on a simple spread sheet. An example of a schedule for our project can be found in the Appendix.

Whooplah	Castle Project												
Castle Modules Project	Date Started	Target Completion	Date Completed	1-Jun	8-Jun	15-Jun	22-Jun	29-Jun	6-Jun	13-Jun	20-Jun	27-Jun	
Curtain Wall													
Research/Reference	1-Jun	2-Jun											
Design	2-Jun	4-Jun											
Model	4-Jun	6-Jun											
Unwrap	6-Jun	6-Jun											
Create Texture	5-Jun	6-Jun											
Apply texture	6-Jun	7-Jun											
Export FBX		15-Jun											
Fixed Bridge													
Research/Reference	1-Jun	2-Jun											
Design	2-Jun	4-Jun											
Model	7-Jul	9-Jun											
Unwrap	10-Jun	11-Jun											
Create Texture	11-Jun	11-Jun											
Apply texture	12-Jun	12-Jun											
Export FBX		15-Jun											
Gate House													
Research/Reference	1-Jun	2-Jun											
Design	2-Jun	4-Jun											
Model	14-Jun	16-Jun											
Unwrap	16-Jun	17-Jun											
Create Texture	Week 6, Class 1	Week 8, Class 1											
Apply texture	Week 6, Class 1	Week 8, Class 1											
Export FBX	Week 9, Class 1	Week10, Class 2											

IMAGE 2.1

The authors of our GDD apparently have done some research into castle design, identifying the modules needed for the game. Our first task, number one on the workflow list, would be to do research into the design of each of the medieval castle elements to design our modules. This research would explore the module's function and how its parameters will influence the design. We would do research seeking visual examples from the real world. After doing some initial investigation into castle construction, I've come up with the following diagram that points out the parts of the castle we will be including in our design.

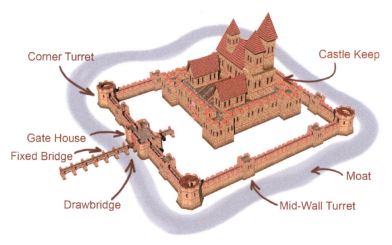

IMAGE 2.2

Using the reference materials from the first step of our workflow, I have completed the second step, the design of the individual modules. Using notes from the GDD about each module and their requirements, I have designed the modules to work with each other in different orientations. Rather than present the designs all together here, I will present the reference materials, parameters and the design of each module as we model them, chapter-by-chapter.

Getting Started with 3ds Max

Open 3ds Max on your computer. If you don't have access to the program, a free 30-day trial subscription is available from Autodesk.com. You should be able to work through the tutorial chapters in this book within the trial period, which will give you a pretty good sense of whether or not you wish to continue. If you are in an academic setting, student or faculty, Autodesk has a program that allows you to use the software for educational purposes for 3 years for free. The details can be found at www. students.autodesk.com.

At the time of this writing, the current version is 3ds Max 2019. As 3ds Max opens, the Welcome Window will appear on the screen. If the Template Window appears, select the "Original Start Up (default)" template. The Welcome Window has slides with some brief introductory highlights related to working in 3ds Max. Please take some time to explore these features, including the last slide, "Next Steps," with links to some startup movies and features. They will help to familiarize you with the user interface (UI) and use of the mouse input device.

Before we start modeling our first project, there are a few set-up items we should take care of. When you're ready, close the Welcome Window. On your computer screen is the default 3ds Max UI, as seen here:

IMAGE 2.3

As with many programs, 3ds Max followed the trend to use a dark, default UI. Many prefer this setting… I guess to some it looks more sophisticated or they feel it is easier on the eyes. Whatever the reason, it is not a great setting when you are trying to learn or teach someone how to use this program. For our purposes, the dark UI creates a problem in that when most buttons are selected, they change from their current dark state to an even darker state. That makes it hard to quickly visually identify what has been selected for the new user and very difficult for instructors to locate an issue while looking over the student's shoulder. For now, while we are learning the program basics, let's change the UI to the lighter environment UI. You can change it back to the dark UI later if you like.

On the top Tool Bar, left-click on the "Customize" tab to open the drop-down menu. Select "Custom UI and Default Switcher…" from the list.

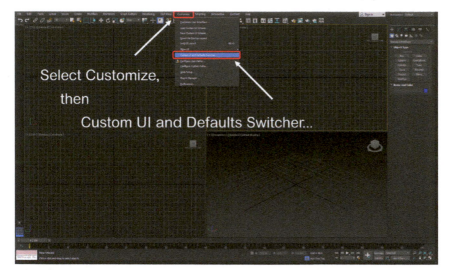

IMAGE 2.4

In the pop-up window that appears, select "ame-light" in the UI schemes list, and then left-mouse click on the "Set" button to initiate the change.

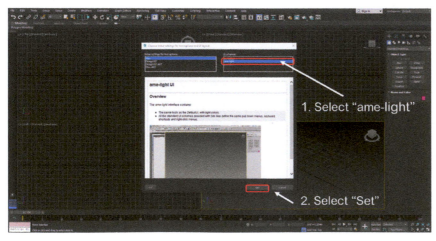

IMAGE 2.5

The screen will change to a lighter UI which is lighter and easier to see. Close the remaining small pop-up windows by selecting "OK."

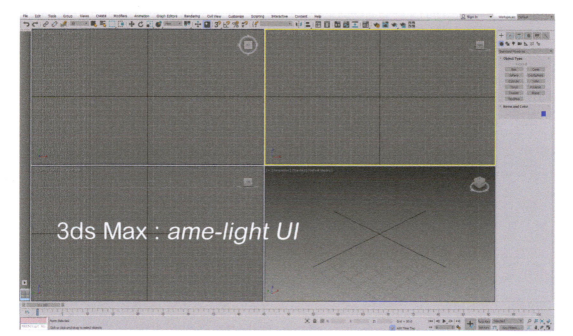

IMAGE 2.6

Autodesk is continually adding new features to upgrade the 3ds Max program. With each upgrade, there are often new features, variations on work flows, new renderers and more. Sometimes the UI gets revamped, and sometimes icon designs are changed. If you are using a different version than 3ds Max 2019, some button icons may be different or located in a different place. If it is one of the basic essential tools, such as the ones we will be using, it will be there somewhere… seek and you will find it. We could utilize several paths available for navigating tool selection: Toolbar, Quad Menu, Ribbon or Hot Key. In this book, for the most part, we will use the Toolbar and Command Panel for our navigation, tool selection and modifications. As you get more comfortable with the program, you can start using the many shortcut keys to speed up your workflow.

Now that 3ds Max is open, first thing we need to do is to save our project. In a video game studio, following the studio's file and object naming conventions is critically important. As stated before, in all likelihood, you will not be the only person working on this file for the project. Developers, programmers and others will be accessing the file for reviews, programming, texturing and other procedures. If an object is named incorrectly, not using the naming conventions established by the company, bad things can happen. Files may go missing or be inaccessible or corrupted, and when implemented in the game, the game engine might not recognize the object. As a result, the game might crash, which is not a good scenario for the studio or for you. Therefore, it is very important to name files and objects correctly. For our projects in this book, we will use a naming convention format for all our models of "last name_object name_01," using all lowercase letters. The "01" indicates it is the first iteration. It might seem silly to comply here, but you might as well get used to what working in a studio will require of you. Naming conventions are number one on the priority list. Every studio I have visited has a horror story about someone not following the basic conventions… it costs time and money.

Save and Save As

From the "File" tab on the Top Tool Bar, select "Save As" to open the dialog box, as with most Windows programs. Create a parent folder where you like on your computer, naming it "3ds Max Basics for Video Games," so that you will know where to find it. At the start of each new chapter where we will be creating a module for the project, create a new folder within the parent folder for that module's files. For our first model, inside that folder create a new folder, naming it "Curtain Wall Module." The name for the first model file we will be creating in the next chapter, the Curtain Wall, will be "last name_curtainwall_01," using your last name where noted. So, my file will be called "culbertson_curtainwall_01."

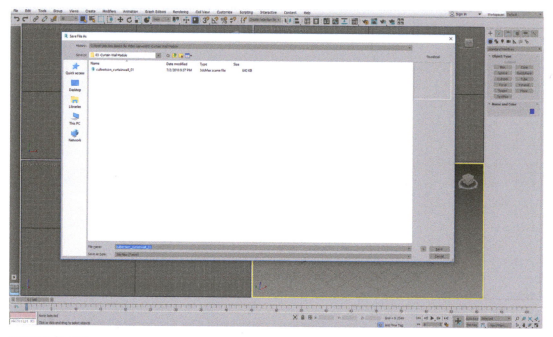

IMAGE 2.7 (Save 2-1)

Note: Above next to the Image 2.8 number, is a green (Save 2-1) notation. The "Save" notations refer to a 3ds Max file that was saved at the time the image screenshot was made. You can use this file as reference to help clarify the process steps that are made. The 3ds Max files can be found on the companion web site as noted in the Appendix.

The "3ds Max Save File As" dialog box has a unique feature. In the lower right corner, just to the left of the "Save" button, is a small button with a plus (+) icon. Game development is an iterative process, meaning, you work on a project, save it, analyze the result and make changes to the next version based on the analysis. Modeling objects works the same way. When you save a scene (the objects), using the "Save" operation, 3ds Max overwrites the existing file with a newer version. However, if you choose to do a "Save As" instead, the Save File As dialog box will open and allow you to click on the plus (+) icon button. When selected, the program will automatically save a new version of the file, adding a sequential number at the end of the file name; in this case, it would change the "01" at the end of the file name to "02." There would be two versions of the file, iterations, with each successive one more developed than the one preceding it. If the file you are working on becomes corrupt and unusable, you can go to the previous save as a backup. If you need to retract to go in a different direction, you'll have a backup to go to. It is important to use the Save As button often.

Auto Backup

There is an autobackup system in 3ds Max as a failsafe for crashes or file corruption. The Autobak files are located in the "My Documents" folder of the "Library" directory. Look for the 3ds Max folder. Inside that folder is a folder called "Autobak." By default, the Autobak saves three versions of the open program in the background, using one of the saves every 5 minutes in sequential order. Five minutes after the third file has been saved, the program overwrites the first file, continuing to cycle through the three as long as the file is open. Check the time stamp for the most recent save. You can change both the number of saves and the time period between saves by going to the Customize > Preferences > Files tabs. It is not recommended to have too many saves as each "save" is a snapshot eating up memory. If you do access a file from the Autobak folder, remember, it will save to that location using the Autobak name. You will need to rename the file and redirect it back to your original file location.

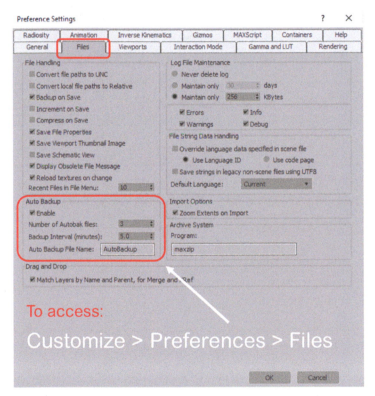

IMAGE 2.8

Warning: Although this program is getting better all the time, 3ds Max will crash or somehow the file can become corrupt without notice, probably at the worst time. Save, save, save! If you find you are performing a procedure correctly but getting unexpected or no results… likely, the program has hit a glitch, bug or crashed. The best option is to do a "Save As" (new iteration), and then restart the program. Open the last good version of the file. Odds are the issue will be fixed.

The last set-up item we should address before we begin to model is the unit set up for scale and measurements. Return to the Top Toolbar to left-click on the Customize tab to open the drop-down menu. From the menu, select "Units."

In the pop-up window, there are several choices for units. Since we will eventually be exporting to the Unity 3D game engine, select the "Metric" radio button and set the units to "Meters." The ratio is: 1 meter in 3ds Max = 1 unit in Unity = 1 meter. When we export the modules to Unity, they should be the correct scale with other objects in the game world. As a check, I created a green 1-meter × 1-meter × 1-meter cube in 3ds Max and exported it to an open Unity file. After bringing it into the Unity scene, I created a gray 1-meter × 1-meter × 1-meter cube using "Create" in the Unity scene to compare them. The image below shows that we are good to go!

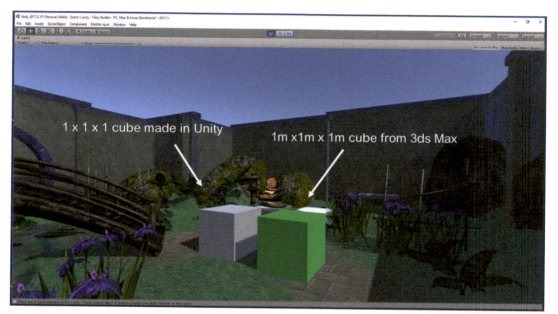

IMAGE 2.9

Save the 3ds Max file. We're finally ready to start modeling!

Curtain Wall Module

Modeling the Curtain Wall

Topics in This Chapter

- Placeholder Art
- World Coordinate System
- Editable Polygon vs. Edit Poly
- Adding Visual Interest to an Object
- Isometric/Orthographic
- Symmetry Modifier vs. Mirror Tool

Concepts/Skills/Tools Introduced in This Chapter

- Scene Explorer
  - Layers
- Perspective Viewport
- Command Panel
- Create Tab

- Geometry
  - Box
- Splines
  - Rectangle
- Utilities
  - Polygon Counter
- Object Color Picker
- Zoom Extents All
- Select and Move Tool Gizmo
- Select and Scale Tool Gizmo
- Quad Menu
  - Convert To:
- Renaming Objects and Changing Color
- Modifier List
- Modifier Stack
- Editable Poly
- Vertex Sub-Object Level Mode
  - Target Weld
- Edge Sub-Object Level Mode
- Polygon Sub-Object Level Mode
- Extrude; Extrude Caddy
- Edge Faces Viewport Setting
- Ctrl-Key, Alt-Key (Multiple Selections)
- Collapse All
- Chamfer Tool
- View Cube Use
- Maximize Viewport Toggle
- Symmetry Modifier
- Polygon Smoothing Groups

The first game asset we will build will be the Curtain Wall module that will be used to create the outer walls around the castle. In each succeeding chapter, we will add another module to our scene, creating more complex objects and utilizing the range of basic tools available in the program.

Going back to our workflow pipeline in developing our models, recall that I have completed the first two steps in the workflow:

- Preliminary research for reference, functionality and style.
- Design development sketches.

Below are three of the images that I used for reference when designing the Curtain Wall. Our GDD also had some parameter requirements for the Curtain Wall that had to be taken into consideration:

- Wall height: between 4 and 6 meters
- Wall length: up to 12 meters
- Wall thickness: 2–4 meters

- Walkway on top of wall: 1.5–2.0 meters wide
- Needs to have "merlon" projections at wall top
- Needs to have a "batter" at the bottom edge (outside castle)
- Hand-painted, shader-textured sides
- Polygon count: under 500

IMAGE 3.1

IMAGE 3.2

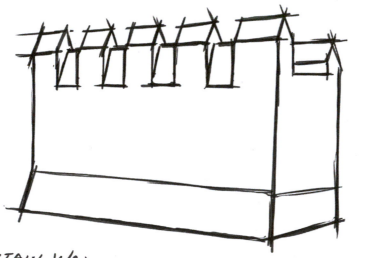

CURTAIN WALL

B. CULBERTSON

IMAGE 3.4

The next step in our workflow pipeline is to create a placeholder or block-out for the programmers on our team to use. Game Development can't wait for the modeler to complete their models. Programmers need to get working too! To meet their needs, modelers provide placeholders or block-outs, rough models that represent the size and shape of what the finished object will be. Placeholders are often updated with more developed models as work progresses. The block-out pieces also allow us to "prove" our design, making sure that all the major requirements will be covered.

Our 3ds Max file will have two mesh models within it: the placeholder (sometimes called the "boxout") and the actual game model. To keep things organized as we work, we can use layers, like the layers in Photoshop, if you are familiar with them. On the MainTool bar, find the "Toggle Scene Explorer." You will notice that there are two toggle Scene Explorer icon buttons next to each other. The one on the left opens a Scene Explorer window on the left-hand side of the user interface (UI), and the other on the right opens a Scene Explorer window at the bottom of the Command Panel on the right side of the UI. Open the one on the left.

Below is a screenshot of the 3ds Max UI with the key areas indicated.

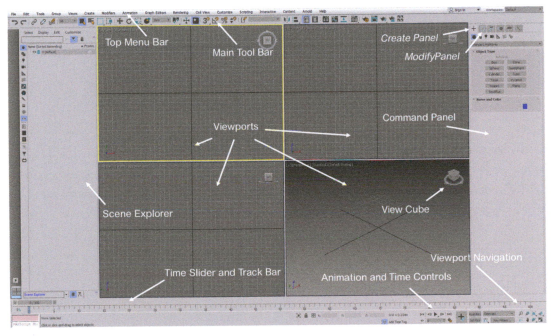

IMAGE 3.5

The Placeholder

Let's start making the Curtain Wall placeholder. If it is not open, please open the file we created in Chapter 2, "lastname_curtainwall_01" in 3ds Max (my file was named "culbertson_curtainwall_01"). If you need to create the file, please do so. In Chapter 2, we set up 3ds Max and our file for this project (Save 2-1).

The Scene Explorer

Along the top of the Scene Explorer is a menu bar with options and selections. The left-hand vertical column has icon buttons for the object types within the scene that can be used to filter which items are shown in the object list. The default layer cannot be changed. Find the "Create New Layer" icon button in the second tool bar row and add a layer. The layer that is "active" is indicated by the green "layers" icon.

Name the new layer "Placeholder." We will build our placeholder model on this layer. All other layers will have grayed out "layer" icons (see the image below). Create another layer, and call it "Curtain Wall Module." The new layer became the active layer, so be sure to click the layer icon for the Placeholder layer to make it the active layer for our next steps. Close the Scene Explorer using the X-out in the upper right corner.

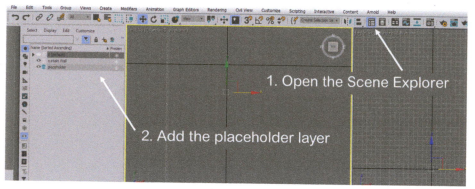

IMAGE 3.6

On the right-hand side of the UI is the area called the Command Panel.

Click on the Create Tab icon in the control panel if it is not already selected. Located just below the Create Tab Icon, left-mouse click on the "Geometry" icon if not already selected (it should be by default) and select the "Box" button in the menu list.

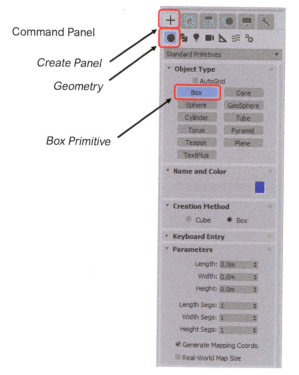

IMAGE 3.7

Creating a Box is a two-step operation with the mouse. First, you create the base footprint, and then add height. In the Top Viewport (the one in the upper left), left-click and drag diagonally to create the base of the box. The size doesn't really matter; we will be inputting exact values in the Parameter rollout shortly.

Release the mouse button, and drag the mouse in the plus Z-axis direction ("up" toward the top of the screen) to give it height.

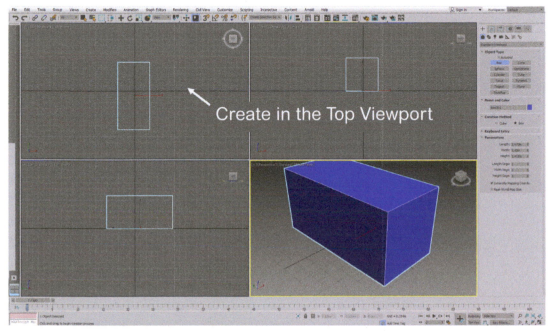

IMAGE 3.8

In the lower right-hand corner of the UI, left-click on the "Zoom Extents All" button. This will center the objects in the scene in each viewport, zooming to include every object in view within the viewport.

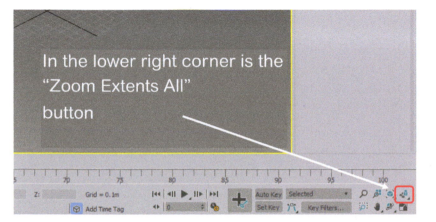

IMAGE 3.9

Next, let's change the size of the box to match the sizes specified in the GDD information. In the Command Panel on the right, find the "Parameters" rollout. Change the numerical values to those shown in the image below.

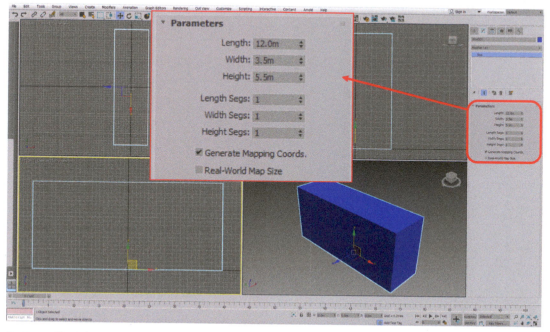

IMAGE 3.10 (Save 3-1)

Click on the Zoom Extents All button again to recenter the box in all the viewports. At this point, this box would suffice for our placeholder. It is a crude approximation of the finished model. Shortly, you will have the skills to make a placeholder with more features. For our game studio, you would save and submit this file to your team's asset folder for access by team members.

Modeling the Curtain Wall

To model an object in 3D, we need a starting point. There are several basic options available to us for this purpose:

- Create a 2D Spline (examples: line, circle, rectangle, ellipse)
- Create a 3D Standard Primitive (examples: box, sphere, cone, torus)
- Use an existing model

We will be using all three methods in the coming chapters. For the Curtain Wall, let's use the first method, using a 2D spline object as our starting point.

The basic modeling workflow is typically to

1. Create a spline, primitive or open an existing model.
2. Convert it to an Editable Poly or Editable Mesh to allow sub-object level access.
3. Manipulate the vertices, edges or polygons in the sub-object level to create the desired shape.

Let's create a spline. In the Command Panel on the right side of the UI, select the "Create" icon if not already selected. In the row below it, select the "Splines" icon next to the "Geometry" icon. Geometry accesses 3D shapes, while Splines accesses 2D shapes. Next, select "Rectangle" from the Object Type list.

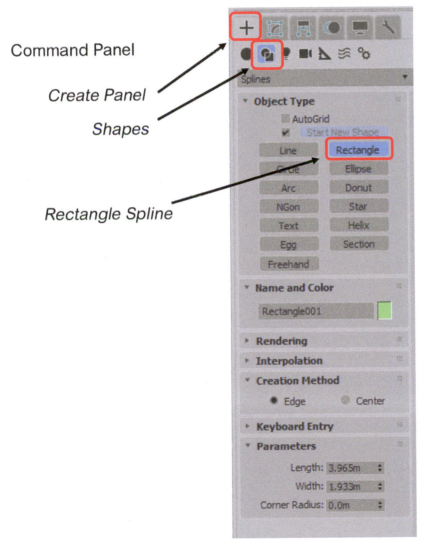

Command Panel

Create Panel

Shapes

Rectangle Spline

IMAGE 3.11

In the "Top" viewport, click in the upper right corner and drag to the lower left corner to create the shape. In the "Parameters" dropdown menu in the Command Panel, change the values to those as shown in the image below.

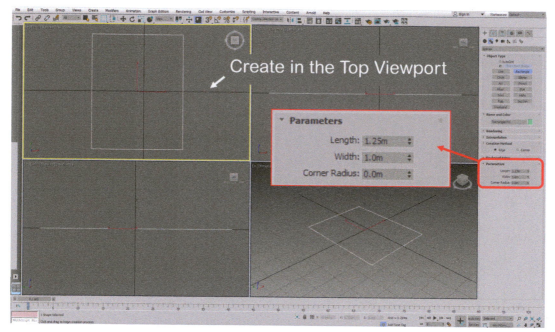

IMAGE 3.12

Note: If you did not create your rectangle in the Top Viewport as I did, the length, width and height orientations will be different. They are based on the orientation of the viewport that object was created in. To avoid confusion, please follow the directions carefully.

Click the Zoom Extents All to recenter the viewports. Why are we making it so small compared to what it needs to be? Because in the development, we will be extruding polygons that will create divisions in the mesh that we can manipulate and expand it to the size we need. It will make sense in a minute.

For the most part, when you create an object, you should center it in the scene at the origin of the World Coordinate System. Next, we will center the object at the 0, 0, 0 coordinates on the lower navigation bar of the UI in the Coordinate Display. Change the X, Y and Z coordinates each to "0." You should get into the habit of doing this for every object/scene. It is important when exporting objects to a game engine, so that objects import correctly relative to the game's origin point.

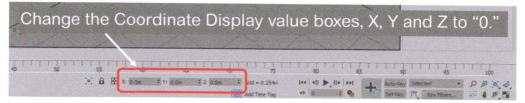

IMAGE 3.13

To build our Curtain Wall from this rectangle, we need to be able to access the sub-object parts, such as the vertices and polygons. To do that, we need to convert the rectangle, a spline object, into an editable object. Left-click on the Select & Move tool on the top tool bar to put the mouse in a selection state.

Select and Move Gizmo

Every object has a gizmo when selected, by default, located at the center of the object's mass.

Selecting the vertical green Y-axis arrow with a left-mouse click and dragging in the direction of the arrow will move the object along the Y-axis, only. Left-mouse click on the horizontal red X-axis arrow and dragging in the direction of that axis will move the object only in the X-axis. Doing the same with the blue Z-axis arrow, when available, will limit movement in the Z-axis only.

This is great for moving along an axis, but what if you want to move freely in any direction? Hover the mouse icon over the translucent yellow square along the horizontal and vertical axes. When it turns a solid yellow, left-mouse click and drag the gizmo in any direction.

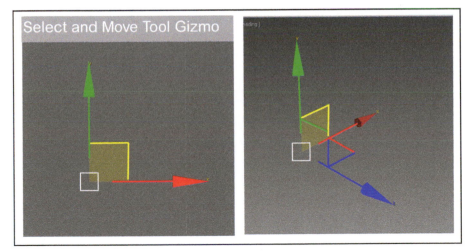

Select and Move Tool Gizmo

IMAGE 3.14

Convert to Editable Poly

Right-mouse click on the rectangle object you created in any of the viewports to open the Quad Menu. This menu is called the Quad Menu because when all of its parts are fully open, it has four quadrants. At the bottom of the menu, select "Convert To:". From the side menu that rolls out of the "Convert To:" menu button, select "Editable Poly." The rectangle has now been converted to a state where we can work in the sub-object level.

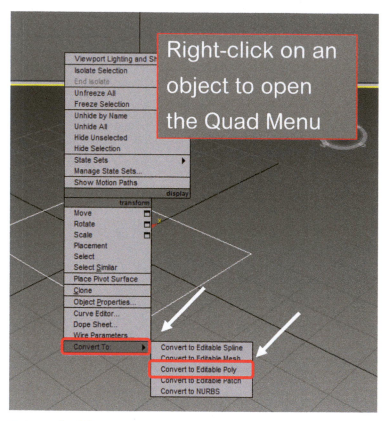

IMAGE 3.15 (Save 3-2)

In the Command Panel on the right side of the UI, you can now see the menu has changed from the Create tab to the Modifier tab. At the top of the list is the objects' name and color. Let's change the name from "Rectangle 001" to "curtain wall." Click on the name box to highlight the name and type in the new name.

Note: If you want to change the object's base color, click on the color picker box in the name and color rollout in the Command Panel. However, it is recommended to not use red as an object's color. In the next few steps, we will be selecting individual polygons on the mesh. When selected, the polygons will be red to indicate they are selected. As you might guess, a red polygon on a red mesh can cause confusion.

Just below the name and color bar is the "Modifier List." Select the arrow on the right side of the Modifier List bar to open the drop-down arrow menu. As you can see, there are many modifiers accessible to us. Click the drop-down arrow again to close the list. Just below the Modifier List is a section called the Modifier Stack, sometimes referred to as the "stack." The Modifier Stack displays the chronological history of an object including creation parameters and any modifiers that have been applied to the object. If sub-objects are available, you can access them from within the stack.

Below the Modifier Stack, you'll find the Selection section. You can also access sub-object parts by selecting the icons arranged in a row here.

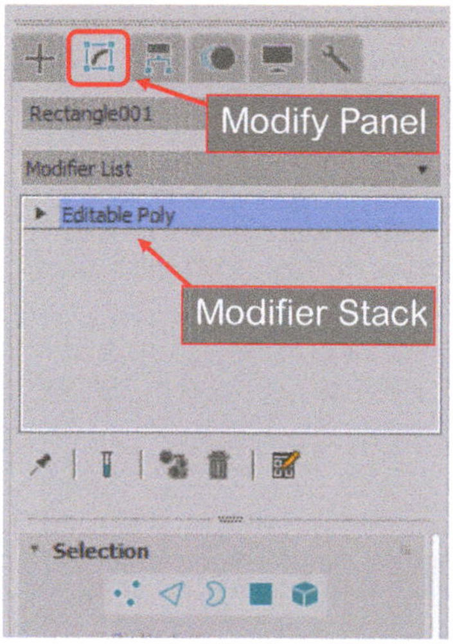

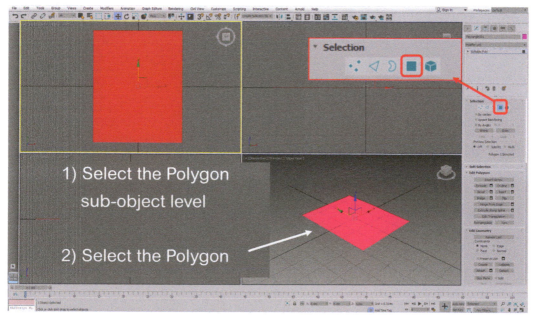

IMAGE 3.16

Select the Polygon sub-object icon in the Command Panel, and then left-click in the middle of the rectangle using the Perspective viewport. The polygon turns bright red indicating it has been selected and the polygon's renderable normal is facing toward us. The other side of the polygon, should you see it, is a darker red, indicating that it is the backside of the normal and will not render.

IMAGE 3.17

Now that we are in the sub-object level mode, we can modify the object.

Extrude the Polygon

We need to add height to the object.

- In the Modify tab of the Command Panel, click on Editable Poly to go into the sub-object level if it is not already selected.
- Select the Polygon icon in the Selection section.
- Next, scroll down to find the "caddy" button for "Extrude." The caddy buttons are the small, square buttons to the right of the rectangle buttons with names. When you select the Extrude caddy, it will open in the active viewport over the selected object. You can move the caddy off the object by dragging the dark rectangle area at the top of it.
- Adjust the middle height value on the caddy to 1.5 meter, and then select the green check mark icon at the bottom of the caddy to accept the change. The caddy will close. If you do not select the green check mark, the modification will not be applied.

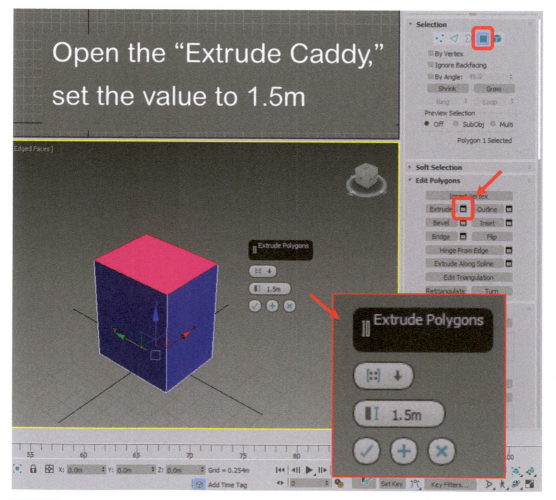

IMAGE 3.18

We just created what will be the lower section of the Curtain Wall. Next, we'll create the middle section. With the top polygon selected, select the Extrude caddy again. This time change the height value to 3.0. Click the green check mark to accept the modification.

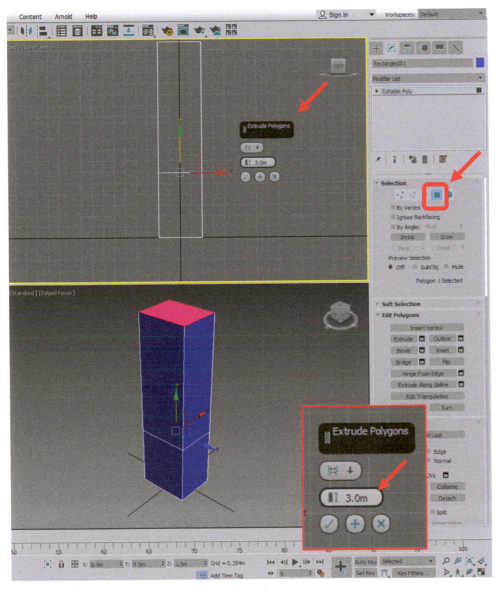

IMAGE 3.19

In the Perspective viewport, it's hard to see the line segments on the model mesh. We can change a setting in the viewport to make them more visible. In the upper left corner of the Perspective viewport, left-click on the "Default Shading" button to expand the rollout. Left-click on the Edge Faces button in the list. When an object is selected with Edge Faces turned on, its segments will be shown in the viewport as white lines.

Let's add some width segments. Select the two polygons as shown by holding the Ctrl-key on the keyboard while selecting. Depressing the Ctrl-key enables you to add to a selection and left-clicking to add more objects. Depressing the Alt-key enables subtracting objects from a selection.

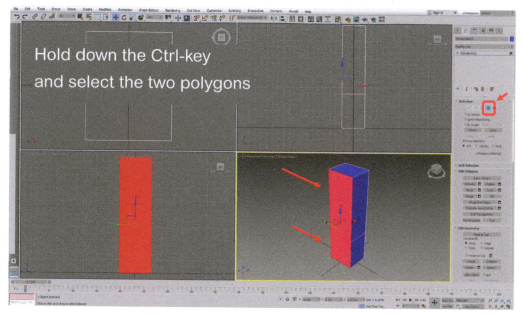

IMAGE 3.20

Select the Extrude caddy again. Change the height value to 0.35 meter for the extrusion. We want to add this extrusion twice, so, instead of selecting the green check mark, this time click the green plus (+) icon. A second extrusion will appear. Now, click the green check mark icon to accept the modifications.

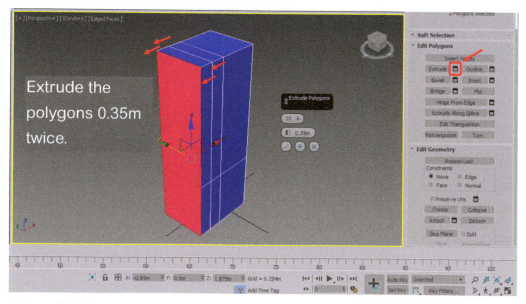

IMAGE 3.21 (Save 3-3)

Next, we will add to the length of the wall to bring it to the required "up to 12 meters" as the GDD calls for. Select the six polygons on the side of the mesh while holding the Ctrl-key on the keyboard as seen below.

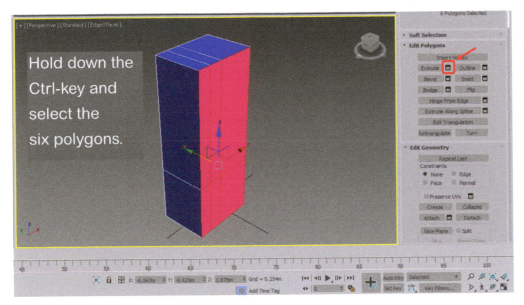

IMAGE 3.22

Extrude these polygons using the Extrude caddy as you have done before, changing the extrusion height to 1.0 meter. Click on the green plus (+) icon to accept the transform.

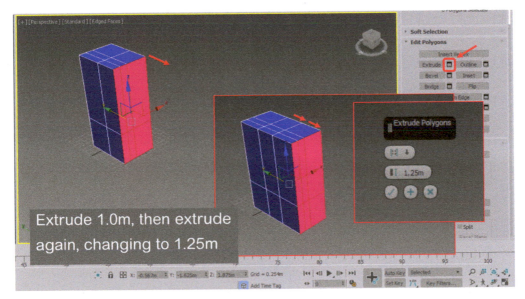

IMAGE 3.23

Extrude the polygons again, and only this time, change the extrusion value to 1.25 meter.

Repeat the previous two steps, alternating between 1.0 and 1.25 meters for the extrusions, three more times each. When finished, the wall will have five 1.25 sections and four 1.0 sections, 10.25 meters in length, which will be acceptable for our GDD requirements. Remember to select the green check mark to accept the modifications after each extrusion.

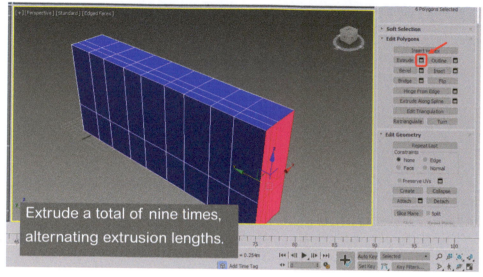

IMAGE 3.24 (Save 3-4)

Are you starting to see the shape we are working toward? Just a few more extrusions to go. The 1.0-meter-width section along the back edge of the top length is going to be our walkway for the player. The two 0.35-meter-width sections will be the top edge of the wall. Holding the Ctrl-key on the keyboard down, select the eighteen 0.35-meter-width polygons along the top of the mesh and extrude them 1.0 meter to create the defensive wall along the top edge of the Curtain Wall.

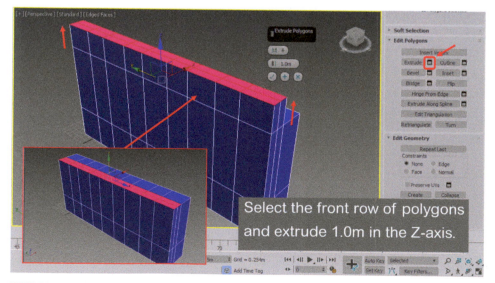

IMAGE 3.25

After clicking the green check mark to accept the modification, press the Alt-key on the keyboard and select every other set of two polygons as shown in the image below (press the Alt-key before selecting). Extrude the selected polygons 0.76 meter to create the familiar castle wall top sections, called "merlons."

Make sure that you haven't inadvertently selected polygons on the backside of the wall, not visible from the current view in the selection process before you do the next extrusion step. Use the View Cube in the upper right-hand corner to turn the scene in the viewport.

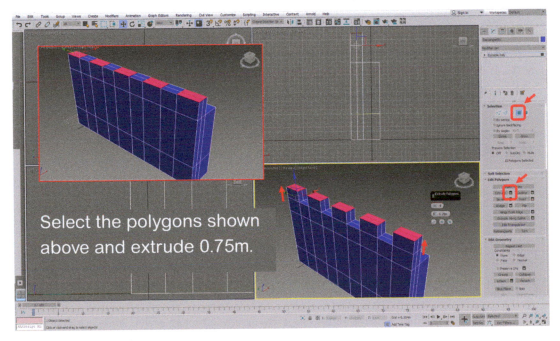

IMAGE 3.26 (Save 3-5)

The View Cube

If you haven't tried to use it, here are some tips for using the View Cube.

IMAGE 3.27

The View Cube is a navigation tool for viewing the scene in different orientations, using the presets or by rotating manually. The View Cube uses a compass for its orientation. Clicking on the little house in the upper left corner orients the viewport in a three-quarter view from above, a neutral position. Left-click the mouse on the cube hot-spots to rotate around the scene, left-clicking the words on the cube will engage the preset orientations described by the words. However, often, these orientations will not be "true." Clicking on the Front preset will reorient the scene view to the front perspective, but it may not be the true Front view. Check the viewport setting in the upper left corner of the viewport. If it says Orthographic, it is not set in a true isometric view that we want (every point in the scene 90 degrees to the plane). You need to make sure you change the viewport back to a true isometric view or your model could become skewed or distorted as you work. If things get too skewed, it could require a total restart of the model.

Caution: Using the View Cube in viewports other than the Perspective viewport can change the viewport setting to Orthographic. When set to Orthographic, some basic operations/tool will not function. Often, beginners fall in love with using the View Cube, using it without controlling it. Their viewport changes to Orthographic as soon as it is used, and they lose use of tools and then are stuck. If the viewport setting has changed to Orthographic, change it back to either Perspective, Top, Front or Left using the dropdown menu located in the top left-hand corner of the viewport.

As designers, we are expected to create models that are visually interesting. Our model, as it is, is perfectly usable for our game. However, it is very plain and not visually interesting. We should add some visual detailing to satisfy the player's visual appetite. To start, let's create angled embrasures on the outside wall. Embrasures are the open areas between the wall's merlons along the top of the wall.

With the Perspective viewport selected, left-mouse click on the Maximize Viewport Toggle button (Alt-W) in the extreme lower right-hand corner of the bottom Navigation Panel. It is the last button in the lower right corner. Now, you are viewing just the active viewport, up close. To get back to four viewports, click the toggle button again (Alt-W).

Back to the modeling, left-click on the Vertex icon in the Selection section of the Command Panel. Now, we will manipulate the vertices of the mesh. Scroll down the Command Panel to the Edit Vertex roll-out section to find and select the Target Weld button. This will allow you to weld two vertices together into one. The way it works is, select a first vertex, and then select a second vertex. If it is an eligible choice, the first vertex will move to the location of the second vertex and the two will become one. Remember, the first vertex moves to the location of the second vertex, so you need to visually plan your moves ahead of time to achieve the desired results.

In the images below, we want to weld the first, #1, vertex to the second, #2, vertex. Click on the #1 vertex and then on the #2 vertex. The two are now welded at the location of the second, #2, vertex.

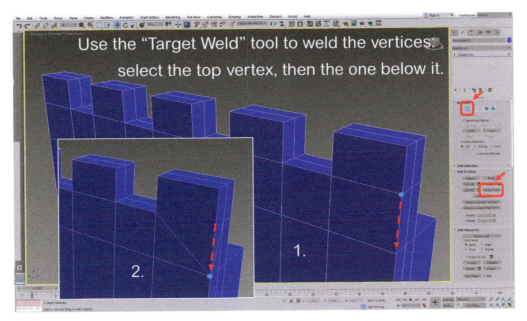

IMAGE 3.28

Continue along the row of vertices, welding the vertices of the upper row to the corresponding vertices in the row below it. Notice how you are creating the angled embrasures between the merlons. Just the addition of these angled polygons makes the model more interesting visually. Let's keep going.

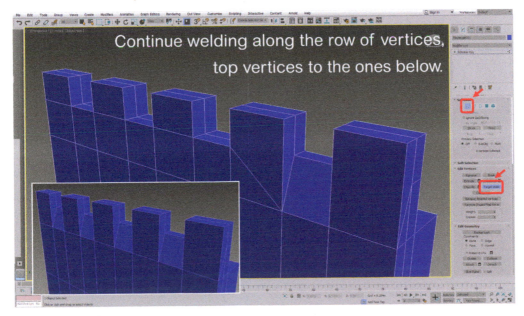

IMAGE 3.29 (Save 3-6)

Make sure to click the Target Weld button again to get out of that mode. You won't be able to do any other operations if it is selected. Hold the Ctrl-key on the keyboard down while selecting multiple vertices, the ones along the top outside of the wall as shown. Release the Ctrl-key, the vertices will stay selected. In the Coordinates on the bottom Navigation Bar, change the Z-Coordinate Display box value to 5.5 meters to create a beveled top.

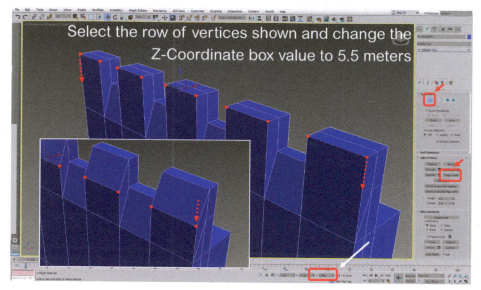

IMAGE 3.30

Rotate the viewport, so you can see the inside of the top wall as shown. Target Weld the top inside vertices to the vertices directly below them to create a beveled top on the inside.

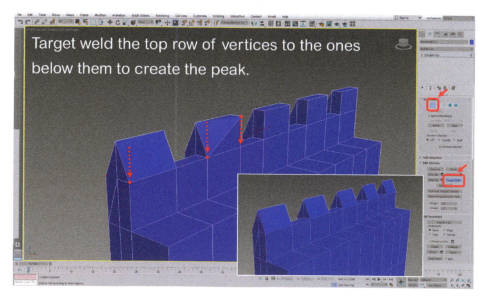

IMAGE 3.31 (Save 3-7)

Chamfer Tool

The peaks create a strong focal point, so strong that they are distracting. Switch to Edge sub-object level mode in the Command Panel, the icon next to Vertex sub-object level mode. Holding down the Ctrl-key on the keyboard, select the five edges along the peak of the wall.

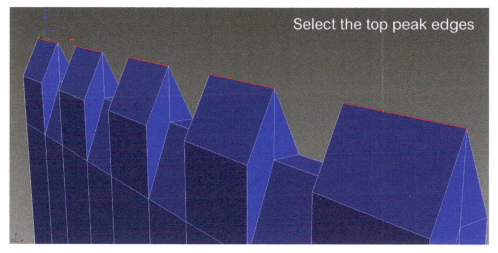

IMAGE 3.32

Find the "Chamfer" tool caddy in the Command Panel Edit Edges section, to the right of the Chamfer tool button and select it. Set the Edge Chamfer Amount value box to 0.05 meter. This will flatten the point a bit, so it is not a sharp knife-edge. "Chamfer" is the rounding of a sharp edge or corner by adding segments.

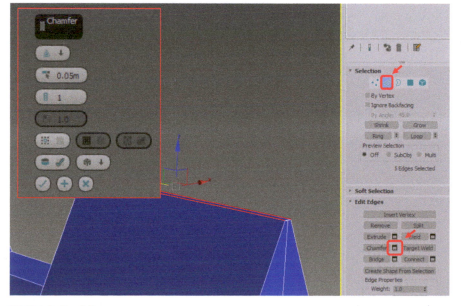

IMAGE 3.33 (Save 3-8)

You might have noticed; our Curtain Wall is not the correct width as specked out in the GDD. We need to double the width. We'll use the symmetry modifier to fix this.

First, we will need to remove all the polygons on the backside of the wall. It will become the centerline of the wall. The symmetry modifier will only work on the open edges of a mesh (having an opening or hole). Rotate the view of the mesh in the Perspective viewport using the View Cube as shown below. Switch to Polygon sub-object level mode in the Command Panel. Holding the Ctrl-key on the keyboard, select the polygons on the backside of the model. Once they are all selected, delete them using the delete key on the keyboard.

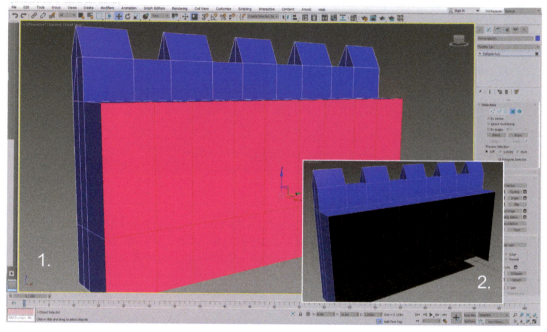

IMAGE 3.34

The polygons on the bottom of the mesh are unnecessary for this model; so, select and delete them too. In the past, a mesh had to be completely closed, no openings or holes, to work correctly in a game engine. Today, engines have progressed to a point that for most game engines, an open mesh is no longer a concern. By removing these polygons, we will lower the polygon count of the mesh. We could delete the end-side polygons too, but there might be a situation when aligning modules in the game that the side piece polygons may be needed.

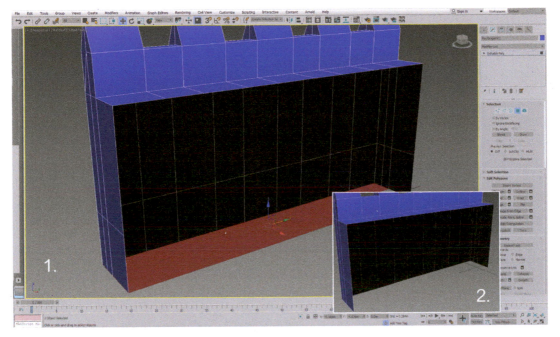

IMAGE 3.35 (Save 3-9)

Now, we have an open edge in the mesh that will allow us to use the Symmetry modifier. For this modifier to work effectively, you should indicate to 3ds Max what side you want the Symmetry modifier applied to. Switch to the Edge sub-object level mode in the selection section of the Command Panel. Now, select any of the edge segments along the opening on the back wall.

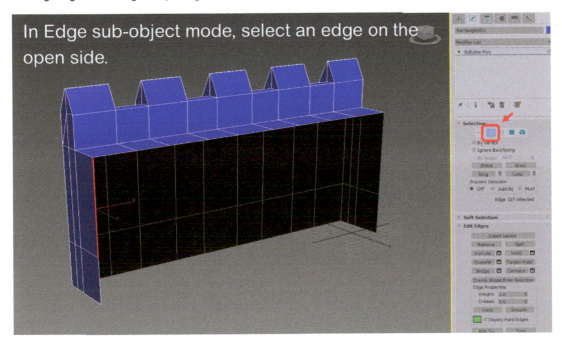

IMAGE 3.36

Symmetry Modifier

Next, open the modifier list roll-down menu above the stack. Scroll down and select the Symmetry modifier. The model in the viewport might disappear or take on a strange shape. This is because we have not set the correct parameters for the mirror axis. In the Command Panel, find the parameters roll out with the mirror axis radio buttons. The default button activated is the X-axis. Try clicking on the Y- and Z-axis radio buttons to see if the model mirrors correctly. For my model to work correctly, I also had to click on the Flip option, along with the X-axis.

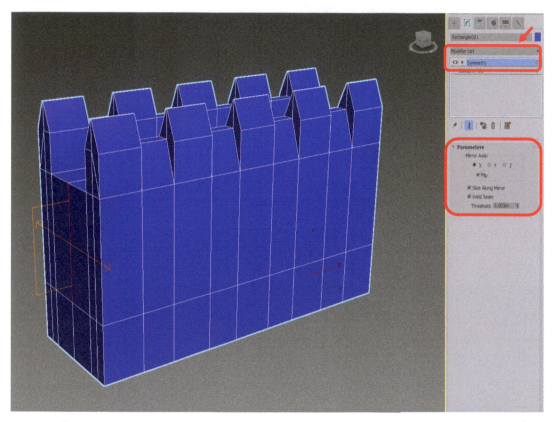

IMAGE 3.37 (Save 3-10)

Note: 3ds Max has another tool like the Symmetry modifier called the Mirror tool. The main difference between the two tools has to do with the center line that gets created. The mirror tool does not weld the vertices along the center line. The Symmetry tool has an option to weld them, keeping the mesh all one piece. The Mirror tool also can create clones or just a mirror image of the object.

With the Symmetry modifier applied correctly, you can see the final size of the wall with the walkway on top for the players to run along.

The wall will have two main sides: one facing the inside of the Castle and the other facing the outside of the Castle. For defensive purposes, the merlons on the outside of the wall need to be tall enough to protect the player from an enemy attack. Merlons on the inside of the wall can be shorter. We could keep working with the Symmetry modifier active; however, we are going to make changes to just one side of the symmetry mesh and not to the other. Because we have added a Symmetry modifier, any changes we do on one side of the centerline will be duplicated on the other. If we want to make the wall tops have different heights, we need to stop the symmetry modifications, but keep the modifications we have already made. Right-click on the Modifier Stack, and select "Collapse All" from the pop-up dialogue box.

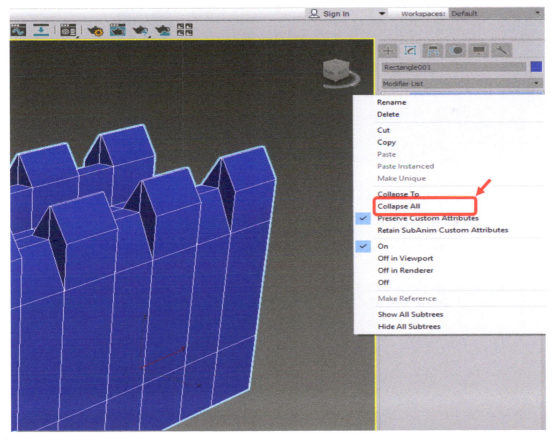

 IMAGE 3.38

A new pop-up window will appear in the middle of our UI. It is a warning telling that once you Collapse All, you will lose the ability to access any of the previous modifications or modifiers after converting them into an Editable Poly. It might be a good time to save the project. With the warning noted, in this case, continuing is alright; clicking on the "Yes" button, the window will close and the stack will collapse leaving an Editable Poly. Note that the mesh is now a simpler equation for the program to calculate in one step, rather than the multiple steps with modifiers before the collapse.

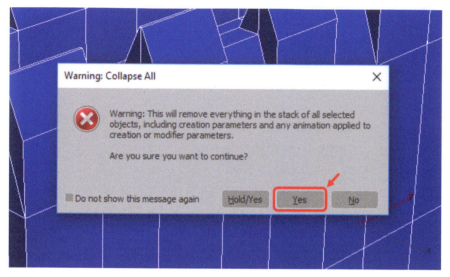

IMAGE 3.39

Switch to the Vertex icon in the Selection section of the Command Panel. In the Front viewport, select the top vertices of the wall on the right side as shown. Use the Select and Move tool to lower them to about one-half the height of the front merlon peaks.

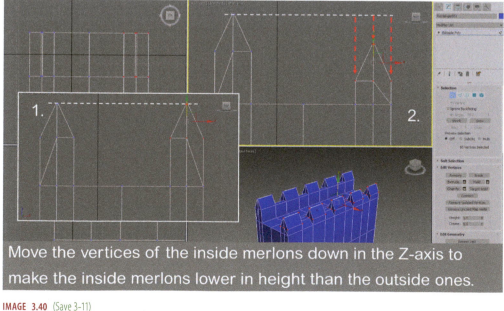

Move the vertices of the inside merlons down in the Z-axis to make the inside merlons lower in height than the outside ones.

IMAGE 3.40 (Save 3-11)

We need to create the batter, the angled base of the outside wall. In the Front viewport, select the bottom corner row of vertices on the left side and move them horizontally to the left on the X-axis, using the green arrow on the Select and Move gizmo. Create an angled wall as shown.

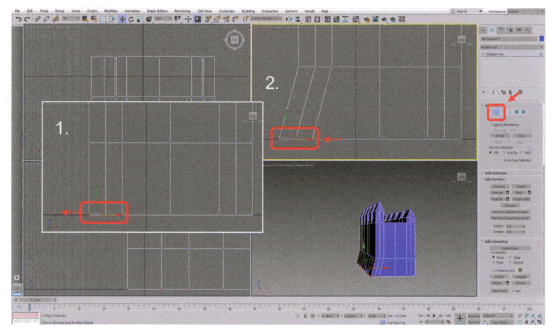

IMAGE 3.41

We should widen the mesh's length on the ends to help compensate for any misalignment we might encounter later when the castle modules are put together. To do this, we will use a new tool, the Select and Scale tool. It is located on the top tool bar, two icons to the right of the Select and Move tool. Select the tool, and then select the mesh in the Left viewport.

Transform Gizmos

The Select and Scale gizmo tool works similarly to the Select and Move tool gizmo. Instead of moving the object, it scales the object larger or smaller. If you locate your mouse in the inner yellow triangular area, closest to the X, Y, Z origin point, click and drag the mouse diagonally from the lower left to the upper right, the object will scale uniformly in all directions. If you locate the mouse over one of the three axis arrow extensions, the model will scale in that axis.

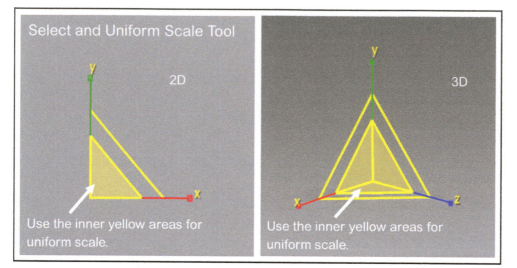

IMAGE 3.42

Change to the Vertex sub-object icon in the Selection section of the Command Panel if not already selected. In the Left viewport, with the Ctrl-key depressed, select the vertices on the left and right ends of the model as shown.

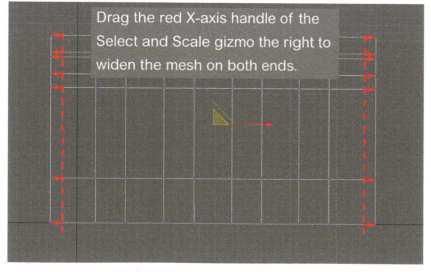

IMAGE 3.43

Clear All

One last thing we should do is to perfom a "Clear All" operation. When the mesh is not selected, you might notice the edges have a soft look, not crisp edges. To sharpen the polygons, we need to remove any "smoothing" being applied by 3ds Max to the mesh. In Ploygon sub-object level mode, select all the polygons in the mesh by draging a selection box around the entire mesh with the Select and Move tool.

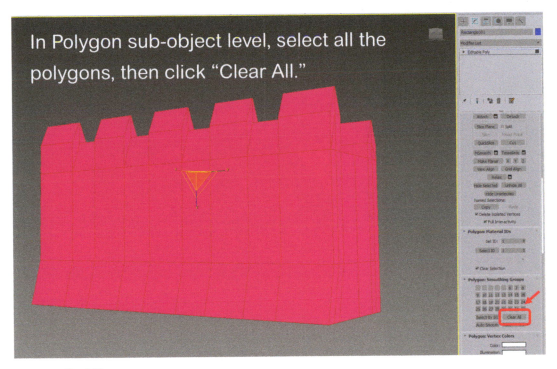

IMAGE 3.44 (Save 3-12)

Scroll way down the Command Panel to the "Polygon: Smoothing Groups" section, and click on the "Clear All" button. All the edges of the mesh will become sharp.

Congratulations, you're all done modeling the Curtain Wall! We can check on the polygon count using the Polygon Counter. In the row of tabs at the top of the Command Panel, click on the last icon in the row, "Utilities." When the tab opens, you'll find a button near the top on the left side called "More." Click it to open a pop-up menu list. Find the Polygon Counter, and open it by selecting it. Select Polygons as opposed to Tris. You can enter a polygon budget, which in our case was 500 maximum. We are in good shape, and our model has 220 polygons, well under the budgeted total.

There is another big step to finishing the Curtain Wall: unwrapping it and texturing it. We will address those two topics, unwrapping and texturing, in a few chapters from now. Below is an image I will share with you of how it is going to look when we do finish it.

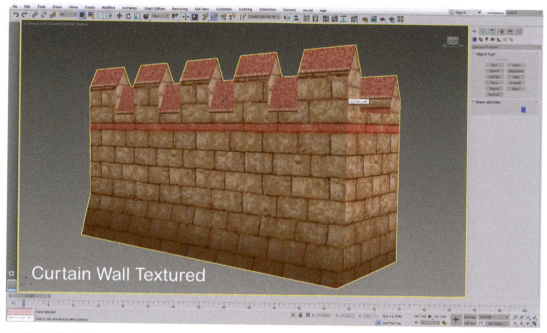

IMAGE 3.45 (Save 3-13)

Let's get some more modeling skills under our belt first. Next, we will model the Fixed Bridge that leads to the draw bridge.

Chapter 3 Exercise: Wood Table and Chair

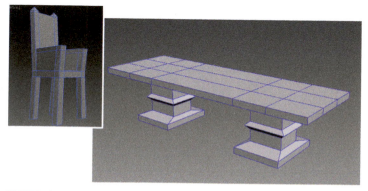

IMAGE 3.46

Model a wooden table and chair to be used in an interior room. Both the table and chair should be single meshes, not multiple pieces. The design of each can be of your choice or you can follow the examples I made. Be sure to do some research to define your design. Both the table and chair were modeled from a Standard Primitive box. Moving vertices and extruding polygons, the models were created. When you complete Chapter 7, Unwrapping the Model, you can return to the finished table and chair models and complete the unwrapping and texturing of your model.

In the companion folder online, you will find the 3ds Max file iterations saves from when I modeled the table and chair along with the texture file, "accessoy_textures.png" for your use.

IMAGE 3.47

Fixed Bridge Module

Modeling the Fixed Bridge

Topics in This Chapter

- Extrude; Extrude Caddy
- Weld; Weld Caddy
- Viewport Templates
- View Align Tool
- Select and Uniform Scale Tool

The second game asset module we are going to create is the Fixed Bridge. The Fixed Bridge crosses over the moat connecting the shore of the moat to the drawbridge. We will be modeling two parts to this module, the bridge section and the end section that receives the drawbridge.

From the GDD, I have noted some parameters that needed be taken into consideration.

Bridge Span module:
Roadway height from ground level: 2 meters
Roadway width: 2 meters
Module width: up to 4 meters
Module length: up to 5 meters
Needs to have a "batter" at the bottom of the piers
Walls lining the roadway with decorative elements
Hand-painted, shader-textured sides
Polygon count: under 150

Bridge End module:
Must have a fitting to receive the drawbridge when it is in the down position.
Drawbridge to be 2 meters wide
Same styling as the Bridge Span module (fits when connected)
Slightly more ornate than Bridge Span module to denote it is the end of the bridge.
Polygon count: under 125

Note: The characters in the game will be scaled to 1.15 meter; short, stocky, fantasy dwarf styling. The structures in the environment should be scaled accordingly.

As with the Curtain Wall, I have done the preliminary research and developed a sketch to work from. Below are three of the images that I used for reference when designing the Fixed Bridge and the final sketch of our model.

IMAGE 4.1

IMAGE 4.2

IMAGE 4.3

FIXED BRIDGE

BRIDGE END

B. CULBERTSON

IMAGE 4.4

Let's get started. Open a new scene in 3ds Max. Create a new file, "lastname_bridgespan_01" (my file will be named "culbertson_bridgespan_01"). We will be using the same 3ds Max setup as we used with the Curtain Wall (units set to meters, etc.). As with the Curtain Wall, we need to create a placeholder for the programmers on the team. Unlike when you made the Curtain Wall, you now have a few modeling skills, so we can make a placeholder that has some shape to it.

In the Scene Explorer, create three new layers: the first called "Placeholder," the second called "Bridge Span" and the third called "Bridge End." Click on the Placeholder layer, the one we will be working on, to make sure it is the active layer.

Looking at our design sketch and the GDD parameters, let's start blocking out a placeholder. From the Geometry tab of the Command Panel, select and create a "Box" in the top viewport as you did with the Curtain Wall placeholder. Change the parameter values in the Command Panel to match the ones as shown in the image below.

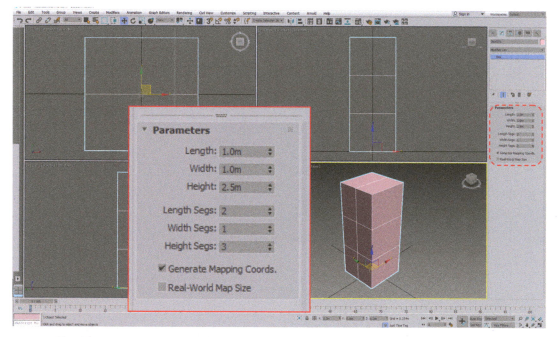

IMAGE 4.5 (Save 4-1)

Next, center the box at the 0, 0, 0 meters for the X, Y, Z coordinates by typing in the values in the Coordinate Display boxes on the lower navigation bar in the user interface (UI). Toggle the Scene Explorer closed using the Scene Explorer button icon on the Main Tool bar to maximize the usable work space for modeling.

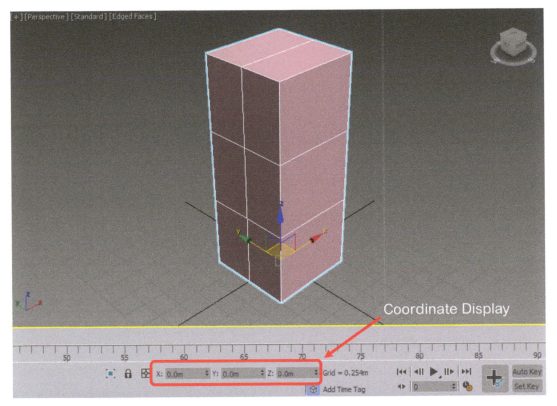

IMAGE 4.6

This box represents the corner pier of the module. We will model half the module and symmetrize it at the appropriate time to finish it. We'll add the bridge span next. Hopefully, you are starting to get familiar with the next few steps. Right-click on the box, and convert it to an Editable Poly. Rename the box "placeholder."

Select the top right polygon on the divided side of the box as shown. With the Polygon sub-object level selected, find the Extrude caddy to extrude the polygon 0.75 meter twice and then make an additional 0.25-meter extrusion.

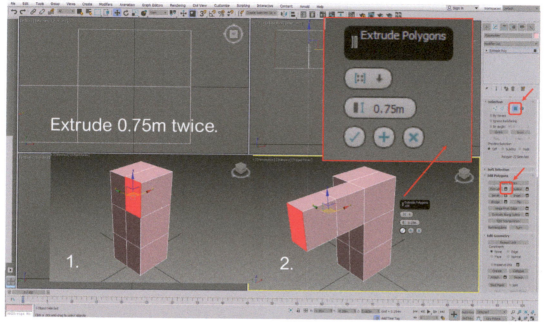

IMAGE 4.7

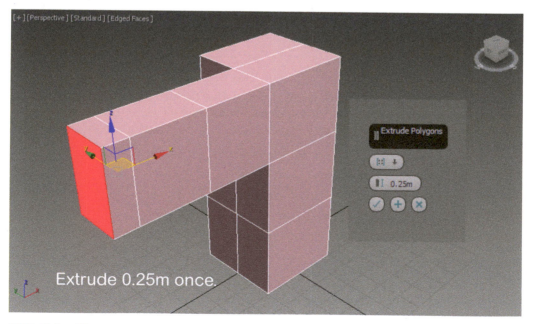

IMAGE 4.8 (Save 4-2)

Next, let's create the roadway, well, half the width of the roadway. Select the four side polygons as shown, and extrude them 1.0 meter using the Extrude caddy.

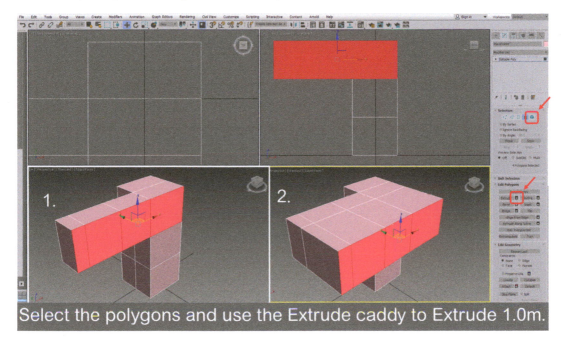

Select the polygons and use the Extrude caddy to Extrude 1.0m.

IMAGE 4.9

The wall along the roadway will be next. Select the top row of vertices as shown, and extrude them 0.25 meter.

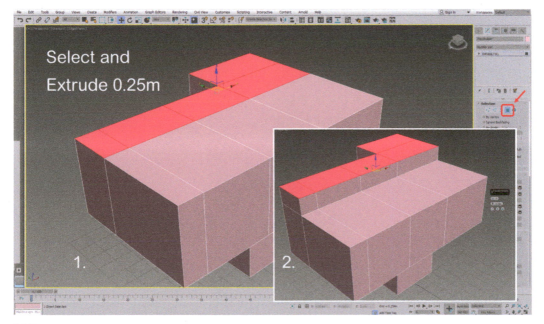

IMAGE 4.10

To finish the pier in the corner, select the two polygons and extrude them 1.0 meter. The center of the span will have a decorative element, extrude the end polygon 0.25 meter as shown.

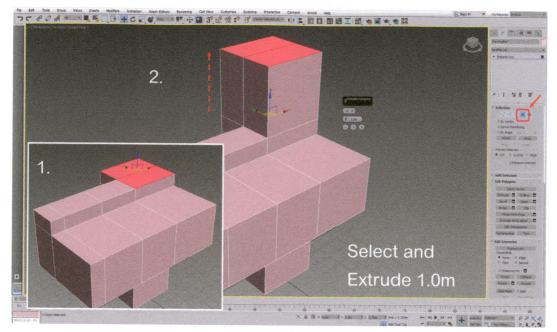

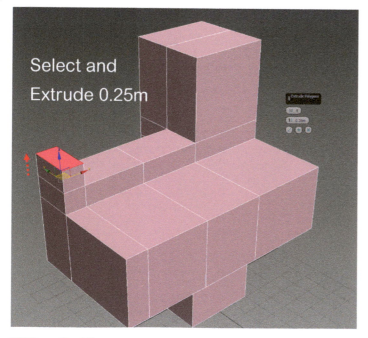

Now, it's time to symmetry the bridge to the full width. Select the polygons along the span, and delete them to create an opening so that the modifier will work. After you delete the polygons, switch to the Edge sub-object level in the Selection section of the Command Panel and select one of the edges along the opening. Remember, you need to tell 3ds Max where you want the Symmetry Modifier to be applied so that it occurs in the right place.

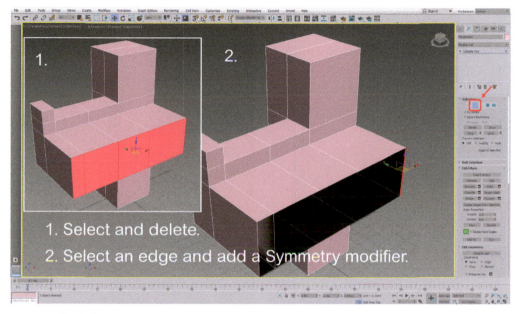

1. Select and delete.
2. Select an edge and add a Symmetry modifier.

IMAGE 4.13 (Save 4-4)

Apply the Symmetry Modifier from the Modifier List in the Command Panel. Click on the various Mirror axis buttons to find the correct orientation. The correct one for my model was the Y-axis. I did not need to use the Flip option.

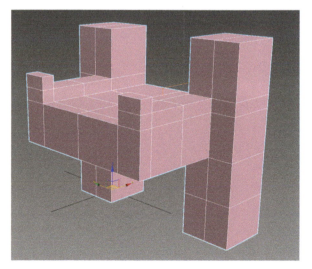

IMAGE 4.14

To complete the span, we will need to collapse the modifier stack to remove the Symmetry Modifier function. Right-mouse click on the Modifier Stack in the Command Panel to open the menu and select "Collapse All." Click on the "OK" button in the pop-up warning window to close it. Now, you can get back into Polygon sub-object level mode.

Select the polygons on the end of the span as shown, and delete them. Switch to Edge sub-object level mode again, and select an edge along the opening you created.

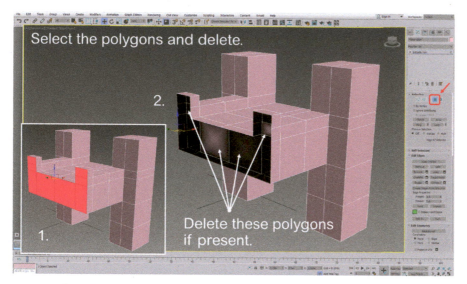

IMAGE 4.15 (Save 4-5)

Apply the Symmetry Modifier to the mesh. The X-axis was the correct orientation for my mesh.

Collapse the Modifier Stack again, to allow us to work at the sub-object level, by right-mouse clicking in the Modifier Stack and selecting Collapse All. Click OK to close the warning window when it pops up.

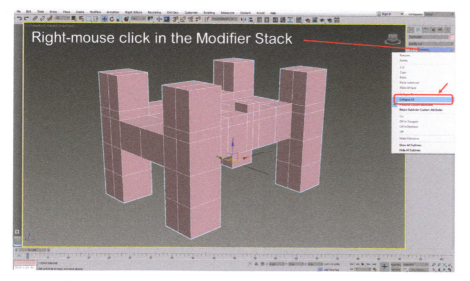

IMAGE 4.16 (Save 4-6)

Recall that we will be making two models for the Bridge module, the Bridge Span and the Bridge End. We will separate one end from the span we created to make the two placeholder modules.

Click on the Zoom Extents All button in the lower right corner of the UI to show all the model.

Selection Tools

Note: There are two option buttons for the selection tools, "The Rectangular Selection Region" and the "Window/Crossing," located to the left of the Select and Move tool icon on the Top Tool bar. With the Rectangular selection region option, anything within the rectangle you create when you drag the mouse diagonally will be selected, even if partially selected. With the Window/Crossing option, only objects that are completely within the selection area box will be selected.

In the Polygon sub-object level mode, using the Window/Crossing selection option, select the polygons on the left end of the model to include the two plers and the roadway between them as shown.

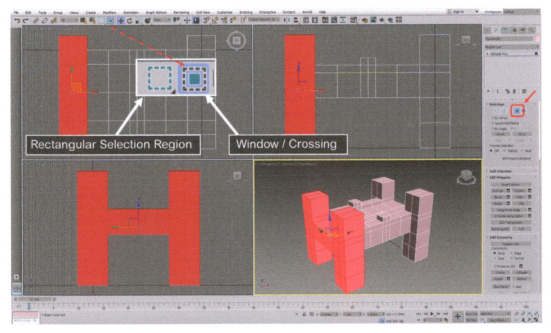

IMAGE 4.17

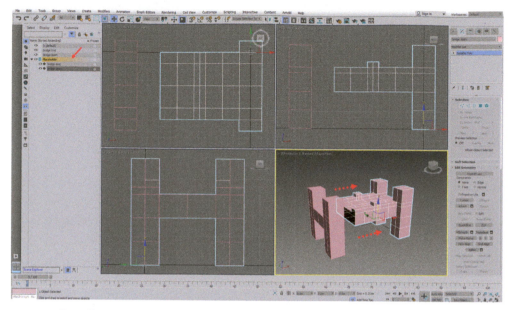

IMAGE 4.18 (Save 4-7)

On the top Tool Bar, toggle the Scene Explorer so that it appears in the UI. On the right side of the UI, scroll down the Command Panel to find and select the "Detach" button. A small pop-up "Detach" dialogue box will appear on the screen. Change the name in the "Detach As:" box to "bridge end." You have created a new, second mesh. The original mesh will still be selected in the Polygon sub-object level mode. Left-mouse click on the Editable Poly listing in the Modifier Stack to deselect it. Then, select the new "bridge end" mesh in the scene with the Select and Move tool, and move it away a short distance from the original mesh. You could also select it in the Scene Explorer as the new mesh likely appeared in the Placeholder level when you detached it.

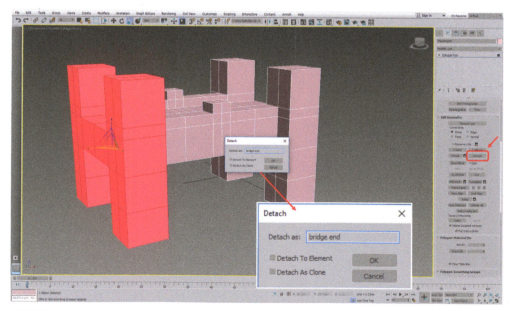

IMAGE 4.19

Rename the original mesh, placeholder, to "bridge span" in the name box at the top of the Command Panel or in the Scene Explorer.

That completes our place holder. We would export this placeholder out to our studio's resource folder for the programmers to use. You probably noticed that creating this place holder was a lot more involved than the previous placeholder we made. You had some modeling skills this time that we could utilize. We can use this placeholder as a start for the final model to save some time.

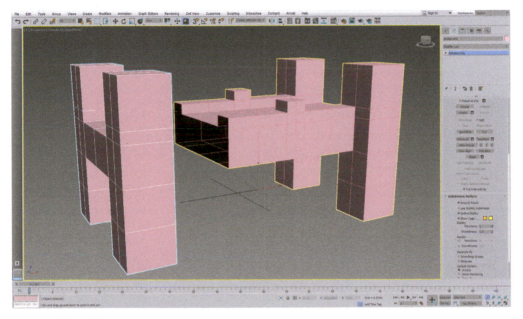

IMAGE 4.20 (Save 4–8)

The Bridge Span

We will start with the Bridge Span again. Right-click on the placeholder bridge span section to open the quad menu. Select the "Clone" button. A Clone Options pop-up window will appear on the screen.

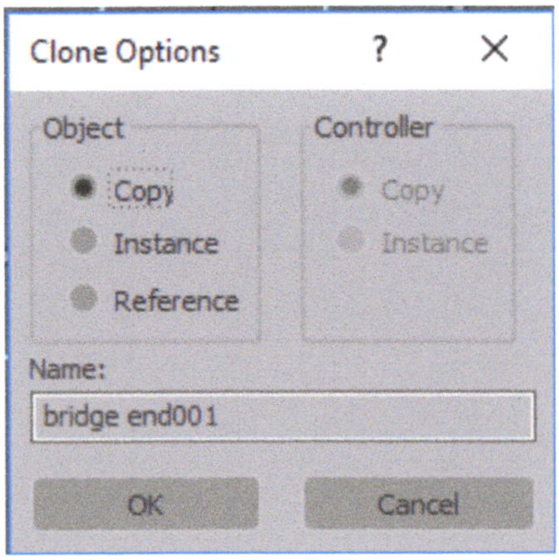

IMAGE 4.21

Clone Options

The clone tool creates a copy, instance or reference of the selected object or objects. There are important differences between the three types of clones.

Copy:

A copy clone will be an identical copy of the original object selected including any transforms. The original and the clone will be two independent objects from each other.

Instance:

An instance clone will be an identical copy that is linked to the original in that any future change or transform made to one of the two objects will happen to the other. For example, if you scale one of the two objects to be 2 meters taller, the other object will scale an identical 2 meters taller.

Reference:

A reference copy is similar to an instance except with a reference; changes to the original object will result in identical changes to the reference clone; however, changes to the reference object will not be made to the original object. Changes are one-way, from original to the clone.

In this cloning case of the Bridge Span, we want to have a Copy. Select the Copy radio button and then the OK button.

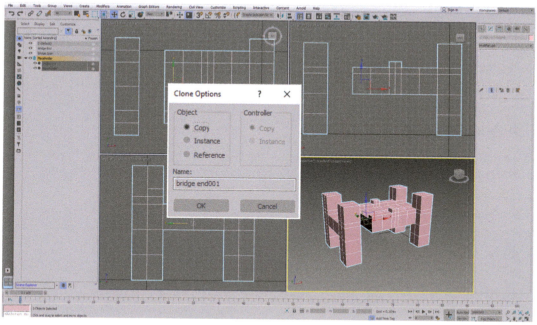

IMAGE 4.22

Notice that in the Scene Explorer window (toggle it "on" if it is off), the cloned object appears in the Placeholder level as bridge span001. Drag the Bridge span001 object in the Scene Explorer up, on top of the Bridge Span layer to move it to that layer.

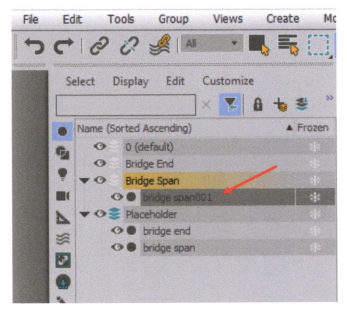

IMAGE 4.23

Repeat the same steps with the bridge end mesh, cloning a copy and moving it to the Bridge End layer in the Scene Explorer.

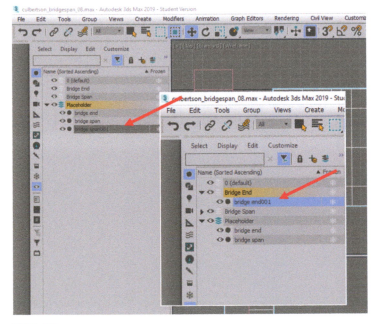

IMAGE 4.24

Now, click on the "eye" icon next to the Placeholder and Bridge End layers to turn those layers off. If we need them, we can turn the layers on to access the meshes. With the Placeholder and Bridge End layers off, we are left with the mesh clone we created and moved to the Bridge Span layer where we will make the game model. Toggle the Scene Editor off to maximize the workspace for modeling.

The mesh we have is a good starting point for the model. We know it is generally the right size. Let's trim it down to its basics and modify the mesh from there. With the object selected, change to Polygon sub-object level mode, if not set there already. Select the left half of the mesh in the top viewport (the upper half) as shown, and delete it.

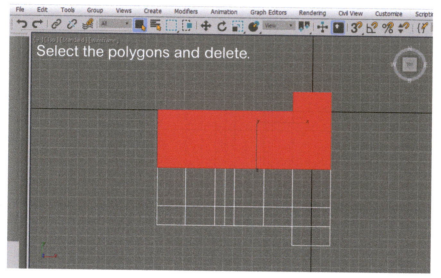

IMAGE 4.25

Next, delete the part of the span that we previously created with the Symmetry Modifier, selecting the polygons shown and deleting them.

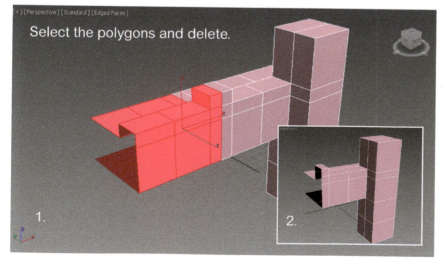

IMAGE 4.26 (Save 4-9)

74

We should be at a good spot to start modifying the mesh into the final bridge span. First let's create the arch under the span from the side view. In the Vertex sub-object level mode, using the Select and Move tool, drag the three rows of vertices individually in the positive Y-axis (up in the screen) like I have done in the image below. Be sure when you drag the gizmo, click directly on the upper part of the vertical green arrow for each set of vertices. This makes the span look much lighter visually. Remember, when you select one of the vertices, you are really selecting three vertices, the one you see and the two directly behind it.

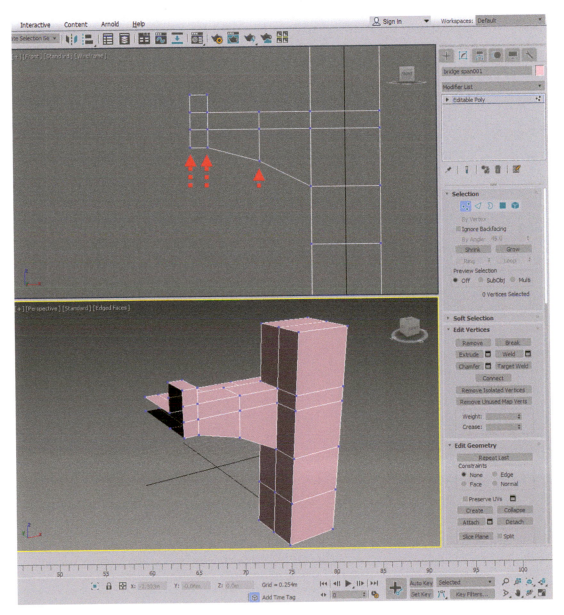

IMAGE 4.27 (Save 4-10)

Next, we'll model the pier. We are going to add a horizontal row of vertices, just below the roadway vertices. This will allow us to do several things. We will be able to add a decorative detail to the side of the bridge span and create a place where the drawbridge can rest when it is in the down position when we make the Bridge End module. While still in the Vertex sub-object level mode, scroll down the Command Panel to find the Slice Plane tool button and select it. You will notice a yellow rectangle appears around the mesh. This yellow rectangle is not an object; it is the Slice Plane tool. Where the Slice Plane tool intersects the mesh, you'll see red vertices. Using the Select and Move tool raise and lower the Slice Plane on the Y-axis. The red vertices that intersect with the Slice Plane move up and down the mesh, with the yellow rectangle, indicating where new vertices would be created. Move the Slice Plane so that it is just below the roadway vertices as shown. To create the new row of vertices, left-mouse click on the button just below of the Slice Plane button, the "Slice" button. Left-mouse click the Splice Plane button again to turn the tool off.

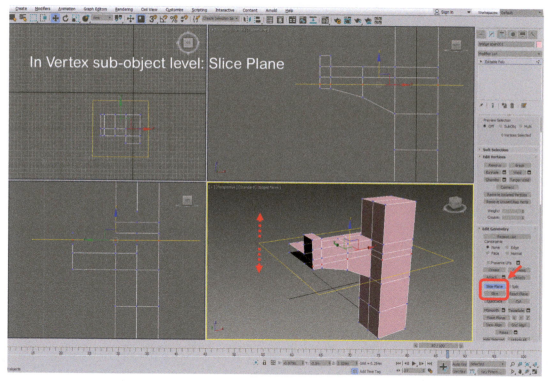

IMAGE 4.28

Visually, the space under the bridge span roadway, between the piers, looks unbelievable. In the real world, the weight of the bridge span would need to be better supported or it would collapse. Making objects in the game look believable is part of good level design.

Switch to the Polygon sub-object level mode, and select the polygon under the span as seen in the image below and delete it.

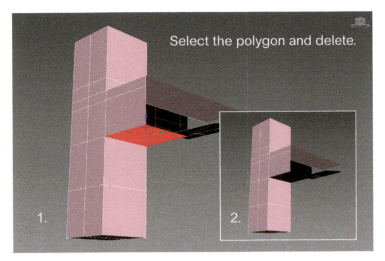

IMAGE 4.29

Select and extrude the two polygons on the inner side of the pier 1.0 meter to fill in the space.

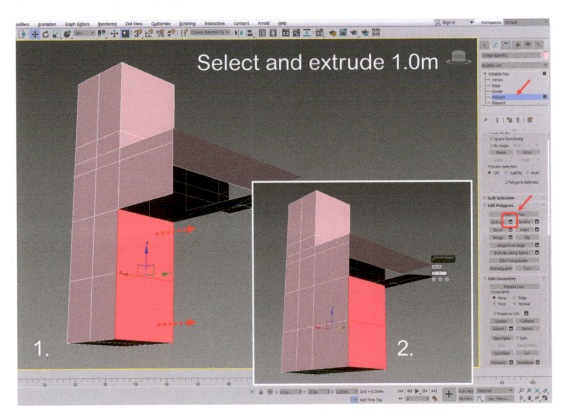

IMAGE 4.30

Next, rotate the viewport enough to see into the opening in the span. You'll see a horizontal polygon that was created with the extrusion. Select it and the two vertical end polygons. Delete these three polygons to create an opening for using the Symmetry Modifier.

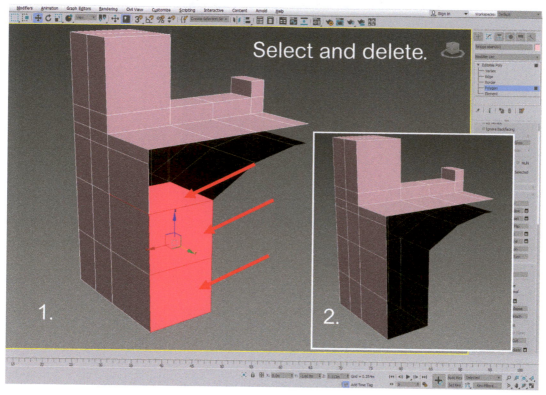

IMAGE 4.31 (Save 4-11)

Knowing we just did the extrusion and deleted the polygons, we are left with four vertices that will require welding. Using the Select and Move tool, select one of the vertices shown in the image below and move it down, away from the upper vertex.

It does not look like it, but there are two vertices on top of each other. Do the same procedure on the other two vertices opposite to these two on the mesh.

Next, use the Target Weld, in Vertex sub-object level mode, to weld the vertices together. Remember, when using the Target Weld tool, the first vertex moves to the second vertex. The reason we moved both lower vertices was to insure the welded vertices would remain aligned with the horizontal row of vertices. If, after welding, your vertices are out of alignment, undo the welding and make the corrections to insure you moved the lower vertices down away from the upper ones before Target Welding them back to the upper vertices.

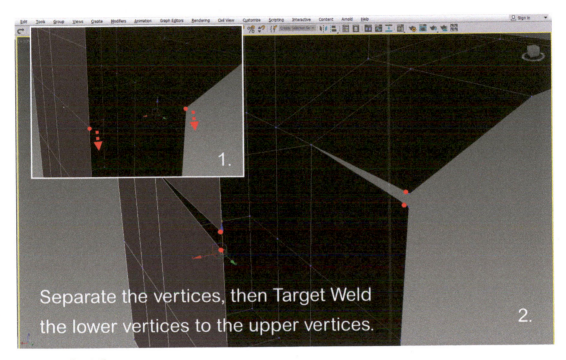

IMAGE 4.32 (Save 4-12)

Moving to the top of the pier, we will model the corner column and learn a new tool, the Border and new extrusion procedure. Rotate the viewport to view the top of the pier as shown. Make sure you are rotating the scene and not the mesh. In Vertex sub-object level mode, select the vertices at the top of the pier column. Lower the selected vertices as shown to create the base of the column.

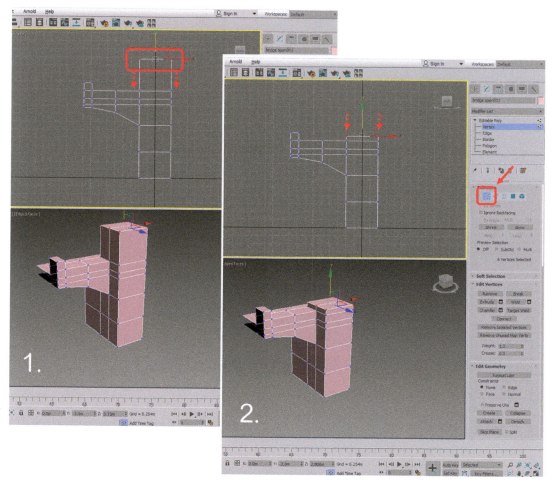

IMAGE 4.33

Select the two top polygons, and in Polygon sub-object level mode, extrude the polygons 0.075 meter using the Extrude caddy.

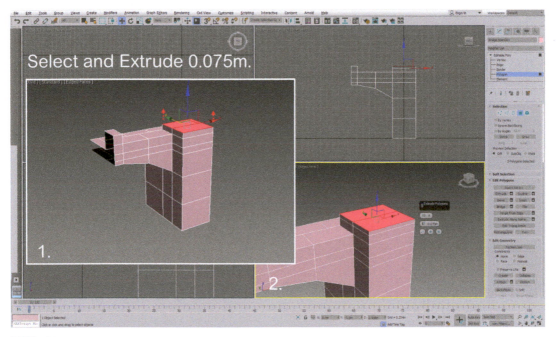

IMAGE 4.34

Next, using the Select and Uniform Scale tool, scale the polygon toward the center of the column, by left-mouse clicking and dragging the mouse, so the corner edges are approximately at a 45-degree angle.

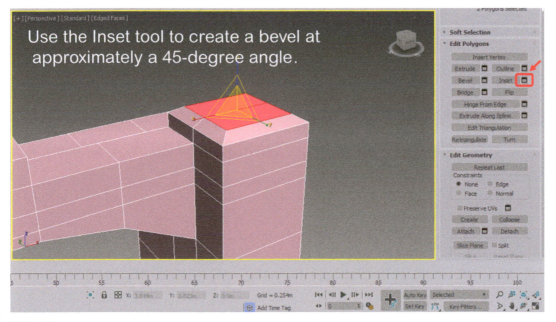

IMAGE 4.35

Extrude the two selected polygons in the up Y-axis 0.50 meter to create the middle section of the column, and then delete the two polygons.

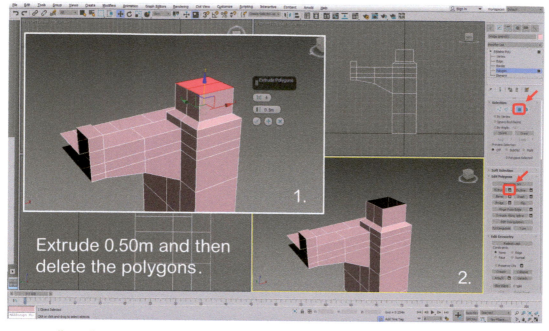

Extrude 0.50m and then delete the polygons.

IMAGE 4.36 (Save 4-13)

Switch from Polygon sub-object level mode to the Border sub-object level mode. Select any segment of the edge of the opening in the top of the column. Notice the entire border is selected, hence, the "Border" sub-object tool.

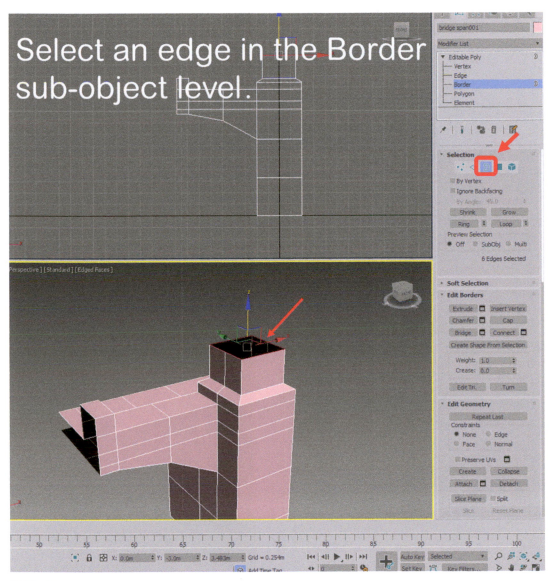

IMAGE 4.37

There is another way to extrude, used exclusively for Edge segment and Border sub-objects. It will not work on polygons. With the Border selected, hold the Shift-key down on the keyboard. Then, use the Select and Uniform Scale tool to click and drag the mouse left or right to extrude the border to create new polygons, tangent to the original edge. Release the left-mouse key, and then release the Shift-key on the keyboard. If you do not click and release in the correct order, it will not work correctly. Create the new border as shown. This will create the bottom of the column cap.

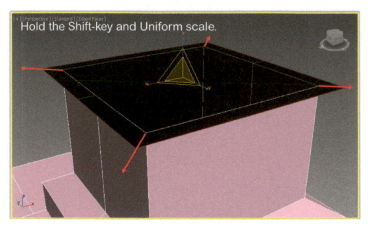

IMAGE 4.38

Change to the Select and Move tool. Hold down the Shift-key on the keyboard first, and then select the yellow vertical part of the blue arrow-head Z-axis. Drag up vertically a short distance as shown to create the side walls of the column cap. Release the mouse and then the Shift-key.

Repeat the steps again, dragging a longer distance, to create another extrusion as shown. This will be the top of the column cap.

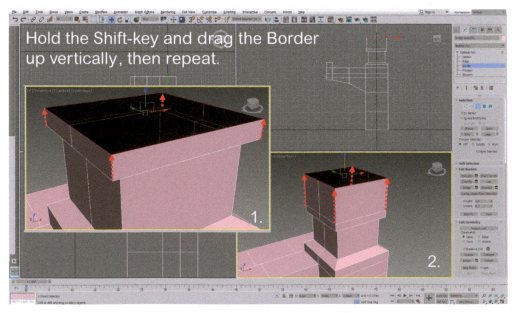

IMAGE 4.39

Switch to the Vertex sub-object level mode and to the Select and Uniform Scale tool. Select the six vertices at the top of the column, and drag them toward the center of the column, being sure to leave a small opening at the tip top. This creates an angled cap.

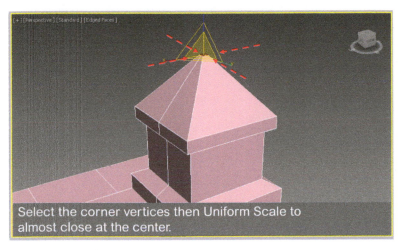

Select the corner vertices then Uniform Scale to almost close at the center.

IMAGE 4.40 (Save 4-14)

We need to weld the six vertices at the top into one vertex. If we use the Target Weld tool, it will be difficult to get the last vertex in the exact center of the column cap. We will weld them using the Weld caddy, located directly above the Target Weld button.

First, select the six vertices at the top of the column cap. Then, left-mouse click on the Weld Caddy button.

Weld Caddy

When the Weld caddy appears in the active viewport, notice the lower dark box area. It has a "Before" and "After" vertex cont. Currently, the numbers are the same. Left-mouse click in the smaller, lighter box above the dark box, and drag the mouse toward the top of the screen, increasing the numbers. As you drag upward, a spherical area of influence around the center of the selected vertices expands. As this sphere of influence expands, selected vertices are included and weld to others inside the sphere of influence. At some point, all the selected vertices will weld, and the "After" value will drop to less than the "Before" value, indicating how many vertices just got welded. In some instances, continuing to expand the sphere of influence will result in collapsing the vertices of the mesh like a black hole, distorting the mesh as it collapses. Use caution, and watch the Before and After values to control the welding.

In this case, after the "After" value number should be five less than the "Before" value number.

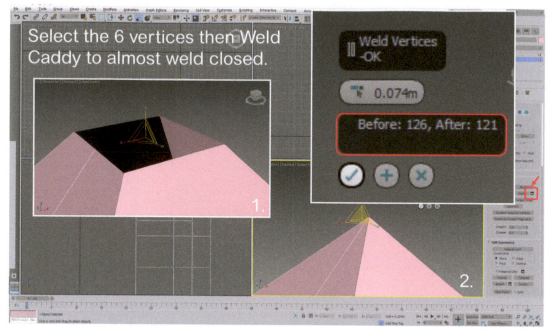

IMAGE 4.41 (Save 4-15)

The next part to model will be the side of the bridge span and the decorative shield shape in the center of the span. Rotate the viewport so that you can view the side of the bridge span. Select the two horizontal polygons shown in Polygon sub-object level mode, then using the Extrude caddy, extrude them 0.10 meter.

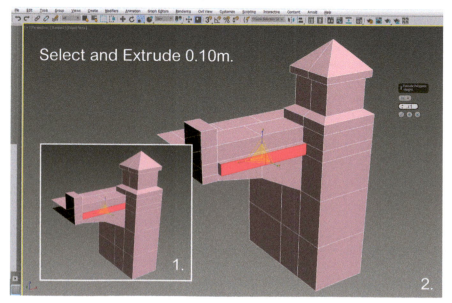

IMAGE 4.42

Switch to Vertex sub-object level mode to model the vertices to shape the decorative shield on the side. For this procedure, you can change the viewport layout to two side-by-side viewports to view the mesh better. One way to do so is to left-mouse click on the lower left-hand corner viewport template button and select the correct choice.

Change the viewport on the left to "Front" and the one on the right side to "Perspective" if they are not already set as such. Zoom in to adjust the view, using the mouse wheel, so you have a good view of the vertices that will be the shield decoration, as shown.

Using the Select and Move tool, move the vertices to form a shape similar to those in the image below. Be sure to use move vertices only in the X- and Y-axes using the red and green arrows of the gizmo, to maintain the clean alignment of vertices (not randomly placed). Keeping vertices somewhat in alignment helps when it comes to unwrapping and adding textures later.

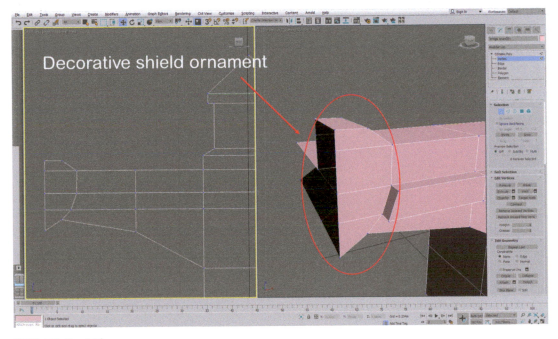

IMAGE 4.43 (Save 4-16)

Next, extrude the polygons on the outside face of the shield to 0.15 meter using the Extrude caddy in Polygon sub-object level mode.

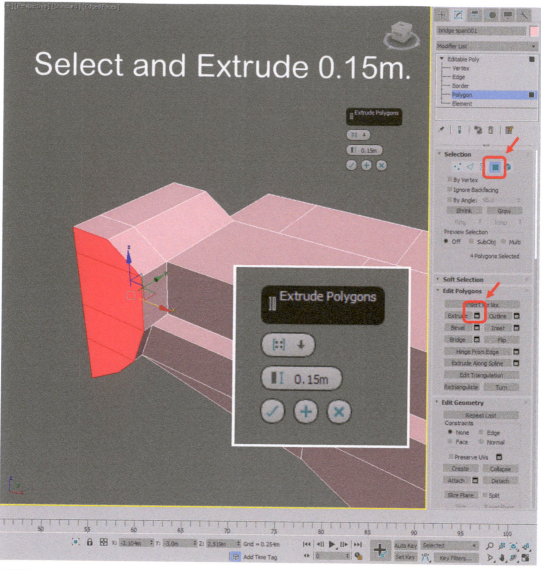

IMAGE 4.44

Rotate the viewport view to view the top of the shield decoration from the end of the span. Visually, the shield should not extend all the way over to the inside of the edge wall. Select the three polygons as shown, and delete them.

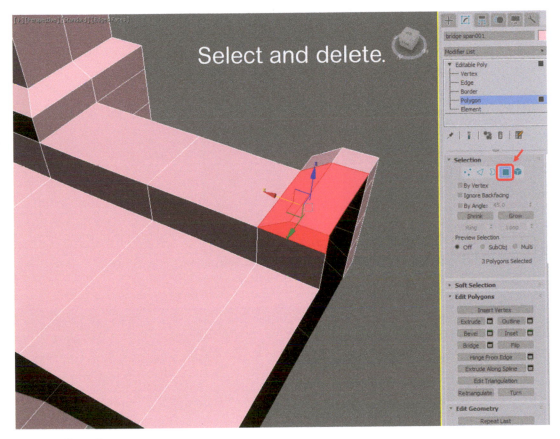

IMAGE 4.45 (Save 4-17)

To close the opening, we just created by deleting the polygons, use the Shift and Drag method of extrusion on an edge.

Switch to Edge sub-object level mode. Hold down the Shift-key on the keyboard, select the edge shown and drag it toward the shield polygons. Release the mouse and then the Shift-key. Switch to Vertex sub-object level mode, and Target Weld the corner vertices to the corresponding vertices on the back of the shield.

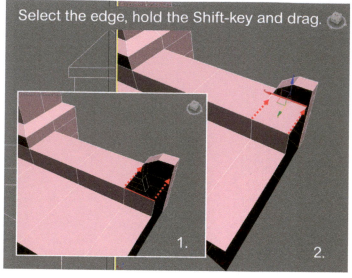

IMAGE 4.46

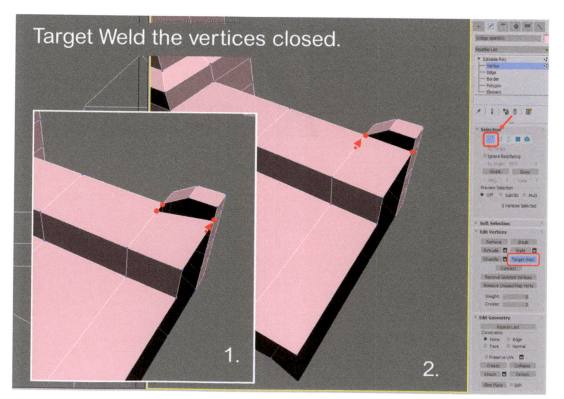

IMAGE 4.47

Next, hold down the Shift-key and select the vertical edge on the shield, and drag it in the direction of the column as shown. Release the mouse and then the Shift-key.

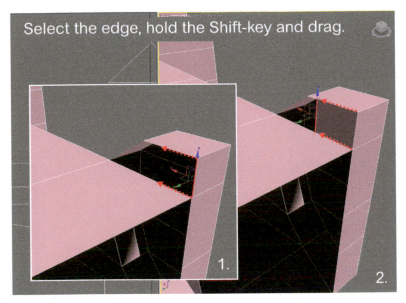

IMAGE 4.48

Target Weld the two corner vertices to the corresponding vertices of the shield to close the gap.

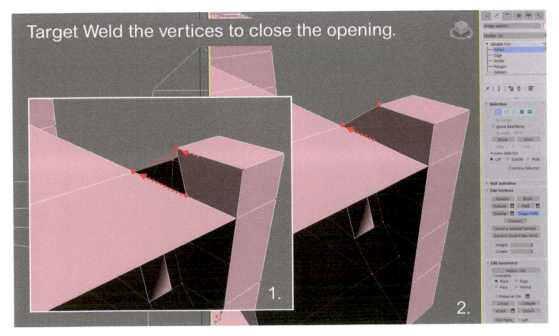

IMAGE 4.49

Select the four end polygons in Polygon sub-object level mode as shown and delete them.

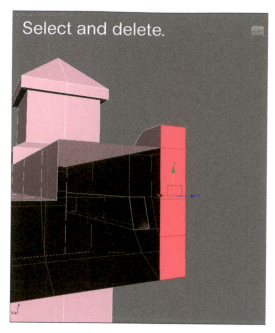

IMAGE 4.50 (Save 4-18)

Inside the mesh, notice that 3ds Max is showing two polygons occupying the same space by trying to render both, resulting in a diagonal stripped pattern. In this situation, we can leave the two polygon faces butting up against each other. There are two more at the opposite end of the decorative trim we added to the side of the span.

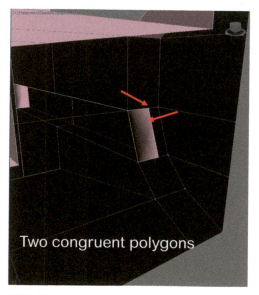

IMAGE 4.51

Switch back to the Quad 4 viewport set up using the viewport layout control in the lower left-hand corner (it is along the left side of the UI, toward the bottom). We have almost completed the modeling of the vertices and polygons. All that is left to do for this module is to use the Symmetry Modifier to fill out the mesh and create the batter at the bottom of the pier.

In Edge sub-object level mode, select an edge along the length of the roadway and add a Symmetry Modifier as you have done before.

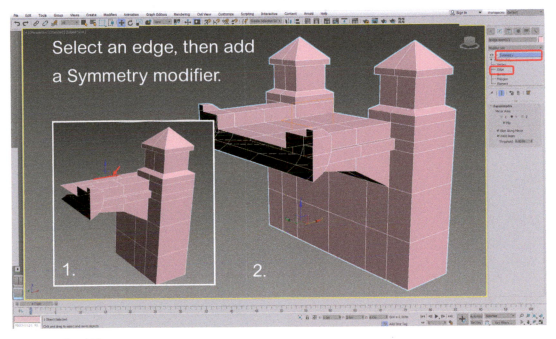

IMAGE 4.52 (Save 4-19)

Collapse the Modifier Stack in the Command Panel so that we can make an adjustment to the base vertices. Right-mouse click in the Modifier Stack, and select the "Collapse All" option. Click "Yes" on the pop-up warning window that appears.

Next, select the bottom row of vertices of the mesh in Vertex sub-option mode. Using the Select and Uniform Scale tool, left-mouse click and drag the mouse to widen the base slightly, creating the Batter as we did with the Curtain Wall. Use the X- and Y-axis handles of the gizmo to control the amount of angle you create.

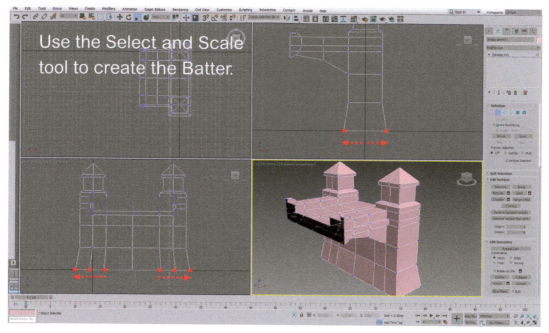

IMAGE 4.53

In Edge sub-object level mode, select an edge along the open end of the roadway and add a Symmetry Modifier. Collapse the Modifier Stack again in the Command Panel.

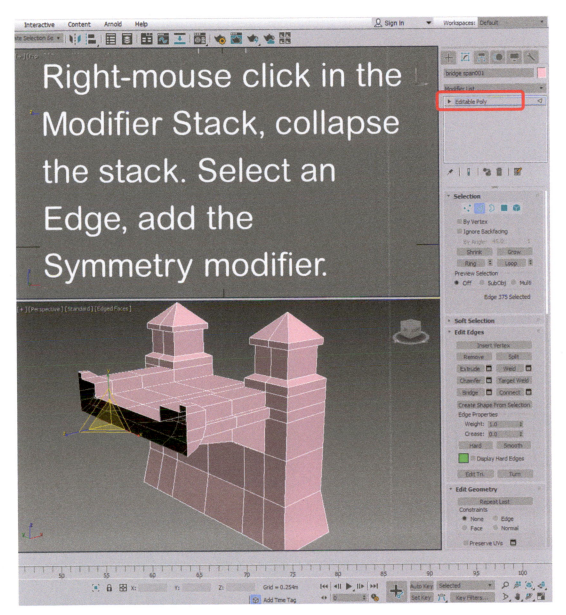

IMAGE 4.54

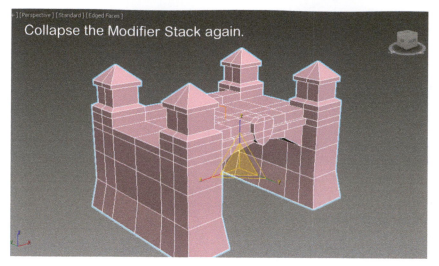

IMAGE 4.55 (Save 4-20)

From this mesh, we will detach one pier end of the mesh to create the Bridge End module. In Polygon sub-object level mode, select the polygons on the left end of the mesh, up to the span as shown. Scroll down the Command Panel, and left-mouse click the "Detach" button. When the Detach pop-up window appears, name the new mesh "Bridge End001" and click "OK."

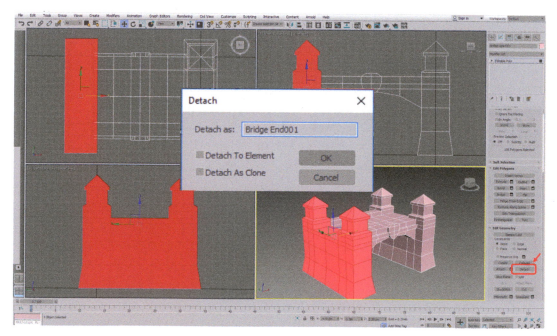

IMAGE 4.56

Toggle open the Scene Explorer. Move the new mesh, Bridge End001 to the Bridge End layer by dragging it over the Bridge End layer name.

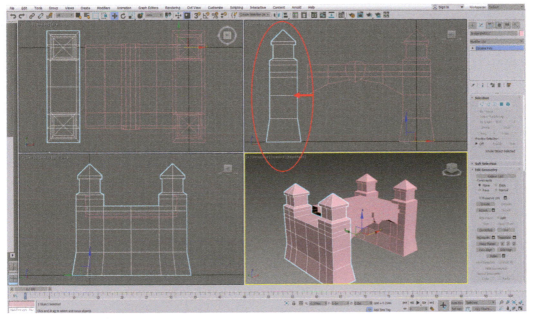

IMAGE 4.57

In the Polygon sub-object level mode, select the polygons shown below. Then, extrude them 0.25 meter using the Extrude caddy. This will create the area for the drawbridge, when we model it, to seat into when it is in the down position.

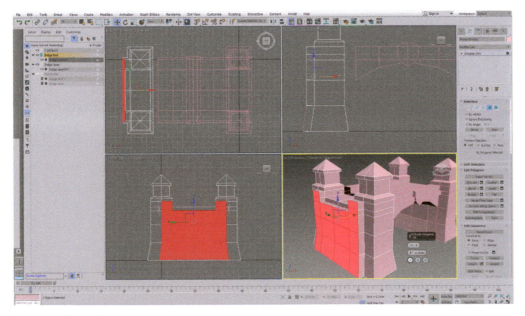

IMAGE 4.58 (Save 4-21)

When the Extrude caddy extrudes a polygon, it does so at a tangent, 90 degrees, to the face. Since the polygons of the batter are angled, the extrusion we just did occurred at an angle. We can fix the alignment, bringing the misaligned vertices back to level with the bottom of the mesh, using the "View Align" tool. In Vertex sub-object level mode, select the three rows of vertices at the bottom of the pier in the Front viewport. Right-mouse click in the Top viewport to keep the selection while changing viewports. We picked the Top viewport because that view is 90 degrees to the view of the row of selected vertices in the Front viewport. In the Command Panel, scroll down, find and select the View Align button.

The View Align Tool

The vertices will realign to be on the same plane, parallel to the plane of the second viewport selected. They move and align to a plane that is the average distance between all the selected vertices. So, you might need to move the vertices to their proper position after using the View Align tool. For the second viewport, always find and select the viewport that is 90 degrees to the viewport with the selected objects or sub-objects.

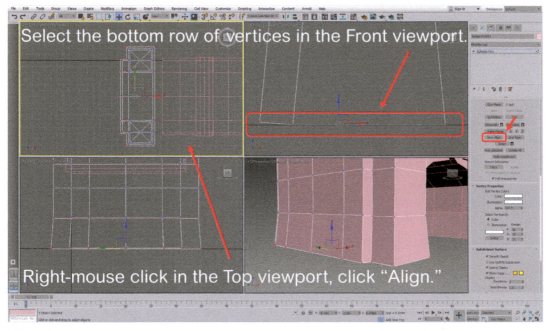

IMAGE 4.59

Repeat the realignment of the five rows of vertices above the row you just realigned to bring them parallel to the bottom row of vertices.

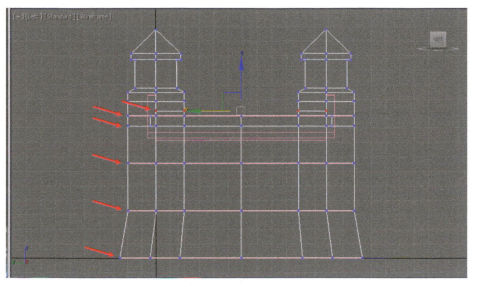

IMAGE 4.60

Next, select the vertices on the column cap, and using the Select and Move tool, drag them up a short distance as shown to make the Bridge End column taller than the Bridge Span columns.

This will help to denote the end of the bridge and give it more visual interest.

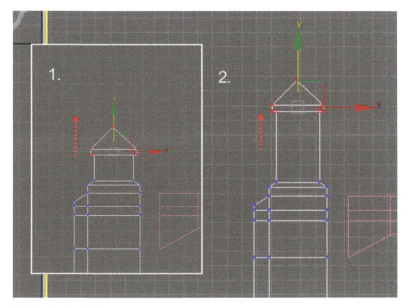

IMAGE 4.61 (Save 4-22)

In the top viewport, use the red X-axis handle of the Select and Move tool gizmo to move the Bridge End mesh a short distance from the Bridge Span module to see the open hole in the mesh.

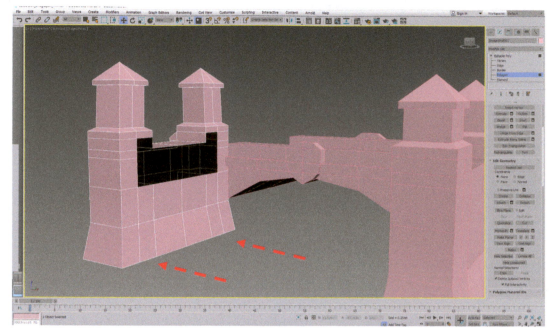

IMAGE 4.62

In Edge sub-object level mode, select the four bottom edges of the opening. Extrude them up by holding down the Shift-key and dragging the Z-axis of the Select and Move gizmo toward the top of the mesh as shown.

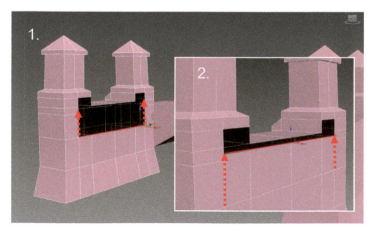

IMAGE 4.63

Use the Target Weld to close the hole along the row of vertices shown in the image. Repeat the extrude, and then Target Weld process to close the remaining holes.

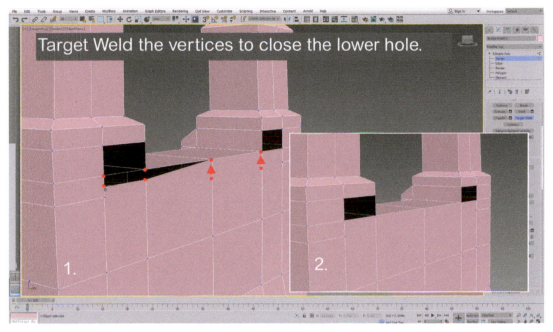

IMAGE 4.64

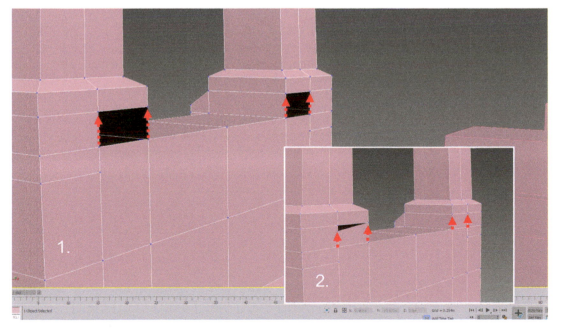

IMAGE 4.65

Toggle the Scene Explorer on. Click on the "eye" icon of the Bridge Span to hide it. Click on the Bridge End (click on "Editable Poly" if necessary) to get out of the sub-object level.

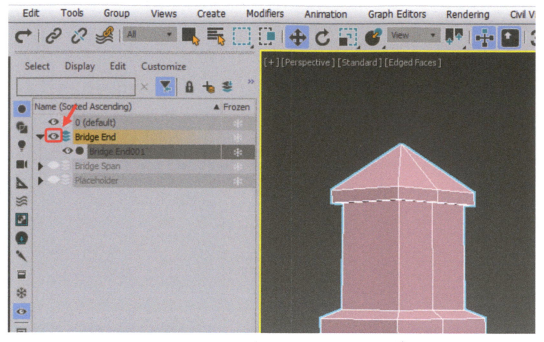

IMAGE 4.66

Notice that the gizmo for the Bridge End is off to the right of the mesh. This is because the Bridge span Pivot Point was located at 0, 0, 0. When we detached this mesh, it inherited the Pivot point location of the Bridge Span. We need to bring the two back into alignment. If we don't, when it is imported in to a game engine, it will not appear where the level developer puts it, it will be off to the side, which will be frustrating for the level developer.

To correct this issue, left-mouse click on the Hierarchy tab at the top of the Command Panel. With the Pivot button at the top selected, click on the "Affect Pivot Only" button. Using the red X-axis handle of the Select and Move gizmo in the top viewport, move the Pivot point to the center of the base of the

Bridge pier (be careful not to move it in the Y- or Z-axis). Click on the "Affect Pivot Only" button again to turn it off. Now, go to the Coordinate Display boxes on the bottom Navigation bar and enter a value of zero for the X-axis. The module mesh should jump to the 0, 0, 0 coordinates.

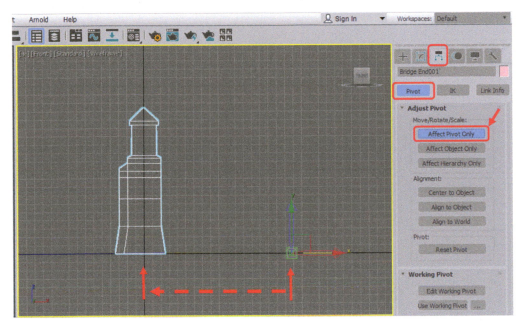

IMAGE 4.67

Toggle on the Scene Explorer if it is off, and click on the eye of the Bridge Span to un-hide it. Move the Bridge End into position at the end of the Bridge Span. The last modeling detail to do is to select the polygons on the bottom of the two meshes and delete them to reduce the polygon count. Delete the bottom polygons on the Bridge End and on the Bridge Span.

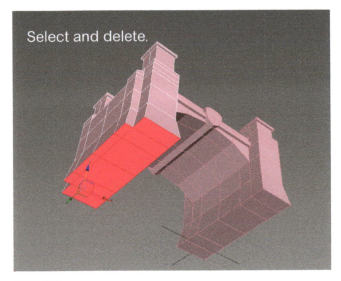

IMAGE 4.68

Save the scene. To see what the modules will look like when assembled, let's clone them using the Select and Move tool. Holding the Shift-key down first, left-mouse click on the bridge span in the front viewport. Drag the mouse to the right on the X-axis. A cloned mesh will follow the mouse. Before releasing the mouse, align the new module with the original Bridge Span to visually connect them. Release the mouse, and then a clone options pop-up window will appear. Select "Instance" as we would want any changes to occur in all copies. It also asks for a number value of how many clones you want. Enter 3 in the box, and click "OK." The clones will appear at a distance equal to what the first clone is from the original. The spans should all line up.

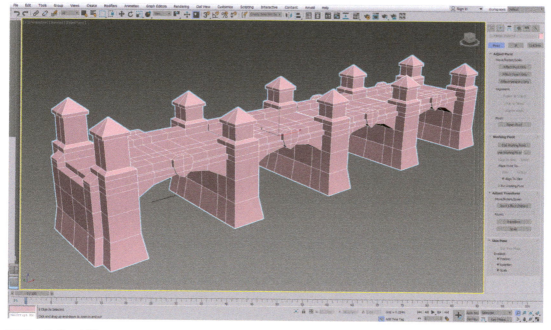

IMAGE 4.69 (Save 4-23)

Congratulations! You modeled a nice-looking bridge.

Next, we'll model the Gate House with the drawbridge. You will get repetitive reinforcement of the tools you have used and learn some new ones, including some basic animation tools.

Chapter 4 Exercise: Wall Torch

Model a wall torch to be used on interior and exterior walls. The model should be on singe mesh. The frame for the torch should have a wall-mounting plate, the torch body and a torch wick for the flame. In the game engine (Unity), a flame can be applied as a particle system. The design can be of your choice or you can follow the example I made. Be sure to do some research to define your design. To help you get started, I created a cylinder and used the Select and Scale tool to model the torch body and wick at the top. Then, I extruded the support arm from the torch body. From the support arm, I extruded and adjusted vertices to create the wall mount. When you complete Chapter 7, Unwrapping the Model, you can return to the finished wall torch model and complete the unwrapping and texturing of your model.

In the companion folder online, you will find the 3ds Max file iterations saves from when I modeled the torch and the texture file, "accessory_textures.png" for your use.

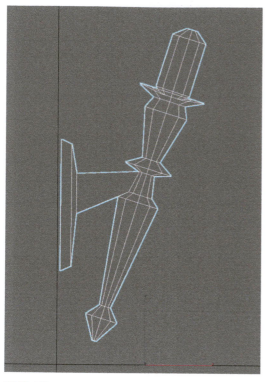

IMAGE 4.71

CHAPTER 5

Modeling the Gate House

Concepts/Skills/Tools Introduced In This Chapter

- Inset; Inset Caddy
- Chamfer Tool
- Using the Coordinates to Move Vertices, Edges, and Polygons
- Ribbon
  - Insert Loop Tool
- Hinge from Edge
- Bridge
- Snaps
- Loops; Insert Loop Tool
- Cut Tool
- Affect Pivot Only
- Cylinder
- Clear All
- Select and Link Transform Tool

- Select and Rotate Transform Tool
- Rotate Gizmo
- Hierarchy Tab
- Torus
- Link Tool
- Mirror
- Cap
- Align
- Array
- Group
- Schematic View
- Animation
  - Auto Key
  - Set Key
  - Auto Tangent
  - Keyframes
  - Time Slider
  - Time Configuration
  - Animation Controls

In this chapter, we will model the Gate House to the castle. This is the main entrance to the castle. On the front side is the drawbridge that, when lowered, the end will rest on the Bridge End module we made in the last chapter. We will model an animated drawbridge that raises and lowers. The Curtain Wall modules we made will connect to the two sides of the Gate House, providing the player access to the structure.

As with the two previous models, I have done the preliminary research and developed a sketch to work from. As before, below are three of the images that I used for reference when designing the Gate House. From the GDD, I also noted some parameters that needed be taken into consideration:

Gate House module:

> *Roadway Height from ground level: 2.5 meters*
> *Roadway width: 2 meters*
> *Module width: up to 12 meters*
> *Module length: up to 8 meters*
> *Needs to have a "batter" at the bottom of the structure*
> *Player access to Curtain Walls on sides of structure*
> *Hand-painted, shader-textured sides*
> *Polygon count: under 1000*

Drawbridge and portcullis:

> *Module width: 2 meters*
> *Module length: up to 3.5 meters*
> *Working drawbridge (ropes must be hidden on retraction into structure)*
> *Cycle animation raising: 180 seconds*
> *Vertical portcullis gate: animated, closing prior to the drawbridge closing (up)*
> *Hand-painted, shader-textured sides*
> *Polygon count: under 350*

Note: The characters in the game will be scaled to 1.15 meter; Short, stocky, Fantasy Dwarf styling. The structures in the environment should be scaled accordingly.

IMAGE 5.1

IMAGE 5.2

GATE HOUSE

B. CULBERTSON

IMAGE 5.4

The Placeholder

Let's get started with the Placeholder. Open a new scene in 3ds Max. Create a new file in 3ds Max, "lastname_bridgespan_01" in 3ds Max (my file will be named "culbertson_bridgespan_01"). We will be using the same 3ds Max set up as before (units set to meters, etc.). As with the Curtain Wall and Fixed Bridge, we need to create a placeholder for the programmers on the team. In the Scene Explorer, create four new layers: the first named "Placeholder," the second named "Gate House," the third named "Drawbridge" and the fourth named "Portcullis." The portcullis is the iron gate that drops down to close the entrance. Click on the Placeholder layer to make sure it is the active layer.

Looking at our design sketch and the GDD parameters, let's start blocking out a placeholder. From the Geometry tab of the Command Panel, select and create a "Box" in the top viewport as you did with the previous placeholders. Remember, the viewport you create an object in determines the orientation of the object's length, width and height. For the directions in this text to correspond correctly with your work, read carefully to make sure you create objects in the same viewport as I do. Change the parameter values in the Command Panel for the box to match those in the image below, and then center the box at the 0, 0, 0 coordinates for X-, Y- and Z-axes, by typing in the value boxes on the lower navigation bar.

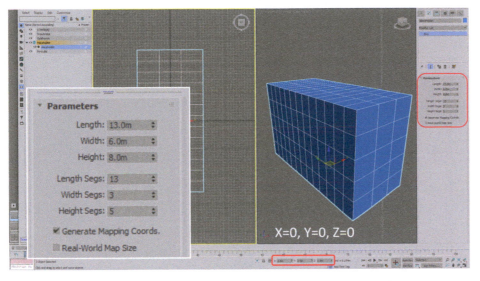

IMAGE 5.5 (Save 5-1)

Looking at the sketch of our model, the Gate House has two tower-like structures flanking the main entrance section. Convert the box to an Editable Poly, and rename it "placeholder."

Select the vertices as shown in the Top viewport. Note, I have changed to a two-viewport template. Using the Scale and Uniform Scale tool, widen the vertices along the X-axis to create the tower shapes.

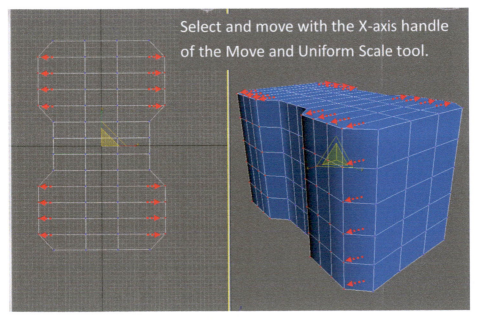

IMAGE 5.6

Next, rotate the viewport so that the front is oriented into view. Select the row of polygons in the middle as shown. Widen the row as in the image to allow a wider front entrance.

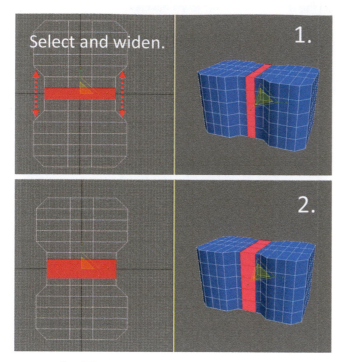

IMAGE 5.7 (Save 5-2)

Select the two polygons on the front side of the mesh, and extrude them -1.0 meter to create an indication of a front entrance door.

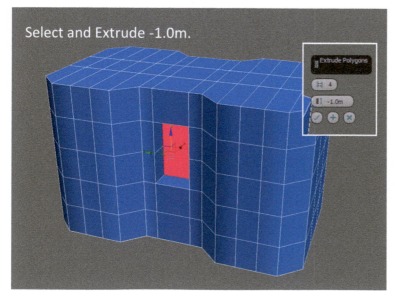

IMAGE 5.8

Rotate the viewport to get a good view of the top, and select the vertices along the front and back. Extrude them 1.0 meter to create a raised wall.

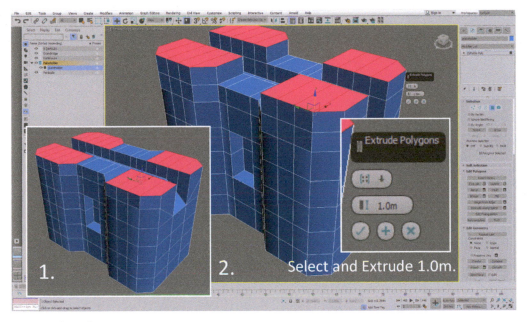

IMAGE 5.9 (Save 5-3)

The player will be able to move from the Curtain Wall top walkway onto the top of the Gate House. We will need a ramp for access since the Gate House is taller. To create a ramp on each end, Target Weld the vertices shown.

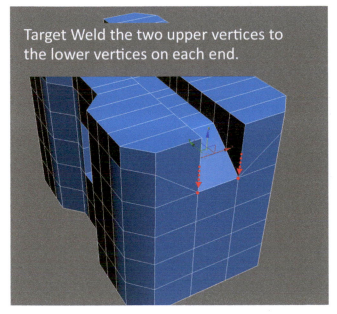

IMAGE 5.10

Lastly, select the polygons on the top and extrude them 1.0 meter to finish roughing out of the tower. This will complete the roughing out of the placeholder.

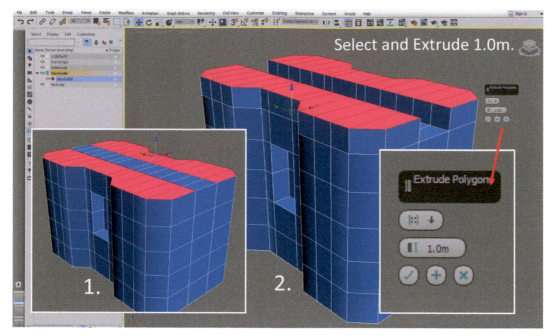

IMAGE 5.11

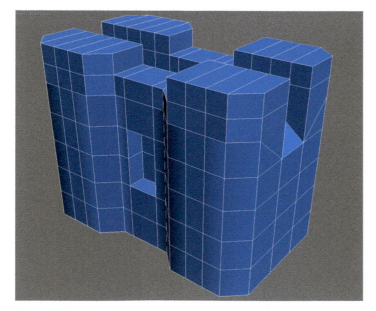

IMAGE 5.12 (Save 5-4)

The Gate House

In the last two chapters, you've modeled the Curtain Wall and the Fixed Bridge. Along the way, the directions have been very specific and detailed. There has been a lot of repetition of the procedures. Did you notice as we made this placeholder, I didn't give you detailed step-by-step instructions? That was on purpose. You should be familiar enough with the basic procedures that we have covered in the previous two projects, for which providing full details shouldn't be necessary. For example, if I ask you to select a polygon, you should automatically know you need to be in the Polygon sub-object level mode to select a polygon. If I ask you to "click" on something, assume it is a left-mouse click unless stated otherwise. For new procedures, I'll try to provide step-by-step details.

To start the Gate House module, switch to the Gate House layer in the Scene Explorer (open the Scene Explorer with the toggle icon button on the top tool bar). In the top viewport, create a box with the parameters as shown in the image below.

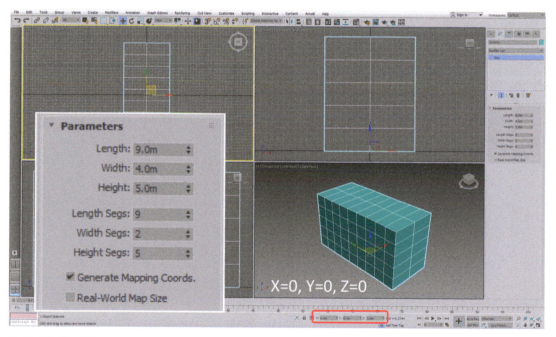

IMAGE 5.13 (Save 5-5)

Toggle the Scene Explorer closed using the Scene Explorer button icon on the Main Tool Bar to maximize the usable work space for modeling. This box will be one quarter of the building. We will use the Symmetry modifier to fill out the building when we finish the modeling of the quarter section. Right-click on the box, and convert it to an Editable Poly.

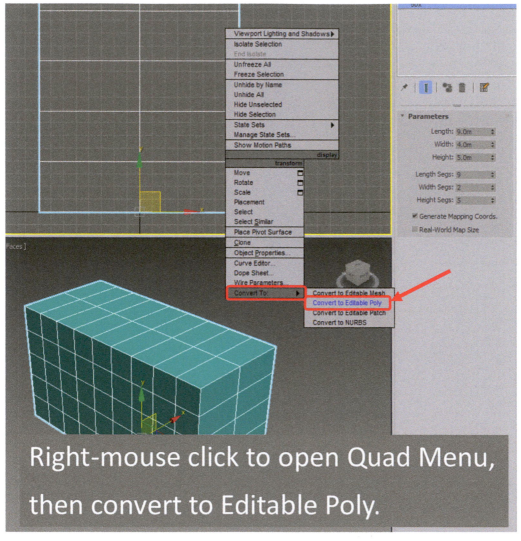

IMAGE 5.14

In the top viewport, select the four columns of vertices on the mesh as shown.

We will move these to create the tower part of the building. We could move the vertices using the Select and Move tool to an approximate location by the eye. However, using the Coordinate Display boxes on the bottom navigation bar, we can move them with more control. In the X-axis box, type in a value of −3.0.

The vertices will move to the new location, creating the desired shape. When entering new coordinates to move something, remember you are entering a value relative to the object's current coordinates from the origin point, not necessarily from the object's World Coordinates, from the origin point.

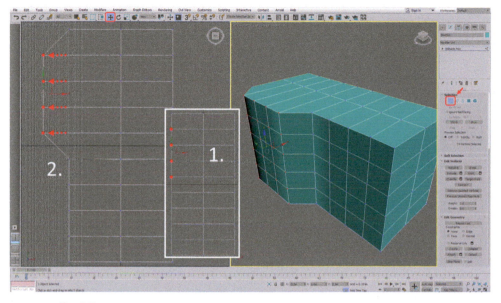

IMAGE 5.15 (Save 5-6)

After moving the vertices out from the wall, you might notice that the wall edges are not sharp/crisp. Since we used a primitive to start the module, 3ds Max, by default, will use smooth edges. To make them sharp, select the whole mesh while in Polygon sub-object level mode. Scroll down the command panel to find, and select the "Clear All" button in the "Polygon Smoothing Groups" section. This will remove all the smoothing associated with the polygons.

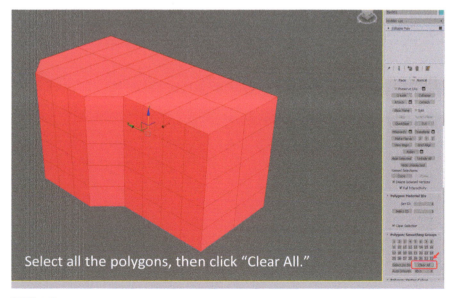

Select all the polygons, then click "Clear All."

IMAGE 5.16

Next, we'll create the wall on the top of the building. In the Top viewport, select the polygons on top of the box as shown. In the Command Panel, scroll down and select the Inset caddy to the right of the Inset button. The caddy will appear in the active viewport on top of the object. The top drop-down list box of the caddy is to apply the inset to the selected polygons as a group or as individual polygons. In our case, "Group," the default setting, is the correct setting. In the next box, the Inset Amount box, change the value 0.5 meter. The Inset tool creates new edges within the polygon, parallel to the border of each polygon selected or inside the outside border of a group of polygons. Click on the green check mark to accept the inset.

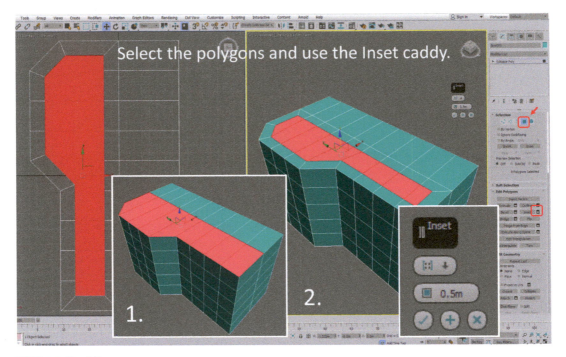

IMAGE 5.17 (Save 5-7)

Now, select the polygons on the end of the mesh as shown.

This is the end of the building that will be the centerline for the Symmetry modifier. The end of the inset of the wall will create short double wall when we extrude it up, creating a divider along the wall. To avoid the hassle of removing it and remodeling the area, let's remove it now. Delete the selected polygons after selecting with the Delete-key on the keyboard. Deleting the extra row of polygons was planned for in the setup.

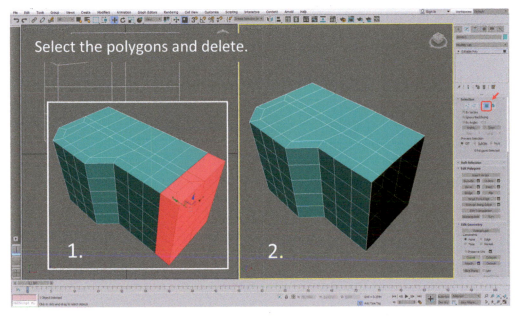

IMAGE 5.18

Change the polygon selection to the ones shown, and extrude them 1.0 meter using the Extrude caddy.

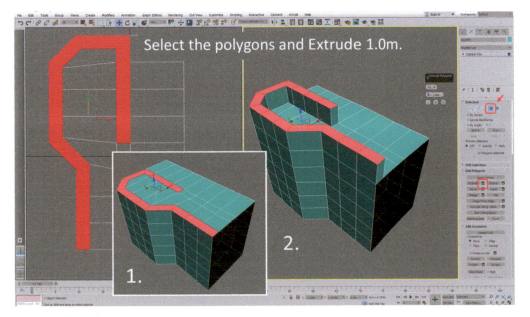

IMAGE 5.19 (Save 5-8)

Rotate the perspective viewport to view the back of the mesh. By extruding the selected polygons shown in the image, –3.0 meters, you will create the interior of the building. Remember to select the green check mark to accept the extrusion.

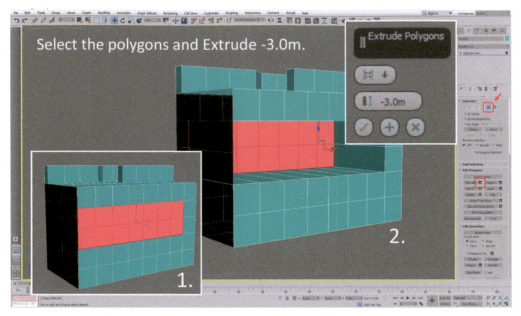

IMAGE 5.20

Select the end polygons shown, and delete them. Removing them will keep the room open as one large room when we use the Symmetry modifier later. Next, select all the polygons remaining on the back side of the mesh and delete them. This will allow the Symmetry modifier to work correctly later when we copy the front of the structure to the back.

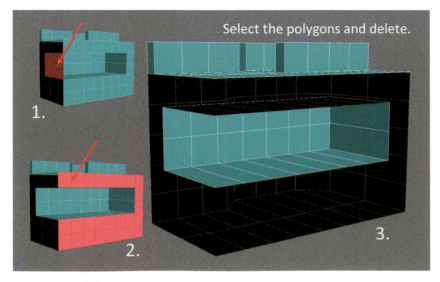

IMAGE 5.21 (Save 5-9)

While we are working on the back side of the mesh, let's create the ramp that will allow the player to access the top walkway on the Curtain Wall when the modules are assembled. The height of the Curtain Wall walkway is 6 meters up from the X-axis. This module has been pre-planned, so we can lower the needed polygons to meet the 6-meter height.

Rotate the viewport to the view as shown to easily select the four polygons shown in Image 5.23. We are going to use a new tool to rotate these polygons to create a ramp for the player to run up and down. While still in Polygon sub-object level mode and with the four polygons selected, scroll down the Command Panel to find the "Hinge from Edge" caddy box next to the "Hinge from Edge" button in the Edit Polygons section and select it. Looking at the caddy, the top value box is the setting for the angle of rotation you want the polygons to rotate. Enter "−14.0" degrees for our ramp. The middle value box is to specify the number of polygons each extruded side is subdivided. Leave this setting at "1." The bottom value box is to select which edge will be the pivot point for the rotation. After a selection is made, the circle next to "Pick Hinge" in the value box will be filled in and the edge ID number will be shown. Click on the "Pick Hinge" value box, and then left-mouse click on the edge indicated in the Image. Sometimes this can be a frustrating tool to work with, getting the hinge orientation to reflect what you are trying to do. Remember, select the polygon(s) first, then the "Pick Hinge" value box, and then the hinge edge.

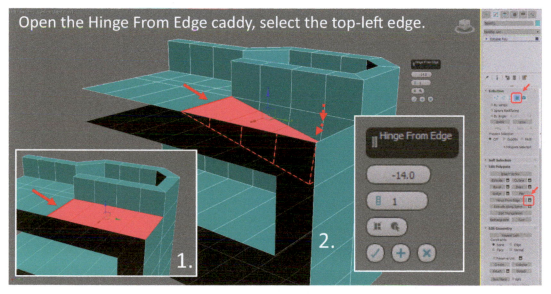

IMAGE 5.22

121

Next, remove the polygons along the back centerline along the new ramp and the two polygons on the end. Besides needing to be deleted, they open up the view of the ramp. Select and delete them as shown.

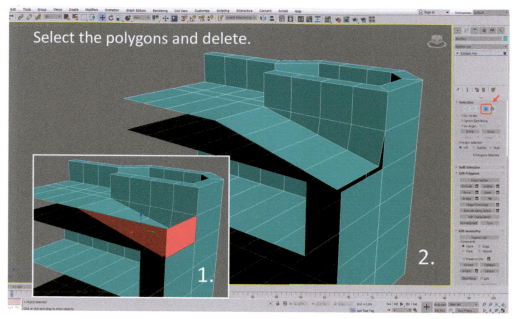

IMAGE 5.23

To finish the ramp, Target Weld the vertices at the bottom of the ramp to the end wall (in that order to keep the end wall straight) to close the gap created.

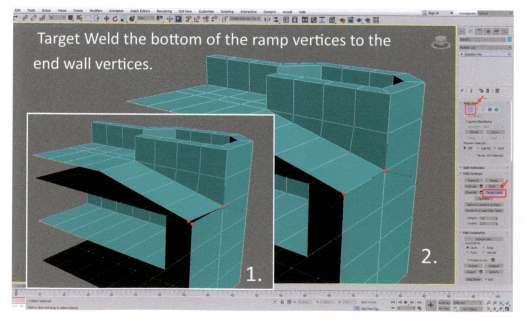

IMAGE 5.24 (Save 5-10)

Next, let's finish the structure for the front of the mesh. Rotate the viewport to select the two polygons as shown. This will be the tower arrow slot window. Narrow on the outside, and wide on the inside. Select the Inset caddy that we used to create the wall on top of the mesh. Set the value of the inset to 0.25 meter.

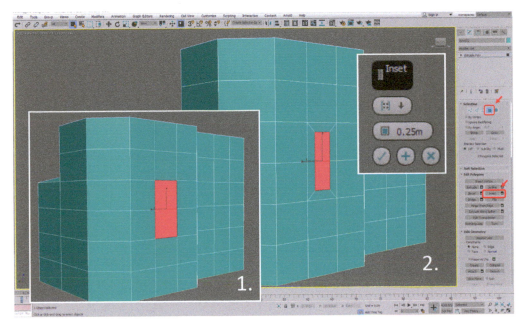

IMAGE 5.25

To create a bevel window frame, change the inset polygons in the X-Coordinate Display value box on the bottom navigation bar from −3.0 to −2.9. When complete, delete the two polygons to create the window opening.

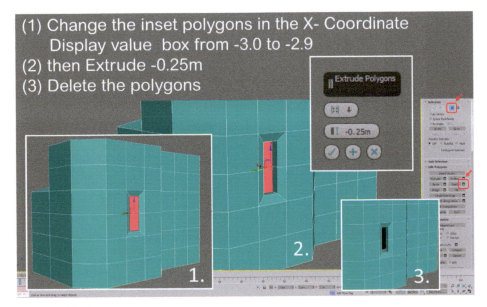

IMAGE 5.26 (Save 5-11)

Now, let's create the inside of the window. Rotate the viewport to view the inside room, and select the two polygons shown and delete them.

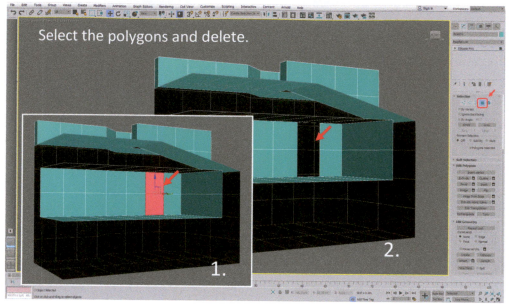

IMAGE 5.27

We need to narrow the distance between the two window openings and then close the gap with polygons. In the Command Panel, change to the Border sub-object level mode (the icon button between the Polygon and the Edge icons) in the Selection section. Next, left-mouse click on the border edge of the inside window opening. Change the X-Coordinate Display value box on the bottom navigation bar from −1.0 to −2.5. This will narrow the distance between the openings.

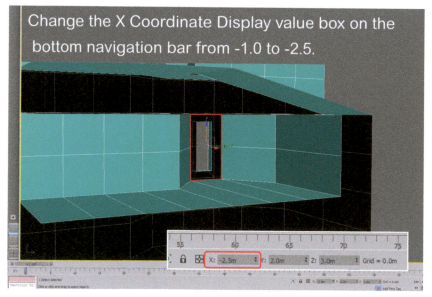

IMAGE 5.28

While still in the Border sub-object level mode, the inside window border selected, hold the CTRL-key and left-mouse click on the border of the outer window opening, so that both are selected. We can connect these two borders with polygons in one-step using the Bridge tool. Scroll down the Command Panel to find and select the Bridge button in the Edit Borders section. The polygons will bridge the gap immediately.

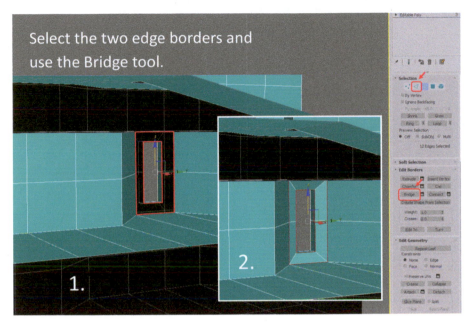

IMAGE 5.29 (Save 5-12)

We should widen the window frame inside to allow the player more room to get close to the opening. Select the six vertices on the inside window frame, and using the Move and Uniform Scale tool, widen the distance between the vertical rows as shown.

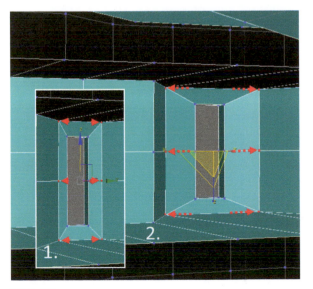

IMAGE 5.30

Rotate the viewport back to the front view. Select the polygon at the base of the window frame. In the Z-Coordinate Display box, change the value to 2.5 meters. This will raise the bottom sill, a design detail.

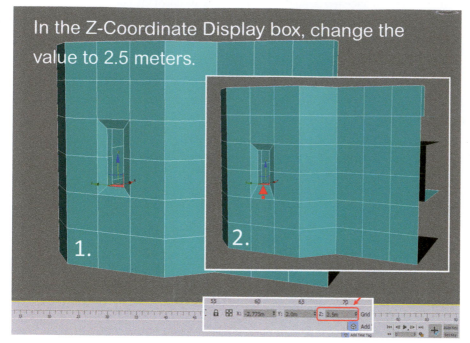

IMAGE 5.31

We will next create the entrance doorway. Select the four polygons as shown (on the outside wall and the inside room wall), and delete them. This creates the opening for the doorway.

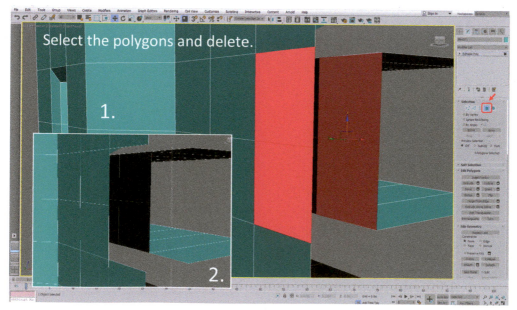

IMAGE 5.32

We'll create the door frame, with a look similar to the window frame. Select the four edges created by the deleted polygons on the outside wall. Then, use the extrude caddy to extrude the edges −0.25 meter.

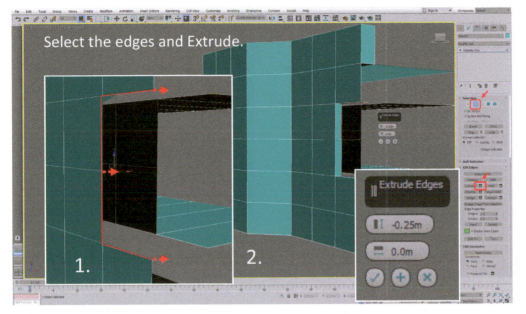

IMAGE 5.33

Select the vertical edges only, and change the value of the Y-coordinate in the Coordinate Display value box from 2.50 to 2.75 to create an angled frame. Select the top edge at the top of the doorway, and change the value of the Z-Coordinate Display value box from 4.0 to 3.75.

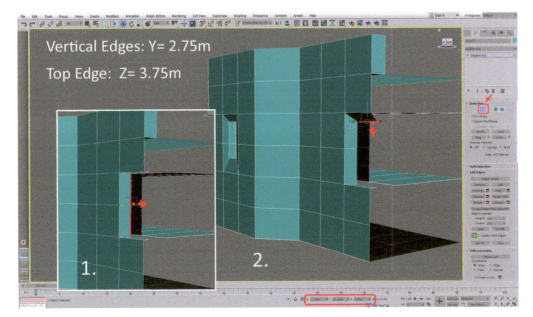

IMAGE 5.34

We'll create a straight, flat part of the door frame next. Select the four edges as shown. Hold down the Shift-key, and drag the X-axis handle of the Select and Move tool gizmo toward the edges of the inside room as shown. We chose not to use the Extrude caddy as the extrusions would come off the edges at a 90-degree angle to the polygons, the wrong direction.

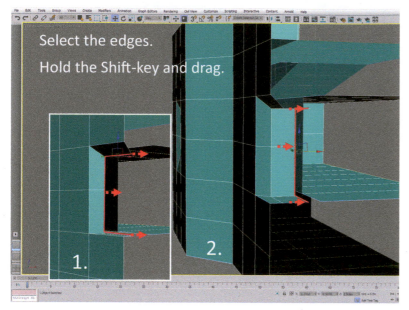

IMAGE 5.35

Now, while still in the Edge sub-object level mode, hold down the Shift-key and select the four edges of the room door opening, so all eight edges of the two openings are selected. Then, use the Bridge tool to connect the edges, closing the gap between the inside and the outside.

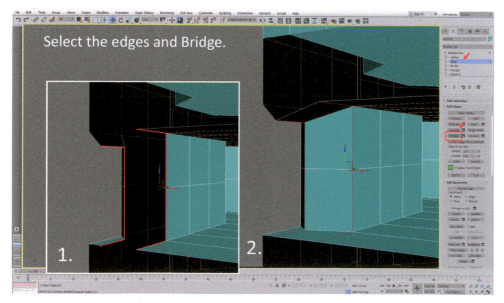

IMAGE 5.36 (Save 5-13)

The vertical wall created by the Bridge tool might be slightly out of "square," not perpendicular to the door opening. In the top viewport, adjust the three vertices on the room side of the polygon by hand, with the Select and Move tool if necessary, to get closer to being square.

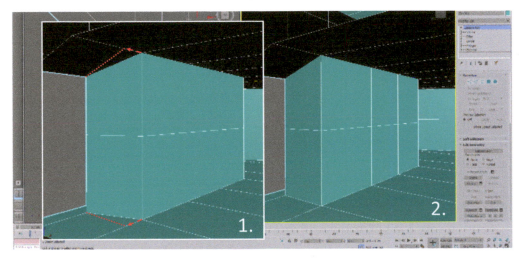

IMAGE 5.37 (Save 5-14)

There is a good amount of space between the ceiling of the interior room and the roof. We can create a cathedral style ceiling in the interior by selecting the centerline vertices and raising them to just below the roof polygons. Move the five on the left first together, and then move the last two individually into alignment, parallel with the ramp above it to create a bevel.

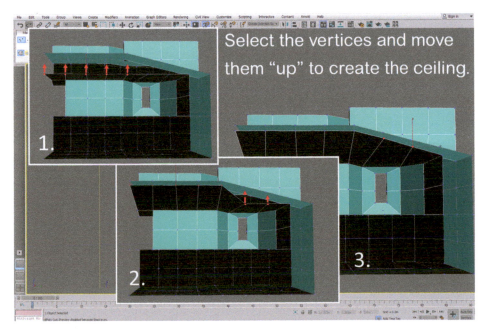

IMAGE 5.38 (Save 5-15)

Tilt the viewport so that you can see the ceiling polygons in color. Notice some of the polygons appear to be two triangles (the colors are slightly different). This indicates that the four vertices that make up this polygon are not in the same plane. As a result, the polygon is trying to bend or twist, creating two triangles.

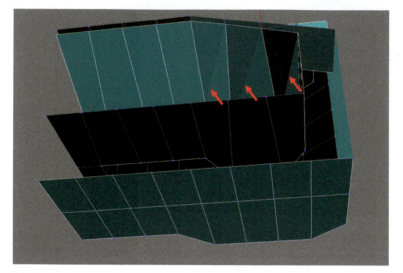

 IMAGE 5.39

This will be an issue when we unwrap and texture this polygon later. The polygon needs to be divided into two triangles that will work well for unwrapping. Rotate the viewport slightly in a horizontal direction to reveal the issue if you are having difficulty seeing the triangles. To fix it now, let's use a new tool, the "Cut" tool.

The Cut Tool

The Cut tool will create an edge between two vertices of a face or polygon. The key to using this tool successfully is to always use Snaps to control it. Right-mouse click on the Snaps Toggle tool icon on the top toolbar. A small pop-up window will open. In the Snaps tab of the window, select the "Clear All" button to reset the options. Then, select "Midpoint" and "Endpoint." Close the pop-up window with the x-out button in the top right corner. You just set up the Snaps, but they are not turned on. Select the Snaps Toggle icon to turn it on. The mouse cursor will now have a yellow wireframe around it indicating that the snaps are on. Now, you are ready to use the Cut tool. In Vertex sub-object level mode, scroll down the Command Panel to find and select the Cut tool button.

With the Snaps on, you should only be able to select a corner vertex on an endpoint of a segment or a midpoint of a segment. This prevents you from accidentally creating a vertex that is not on a segment, which the Cut tool can do with the Snaps off. When working without the Snaps turned off, especially in the

Perspective viewport, you might click on what you think is an endpoint, but, in virtual reality, you might be creating a vertex located 10 meters away. You will discover the mistake when you change viewports and see a vertex out of place. Remember, it's 3D!

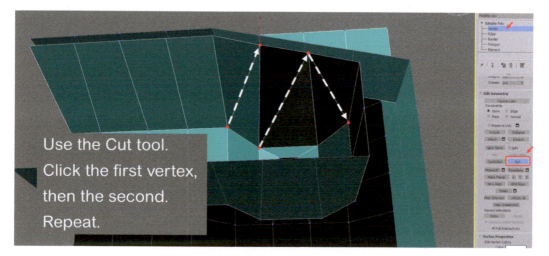

IMAGE 5.40

So, set the Snaps settings as described above and turn on the snaps. Using the Cut tool, click on the first vertex in the corner of the polygon, and then the one in the opposite corner as shown. This will create an edge, separating the two triangles, fixing the issue. Repeat the procedure on the three other polygons in the ceiling exhibiting the "bending" polygon issue. This will finish the interior room. Remember to turn off the Snaps!

IMAGE 5.41 (Save 5-16)

We will finish the top wall modeling next, adding the embrasures and merlons. Select the polygons shown in the image below along the top of the wall.

Next, open the ribbon tool bar by clicking on the ribbon Toggle icon on the top tool bar. In the main Modelling tab, find the "Insert" button in "Loops" and select it once. This added a row of edges along the center of the selected polygons and continued them until it hit an end edge. This row of edges will allow us to get creative with the merlons after we extrude them.

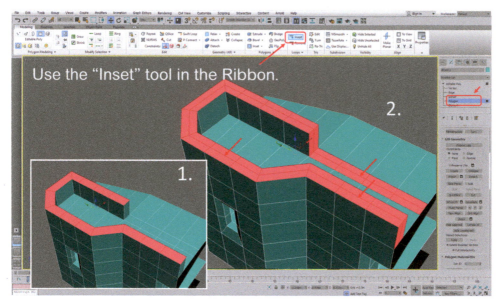

IMAGE 5.42

Select the pairs of polygons as shown in the image. These will be the merlons. Once selected, extrude them 0.5 meter.

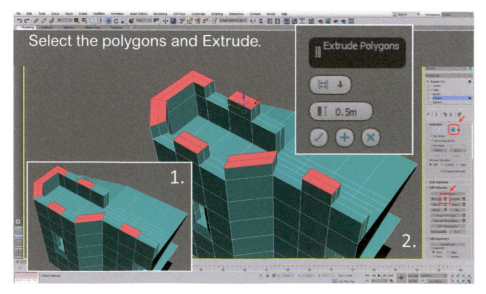

IMAGE 5.43 (Save 5-17)

The next step will create a bevel on the embrasures, the areas between the merlons. Select the horizontal row of edges on the outside walls only as shown. In the Z-coordinate value box, change the value from 6.0 to 5.5 meters. This will create the bevels.

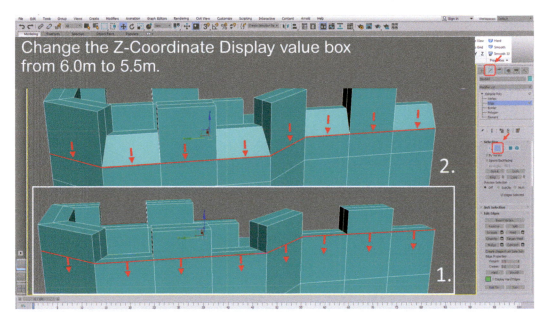

IMAGE 5.44

Our sketch shows a peaked top for the merlons. Select all the center edges along the top of each merlon together, and using the Select and Move tool, drag the Z-axis handle of the gizmo up to create a peak. Move it so that the angle is about the same as the embrasure angles below them.

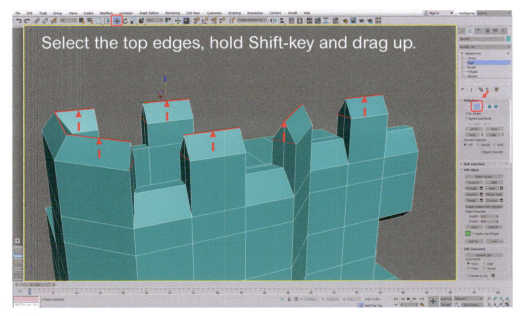

IMAGE 5.45

The peaks create a strong visual dominance, too hard of an edge. While the peak edges are still selected, find the "Chamfer" tool caddy in the Command Panel Edit Edges section, to the right of the Chamfer tool button and select it. Set the Edge Chamfer Amount vale box to 0.05 meter. This will flatten the point a bit, so it is not a sharp knife-edge. "Chamfer" is the rounding of a sharp edge or corner by adding segments.

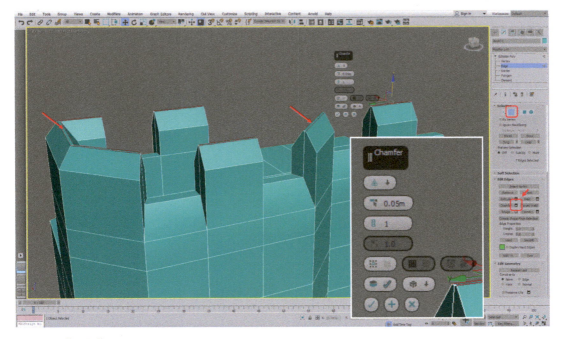

IMAGE 5.46 (Save 5-18)

To finish the tower look, we need to make the top of the tower a bit taller. Select the vertices shown in the image (it might be easiest to select in the left viewport). We want to just raise the merlons and embrasures on the tower part. In the Z-coordinate value box on the lower navigation bar, change the value by adding 0.50 meter to whatever number it is currently. My "Z" value was 6.52 meters, so I made it 7.02 meters, raising the vertices.

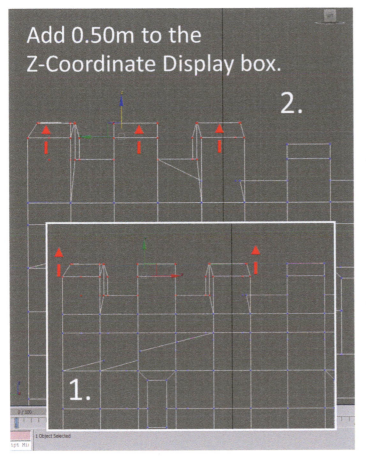

Add 0.50m to the
Z-Coordinate Display box.

2.

1.

IMAGE 5.47

Now, select the three polygons on the walkway as shown. In the Z-Coordinate Display box, change the number from 6.0 to 6.5 meters. This will create a ramp and keep the walking surface rise even with the height added to the tower wall.

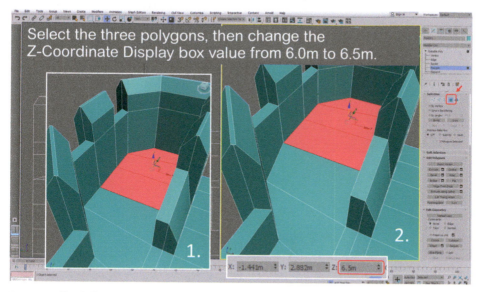

IMAGE 5.48 (Save 5-19)

Before we leave the roof area, we need to adjust the width of the ramp that leads to the Curtain Wall. It needs to be less than 2 meters wide in the final structure, so it should be less than 1 meter in this quarter mesh. Switch to the Windows/Crossing selection tool on the top tool bar. In the Top viewport, drag the selection box over the middle wall on the top of the roof as shown. Because of the mesh vertex positions, only the parts we want to move will be selected. Change the X-Coordinate Display value box to 1.0 meter. Since the coordinate is from the center of the wall, we will be safely within the 1-meter limit.

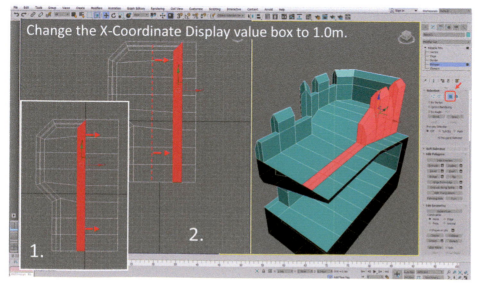

IMAGE 5.49 (Save 5-20)

We will need to model a place for the Drawbridge to go so it looks like it is part of the Gate House structure. On the front side, select the five polygons shown and extrude them 0.75 meter.

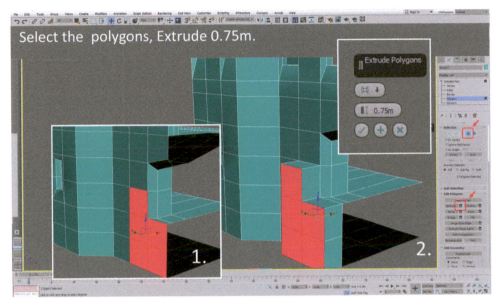

IMAGE 5.50

The drawbridge will be located on top of the vertical row of polygons closest to the centerline. Select the three polygons next to those as shown, and extrude them 0.50 meter.

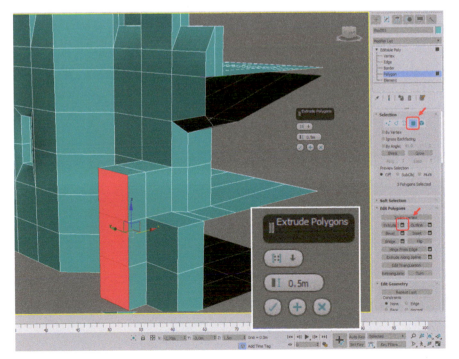

IMAGE 5.51

Select the polygon as shown at the top of the extrusion. Change the Z-Coordinate Display box value setting from 3.0 to 2.25 meters, creating a bevel that relates to the beveled faces on the top wall.

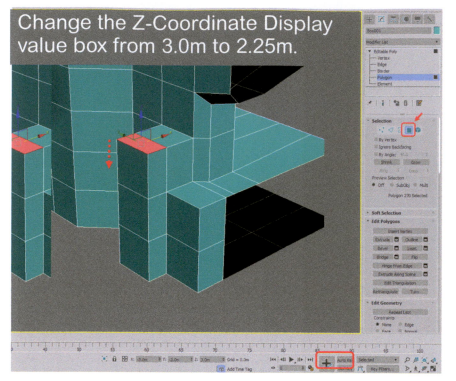

IMAGE 5.52

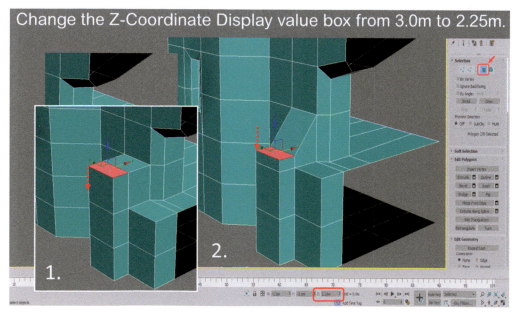

IMAGE 5.53 (Save 5-21)

Select the two polygons on the centerline as shown, and delete them.

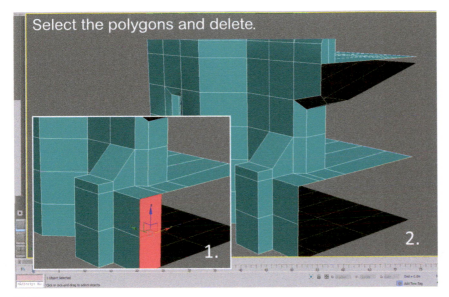

IMAGE 5.54

When we originally started to make the Gate House, the measurements I gave you were 0.5 meter, too short for the box we started with. Now is a good time to fix the mistake. Rotate the view to the bottom of the mesh, and select all the polygons there. In the Z-coordinate value box, change the value to −0.50 meter to lengthen the bottom row of vertices. This will align the bottom of the structure with the bottom of the fixed bridge, so the drawbridge will be the same height as the roadway. After adding the −0.50 meter to the mesh, it now extends below the X-axis on the viewport grid. Let's move the mesh back up to the X-axis so that the bottom row of vertices for all the modules we make will be on the same plane. Select the mesh, and change the Z-axis value box for the coordinates to 0.50 to raise it.

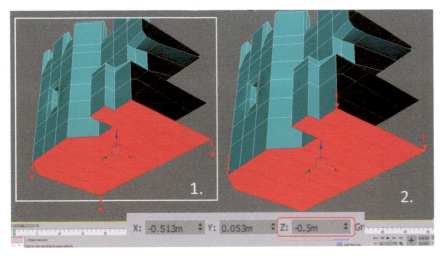

IMAGE 5.55

You might have noticed that some polygons of the model have smoothing on them. To get back to the crisp edges, select the entire mesh in the Polygon sub-object level mode. Scroll down the Command Panel to find the "Clear All" button, and select it.

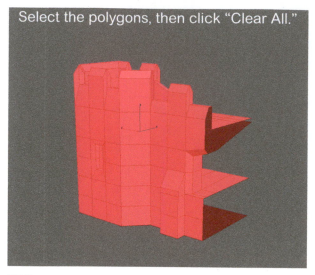

IMAGE 5.56

Select the bottom polygons as shown below. The selected polygons are not needed for the model, and the floor is raised; so, delete them to reduce the polygon count.

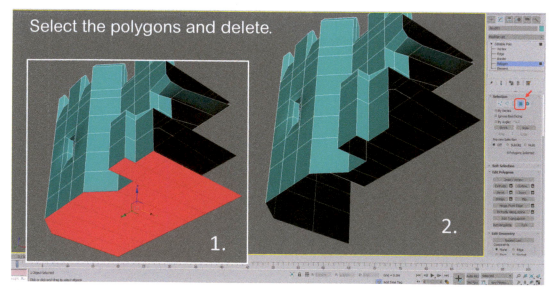

IMAGE 5.57

In this view, you can see two polygons on the top end wall that need to be deleted for the Symmetry modifier to work correctly. Select and delete them.

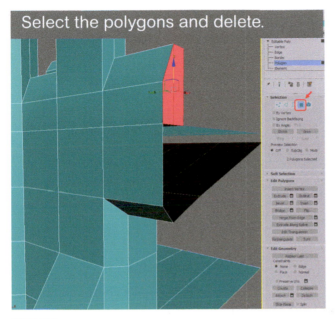

IMAGE 5.58

There are a few minor things to wrap up. To complete the quadrant of the gate house, the arch of the front entrance needs to be created. Select the two vertices that will be on the top of the door frame, the centerline of the symmetry as shown. Change the value currently shown in the Z-coordinate box to 5.0 meters, and then adjust the lower vertices slightly to make the two edges leading to the vertices parallel.

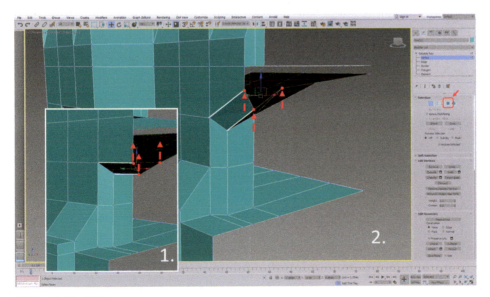

IMAGE 5.59 (Save 5-22)

One last thing we should do is check our polygon count. To check the polygon count, left-mouse click on the last icon on the right at the top of the Command Panel, the Utilities tab. Next, select the "More" button. From the pop-up window, select Polygon Counter. In the Polygon Counter, switch to Count Polygons.

My mesh has 253 polygons. This is one quarter of the total it will be after we use the Symmetry modifier. So, my final Gate House structure will have 4 × 253 or 1012 polygons. I'm 12 polygons over the 1,000-polygon limit stated in the GDD for this part of the module. Let's look at the model to find ways to reduce the polygon count.

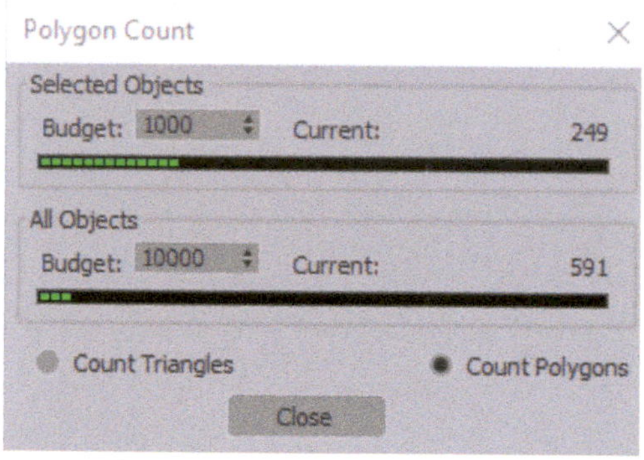

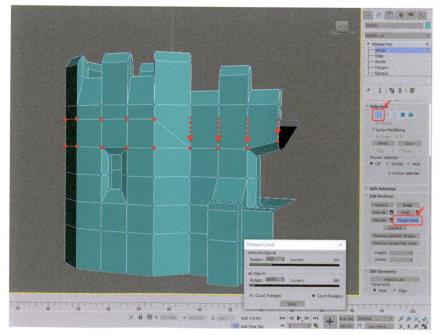

IMAGE 5.60

So, we need to reduce at least three polygons from the quarter model. On the roof, there are some we can reduce. I'm going to Target Weld the extras together, making sure that the reductions do not change the shape of the model.

There is an entire horizontal row of polygons above the outside window that extends around to the ramp that can be reduced.

IMAGE 5.61

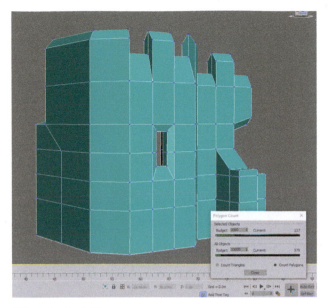

IMAGE 5.62 (Save 5-23)

After eliminating those unnecessary polygons, the polygon count has dropped to from 253 to 237 for the quarter section. That will give us a total of 948 for the full mesh, below the 1,000-polygon limit. It doesn't seem like much, but it will help the game performance. We could go back and look for more possible reductions to further reduce the count. Feel free to on your own.

Save an iteration of the Gate House at this point in case changes to the structure need to be made later. Now, let's complete the structure. Select an edge along the X-axis centerline, and then add a Symmetry modifier. Find the correct "Mirror Axis."

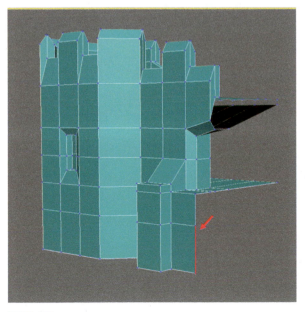

IMAGE 5.63

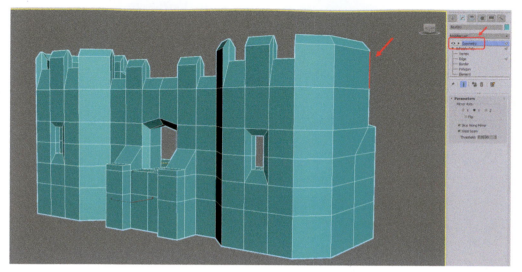

In the modifier Stack of the Command Panel, switch back to the Edge sub-object level mode and select a vertex on the back side along the Y-axis centerline. Add another Symmetry modifier.

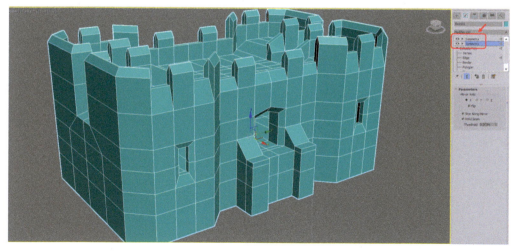

IMAGE 5.65 (Save 5-24)

Next, we will add the drawbridge to the Gate House.

The Drawbridge

Toggle open the Scene Explorer. Change the active layer from the Gate House layer to the Drawbridge layer. Now, we will be working on that layer only.

In the top viewport, create a box to start the drawbridge element with the parameters shown in the image below.

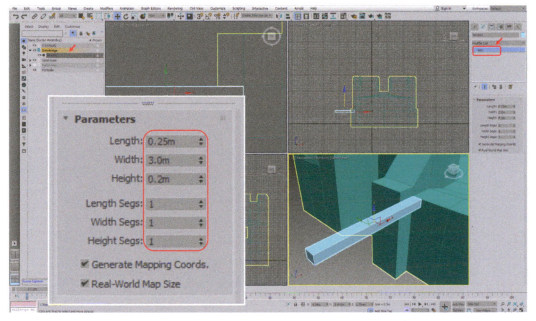

IMAGE 5.66

Add width to the drawbridge by extruding the side polygon 1.75 meter as shown. Then, extrude another 0.25 meter to keep the symmetry of the mesh. The Drawbridge will now be 2.0 meters wide, the width of the opening we created for it on the Bridge End module and on the Gate House.

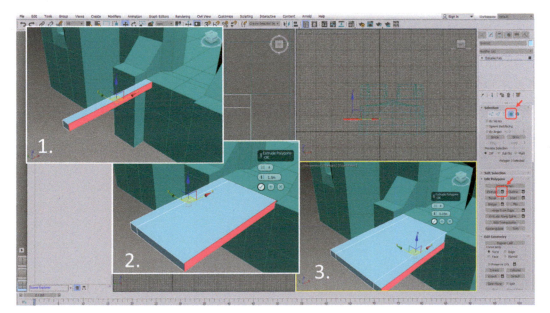

IMAGE 5.67

Next, extrude the two narrow polygons on the top 0.25 meter as shown. These will create a short side-wall detail. To finish it off, select the four top end vertices as shown and use the Select and Uniform Scale tool to move them toward the center a short distance to create an angle on the ends of the side walls. Another subtle detail addition to the model to add visual interest.

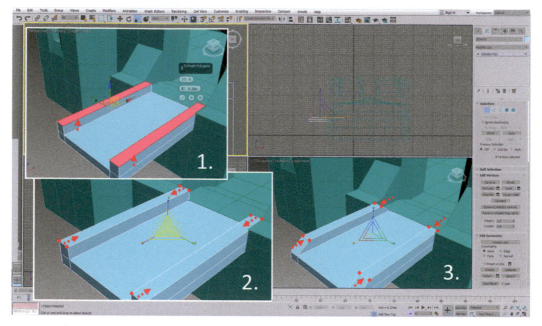

IMAGE 5.68 (Save 5-25)

Left-mouse click on the Editable Poly object in the modifier list to get out of sub-object level mode. The drawbridge will still be selected. Switch from the Select and Uniform Scale tool to the Select and Rotate tool next to the left of the scale tool. The Rotation gizmo appears in the center of the mesh. Try rotating the mesh using the gizmo.

Rotate Gizmo

The Rotate gizmo works like a virtual trackball. The gizmo can rotate an object freely, about the X-, Y- or Z-axis, or about an axis perpendicular to the viewport.

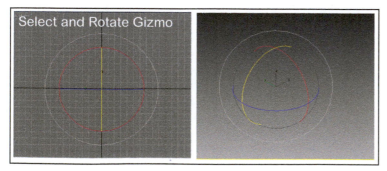

IMAGE 5.69

Drag anywhere on one of colored axis arms to rotate the object about that axis. As the gizmo rotates about the X-, Y- or Z-axis 3ds Max will show a transparent shaded area showing the direction of the rotation. 3ds Max also displays measurement of the rotation in degrees.

If you click and drag inside the Rotate gizmo or click and drag on the outer edge of the gizmo will rotate freely.

The outermost gray circle of the gizmo is the Screen handle. With it, you can rotate the object on a plane parallel to the viewport.

When you rotate the mesh using the gizmo, the mesh will rotate around the gizmo in the center of the mesh. Not rotating at the end of the mesh, how a drawbridge in real life works. Use the undo button to reset the mesh to where we created it if necessary. We can correct the rotation by moving the Pivot Point. To do this, switch to the Select and Move tool, and then select the Hierarchy tab at the top of the Command Panel (to the right of the Modify Panel tab). The Pivot button should be selected by default. Below it is the "Affect Pivot Only" button. Click it to activate it. When you select it, the Select and Move tool Gizmo will change to one with doubled-up lines making it look bigger. While in Affect Pivot Only mode, you are limited to making changes only to the pivot point of the mesh. An object's pivot point is generated when an object is created. It is automatically located at the center of mass of the object. While in the Affect Pivot Only mode, we can move or rotate the gizmo. Scaling does not affect the pivot point. Move the gizmo to the end of the bridge mesh closest to the castle, at the intersection of the angled ramp and the top corner of the bridge bed walking surface as shown. This is where we want the drawbridge to hinge from as it is drawn up to reveal the moat. Click the Affect Pivot only button again to deactivate it. Now, rotate the bridge mesh using the Select and Rotate tool. It should pivot correctly. Undo the rotations if necessary to return the bridge to the horizontal position.

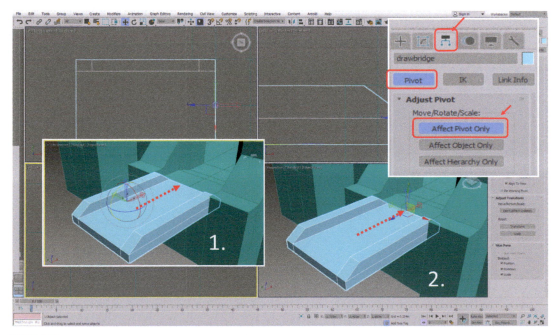

IMAGE 5.70

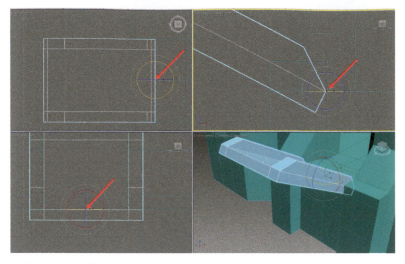

IMAGE 5.71 (Save 5-26)

Next, we will animate the drawbridge. First, make sure that the drawbridge mesh is selected. To animate an object in 3ds Max, you must be in Animation Mode. Click on the "Auto Key" button on the lower navigation bar on the right side. When selected, it will turn red as will the Time Slider bar above it. You will also notice that the active viewport outline has changed from yellow to red. All the red indicates you are in Animation Mode. Almost everything in 3ds Max can be animated, from movement and scale to color changes. It is really a powerful feature in the program. Because so many things are animatable, the red indicaters are there to remind when you are in Animation Mode.

As you are working, it is easy to forget to turn off the Animation Mode button and continue working only to realize you have been animating things without realizing it. It happens to everyone at some point. Another good reason to do frequent backups.

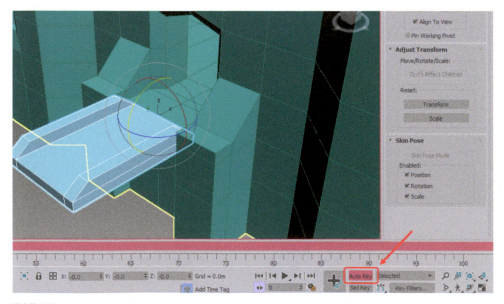

IMAGE 5.72

If the Time Slider is not at the "0" frame, all the way to the left, move it there. With the drawbridge selected, click on the "Set Key" button to the left of the Auto Key button. This will add a keyframe to the timeline at the location of the Time Slider, in this case, at the "0" frame. The drawbridge will be in its current position at frame "0."

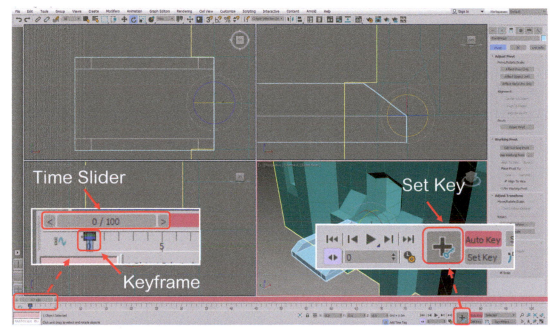

IMAGE 5.73

Move the Time Slider all the way to the right to frame 100. Rotate the drawbridge to a vertical position (90 degrees) as shown. When you moved the object, you immediately created a new keyframe at the location of the Time Slider. So, to insure you do not overwrite an existing keyframe by mistake, but make sure you move the Time Slider prior to making any changes to the object.

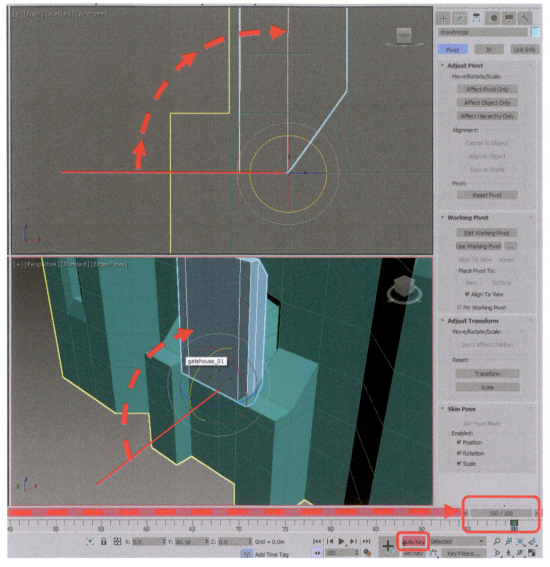

IMAGE 5.74

Drag the Time Slider back to the "0" frame. The drawbridge should rotate back down. Next, click on the "Play" button to the left of the Set Key(s) button. The animation will play in the active viewport. If it is happening really fast, you need to make an adjustment to the playback speed. To do that, click on the Time Configuration Button to open its window. In the Playback section of the window, select the "Real Time" tick box. Close the window, and try the play button again. By default, in 3ds Max, real time is 30 frames which is equivalent to 1 second. This can be modified if necessary.

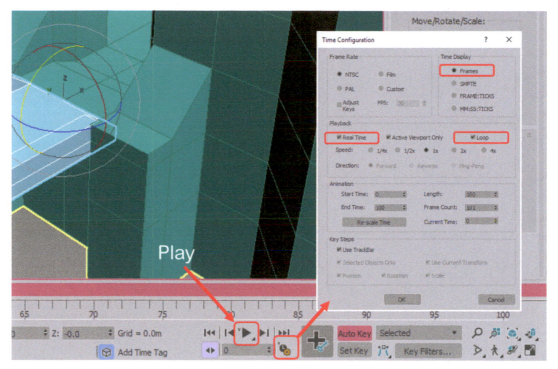

IMAGE 5.75

Right now, the raising of the bridge looks very mechanical, not natural. To give the bridge the appearance that it is very heavy, that it has weight, lets adjust the movement. Move the Time Slider to 50. The mesh is half-way through its motion path. Rotate the mesh half-way back to the down position so that it is 25 percent along the rotation motion path it takes. Now, it will travel 25 percent of the distance in half of the time and travel the remaining 75 percent of the distance in the other half of the time. It will rise slowly and then accelerate, as if momentum was involved. Play it to see if it looks more realistic.

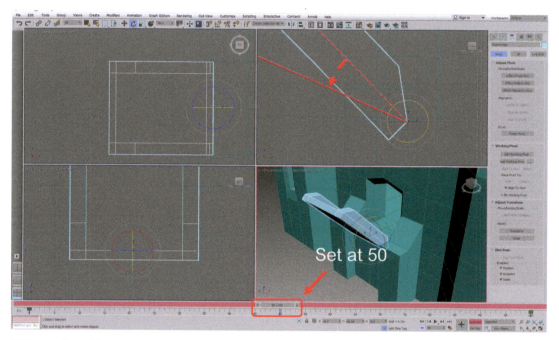

IMAGE 5.76 (Save 5-27)

Move the Time Slider back to frame zero. Next, we will create the detail pieces of the model. The hinge that the bridge rotates on will be first. At the pivot point, in the Front viewport, create and position, as shown (centered in the raised side wall of the mesh), a cylinder with the following parameters:

> *Radius: 0.40 m*
> *Height: 0.20 m*
> *Height Segments: 1*
> *Cap Segments: 2*
> *Sides: 8*

I rotated mine a little to align a spoke segment with the angled bevel segment of the Bridge mesh.

Notice the cap segment creates an inner ring of segments on the flat ends of the cylinder. Select the inner circle of polygons on the inside end of the cylinder, and extrude them 0.10 meter. This will create the look of an axle rod.

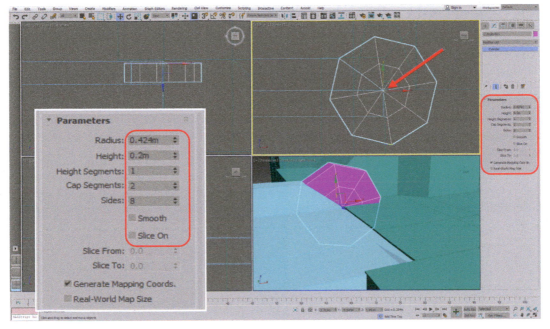

IMAGE 5.77

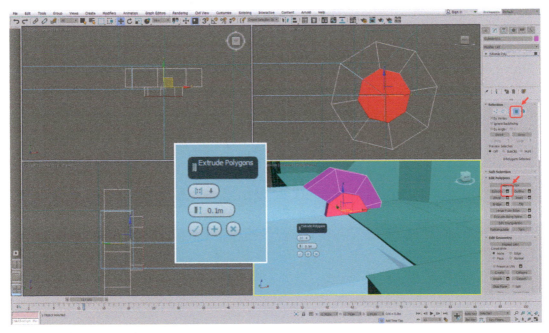

IMAGE 5.78

If you scrub the Time Slider horizontally, the drawbridge will move, but the hinges do not. To get the hinges to move with the bridge mesh, we will use the Select and Link Tool, the third button from the left on the Main Tool Bar.

The Select and Link Tool

The Select and Link tool creates a hierarchical relationship between two objects. With the tool selected, left-mouse click on an object, the child, if it is not already selected. Drag the dashed line created from the child to the parent object, releasing the mouse button. The second object's (the parent) edge segment will flash white to indicate that that object has been selected as the parent in the relationship between the two objects. The child object will "listen or follow" the parent object, keeping a position relative to the parent, when and wherever the parent moves. However, the child can be moved freely in any direction without effecting the parent's location. As soon as the parent is moved, the child will immediately follow, relative to the parent from wherever it is. The child will also inherit scale and rotate transformations applied to the parent.

Parent/Child relationships can be viewed in the Schematic View, accessible from the main menu bar. The window shows every object in the scene and their relationship to all the other objects. Take a peek, we won't be utilizing its capabilities this early in the learning process. With rigging and some other operations, it is extremely useful.

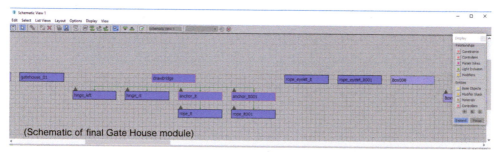

IMAGE 5.79

Select and link the hinge to the drawbridge as directed in the previous paragraph. Remember, link the child to the parent, not the parent to the child. A way to remember, like in real life, the child follows the parent. Now when you rotate the drawbridge, the hinge should rotate with it.

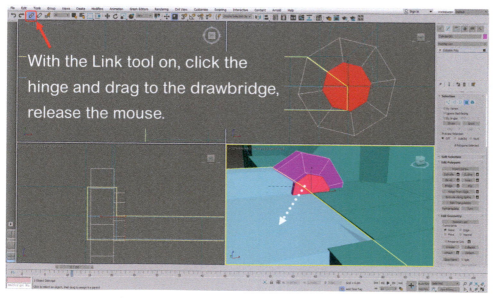

IMAGE 5.80

To create the hinge for the other side of the bridge, let's clone it. With the hinge selected, click on the "Mirror" tool icon on the top menu bar. In the pop-up window that will appear on the screen, select "Instance," so whatever modifications you make to one will happen to the other. Select the six options from the top "Mirror Axis" section list until you find the correct one, or you can go through the logical process of determining which would be the correct one. For me, I just click until I like what I see! In my case, it was the Y-axis (which wasn't hard to deduce…). Move the cloned hinge into position as shown. Rename the first hinge piece "hinge_lt" and the second one "hinge_rt."

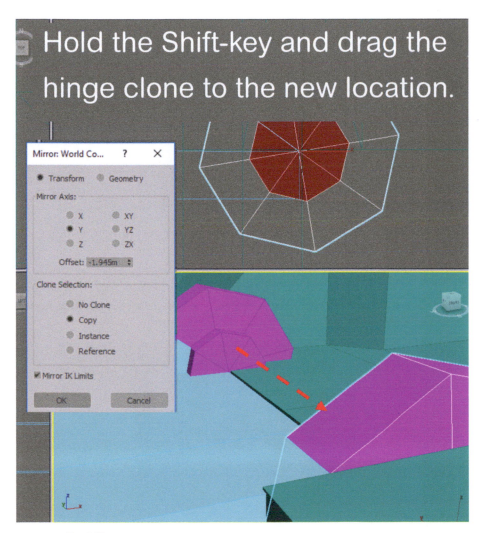

IMAGE 5.81 (Save 5-28)

We will add the rope assembly to "lift" the drawbridge next. We could model a chain to do the lifting, but a heavy rope will work better for us at this basic stage. The rope will be "pulled" through a hole in the Gate House wall above the front entrance. First, let's make the "hole" for the rope to go through on the wall, the "eyelet." On a ship, the anchor line goes through a hole in the ship's hull called a "hawsepipe." We will call it an eyelet, but it does the same thing as a hawsepipe. From the Standard

Primitives list, create a Torus shape in the front viewport, roughly where I have created one. To use the Torus (a doughnut shape), click, drag, release the mouse button and drag again, three steps. Set the parameters after you create it to those shown below.

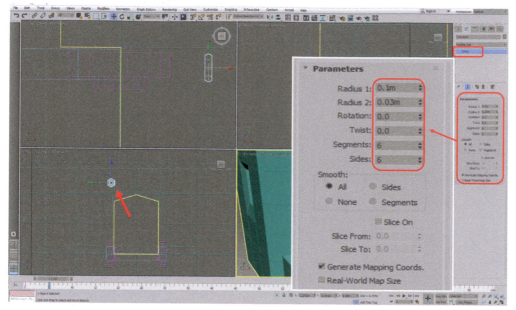

Position so that it is mounted on the wall. Rename the torus, "rope_eyelet_lt."

Select one of the torus eyelets, and with the Angle Snaps on, rotate it so you can see the back side. Convert it to an Editable Poly, and then select the polygons on the back and delete them.

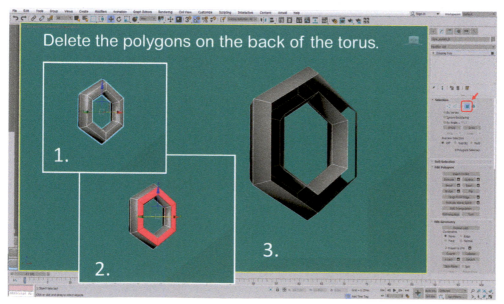

Select the inner border edges with the Border sub-object level, and then click on the "Cap" tool in the Modifier Panel. Then, rotate it back to the front position.

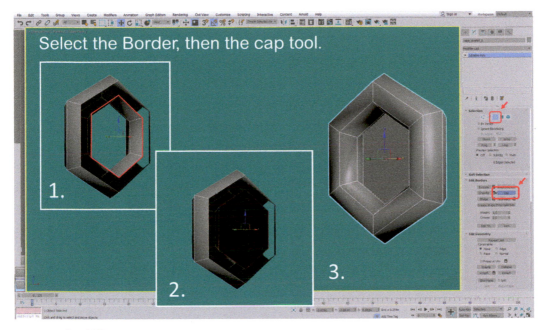

IMAGE 5.84 (Save 5-29)

Next, make the anchor point for the rope at the far end of the drawbridge by creating a cylinder, similarly to the Hinge piece, with parameters as shown and locating it as in the image.

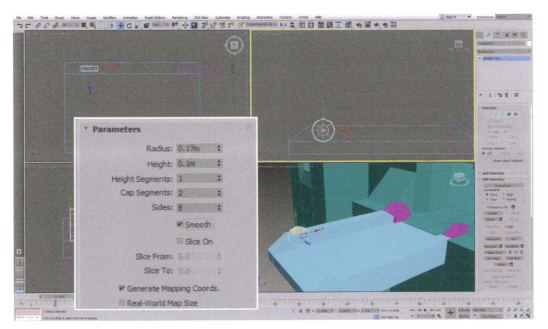

IMAGE 5.85

Convert to an Editable Poly, and select the inner circle of polygons on the flat side as you did with the hinge. In the Front viewport, scale the circle to a smaller size as shown so that it is within the side wall of the bridge.

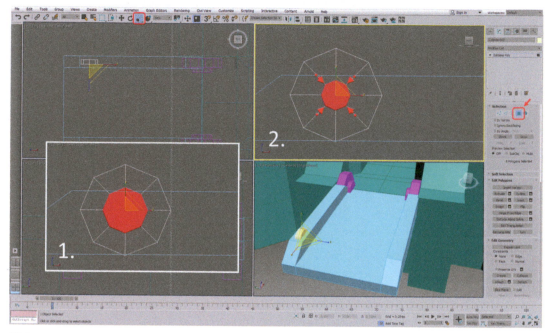

IMAGE 5.86

Next, extrude the polygons 0.1 meter to create an axle that pokes through the inside wall. Rotate the viewport to a back view of the cylinder anchor, and repeat the two steps on the opposite side of the anchor piece, scale the inner edges smaller and extrude to create an axle. Rename the cylinder, "anchor_lt."

Link the anchor_lt to the drawbridge using the Select and Link tool. Click on the anchor_lt (the child), and drag the line with the mouse to anywhere on the drawbridge. Release the mouse button. The drawbridge segments will flash white, indicating the link has been made.

Time to create the ropes that "lift" the bridge. This will be a bit trickier: have patience, work methodically and carefully… it will work.

Create a cylinder in the top viewport with the parameters shown in the image below.

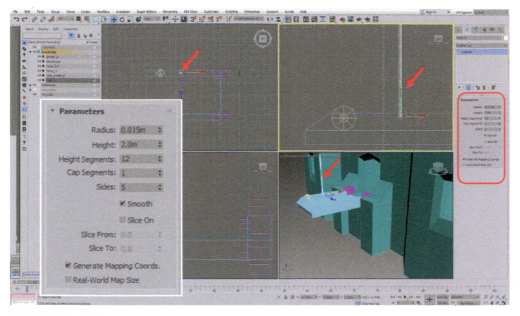

IMAGE **5.87** (Save 5-30)

Rename the cylinder "rope_lt." The pivot point for this object is at the bottom of the mesh. We will want the pivot point to be at the center of the anchor_lt. With the rope_lt selected, click on the "Align" tool on the Main Tool Bar. Next, click on the anchor_lt to initiate the Align selection window. With the settings as shown, the rope_lt will jump to the anchor_lt, with its pivot point at the center of the anchor_lt.

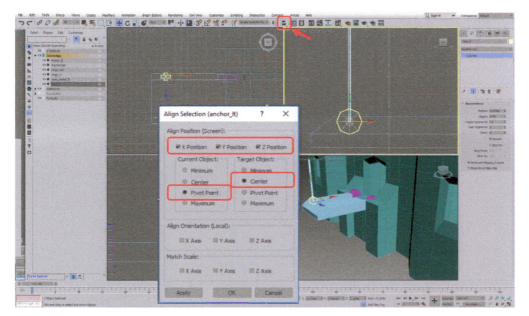

IMAGE **5.88**

Link the rope_It to the anchor_It. Now when you rotate the anchor_It, the rope will rotate around the anchor_It's pivot point.

Rotate the anchor_It so that the rope moves toward the eyelet on the Gate House wall. With the rope pointed at the eyelet, change the Height Parameter (the length) of the rope_It so that it just passes through the hole in the eyelet. Remember, lengthen the rope and rotate the anchor, but do not rotate the rope.

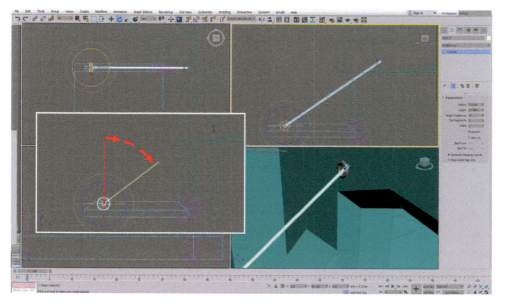

IMAGE 5.89 (Save 5-31)

Once you have it positioned properly, convert the rope to an Editable Poly. Now, add a "Bend" modifier to the rope_It object in the Modifier Stack. Set the Angle Bend to −20.0 degrees and the Bend Axis set to "Z." Rotate the anchor_It so that the rope_It fits back into the eyelet on the wall. The rope should rest on the bottom of the hole in the eyelet like it would in the real world. The rope now has a natural sway to it as if gravity was pulling down on it.

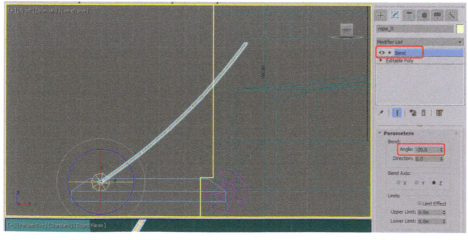

IMAGE 5.90

Now for the tricky part… turn on the Auto Key button to enter the Animation Mode. The red lines appear above the Time Line and around the active viewport. Move the Time Slider all the way to frame 100, the end of the animation as we did for the drawbridge. Even though the drawbridge is not selected, it moves since we animated it.

Because the rope is linked to the anchor, and the anchor to the drawbridge, the rope moved relative to the drawbridge and now is pointing down.

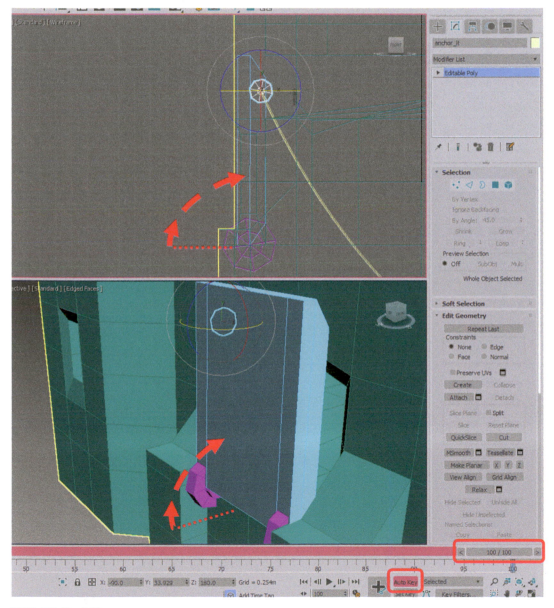

IMAGE 5.91 (Save 5-32)

Rotate the rope anchor so that the rope once again is resting on the bottom of the inside hole of the eyelet.

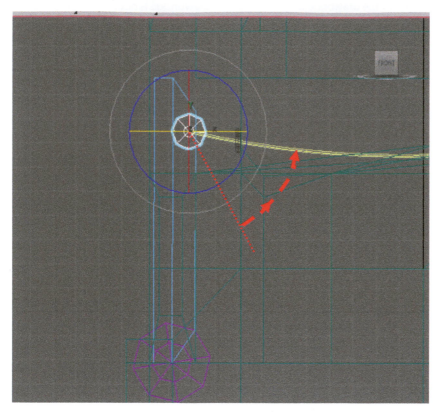

If you scrub the Time Slider back to frame zero, the rope will move away from the eyelet and eventually return to it when the slider hits frame zero. It is moving like this due to the animation algorithms that 3ds Max has, trying to ease in and ease out of keyframes with motion mimicking the real world (moving from point to point in the space). What we need to do is to add more keyframes to control the movement.

Move the Time Slider to 50. You can also manually enter frame numbers in the value box below the Play button on the lower navigation bar. Next, rotate the anchor to bring the rope_lt back to the bottom of the hole in the wall eyelet.

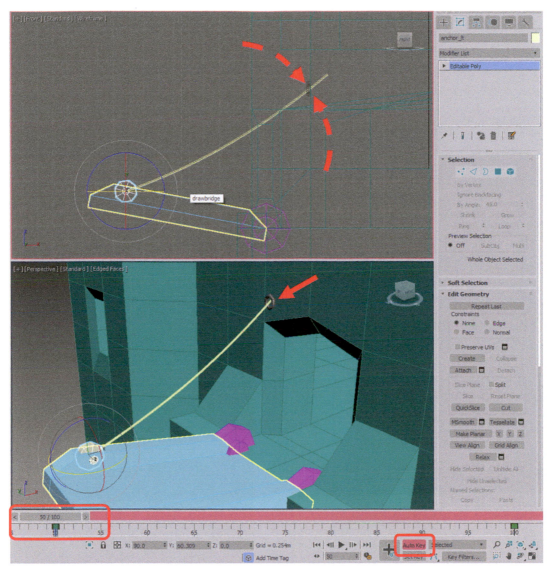

IMAGE 5.93

Scrub the Time Slider from 0 to 100. The rope appears to lift the drawbridge. Where is the rope going when it goes inside the building? It is supposed to go inside the Gate House in the open space between the ceiling of the interior room and the roof. We could have animated the rope getting shorter just as easily. However, an animation of a transform that changes the length of an object will not readily export with the model to our game engine, Unity. We are hiding it in the between the ceiling/roof space of the structure.

My animation has one problem at the end of the animation though, the rope_lt end dips through the ceiling, down into the interior room and would be visible to the player.

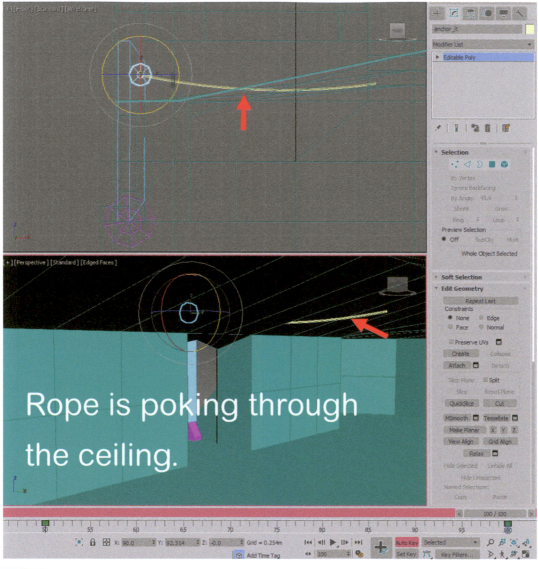

IMAGE 5.94

To fix it, I moved the Time Slider to 85, a frame before the rope dips into the room and clicked on the Set Key(s) button to make a new keyframe.

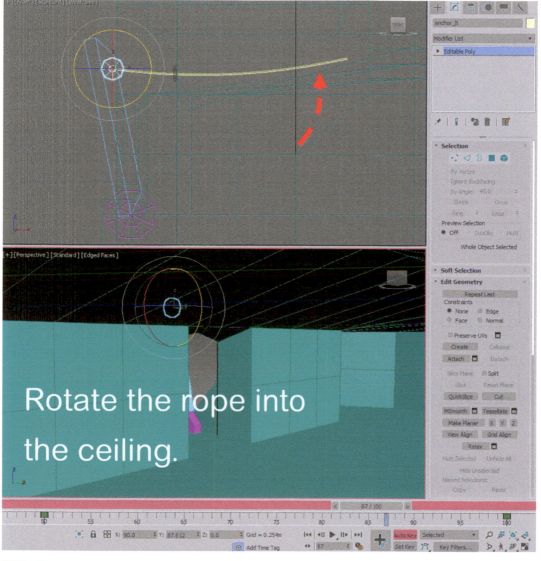

IMAGE 5.95

Then, I moved the Time Slider to frame 100 and rotated the anchor to move the rope_lt up into the hidden area between the ceiling and roof. Hit the play button to view the rope's motion path to see if it is working properly. If yours is not, go back to the last save and try again. You might have missed one small step that can throw it off track.

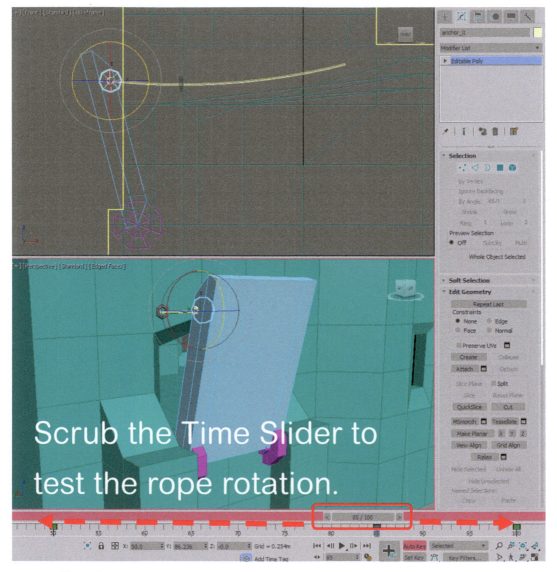

IMAGE 5.96 (Save 5-33)

Turn off the Auto Key button to get out of Animation Mode. Hold the Ctrl-key down, and select the eyelet_ly, rope_lt and the anchor_lt. Now, hold the Shift-key down and use the Select and Move tool to drag a clone copy of these objects to the other side of the drawbridge. Select Instance as the clone option from the pop-up window. Rename the new cloned pieces, eyelet_rt, rope_rt and anchor_rt, respectively. Play the animation to see if everything is working correctly.

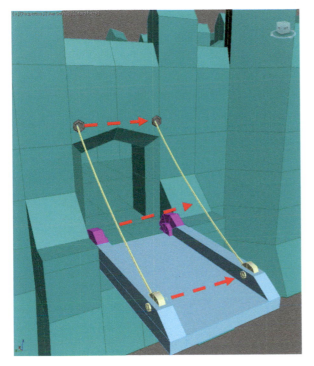

IMAGE 5.97 (Save 5-34)

The Portcullis

The metal grill gate that drops down from the top of the entrance way is called the portcullis. Defensively, it is more secure than the drawbridge. Sometimes its weight was used as a counterweight to open and close the drawbridge.

To make our portcullis, start by changing to the portcullis layer in the Scene Editor. Then, create a box with the parameter shown in the image below. Convert the box to an Editable Poly. Move the vertices in the center of the mesh toward the bottom of the mesh. We are making a point on the end.

Select the bottom row of vertices, and open the Weld caddy from the Command Panel. Raise the number in the value box so that all the vertices weld into one vertex. The "After" value will drop to 13.

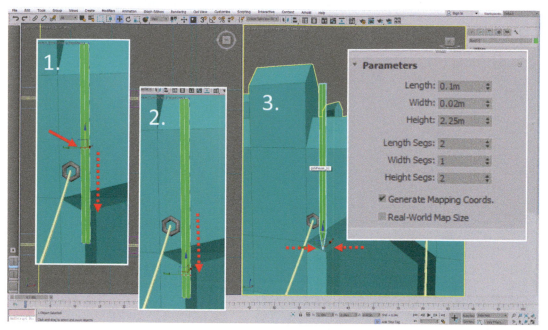

IMAGE 5.98

Click on the Editable Poly in the Modifier Stack to get out of sub-object level mode. We will use a tool called Array to create the gate. From the Tools tab on the Top Tool Bar, select Array.

The Array Tool

The array tool clones an object multiple times, offsetting each object a set increment of distance, rotation and/or scale. In the pop-up window, change the value of the appropriate boxes to move (distance), rotate (degrees) or scale (percentage) the cloned objects. Select the type of clone, Copy, Instance or Reference. Select how many clones are to be generated. With the Preview button on, you can make adjustments before committing.

In the Array Window, in the Y column, change the Move value to −0.25. In the Count value box, change the 1D value to 6. Click on the OK button to accept.

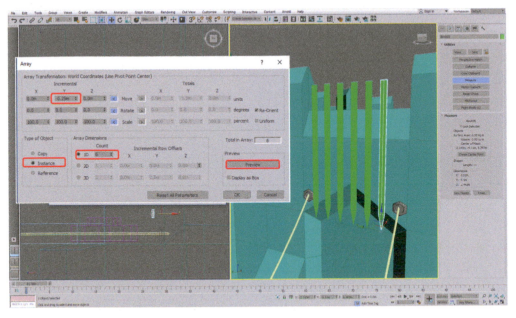

IMAGE 5.99 (Save 5-35)

Next, we need the horizontal cross bars to finish the gate. In the Top Viewport, create a box and position it with parameters as shown in the image below.

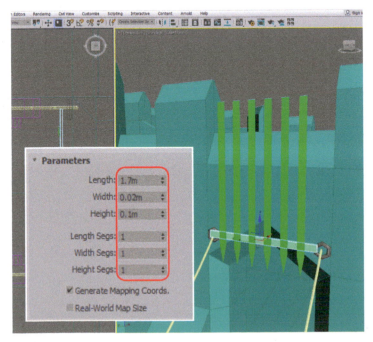

IMAGE 5.100

Open the Array tool, and change the Move value boxes in the Y column to 0.0 and the Z column to 0.3. With the preview button on, check that the bars look acceptable and click OK if they are.

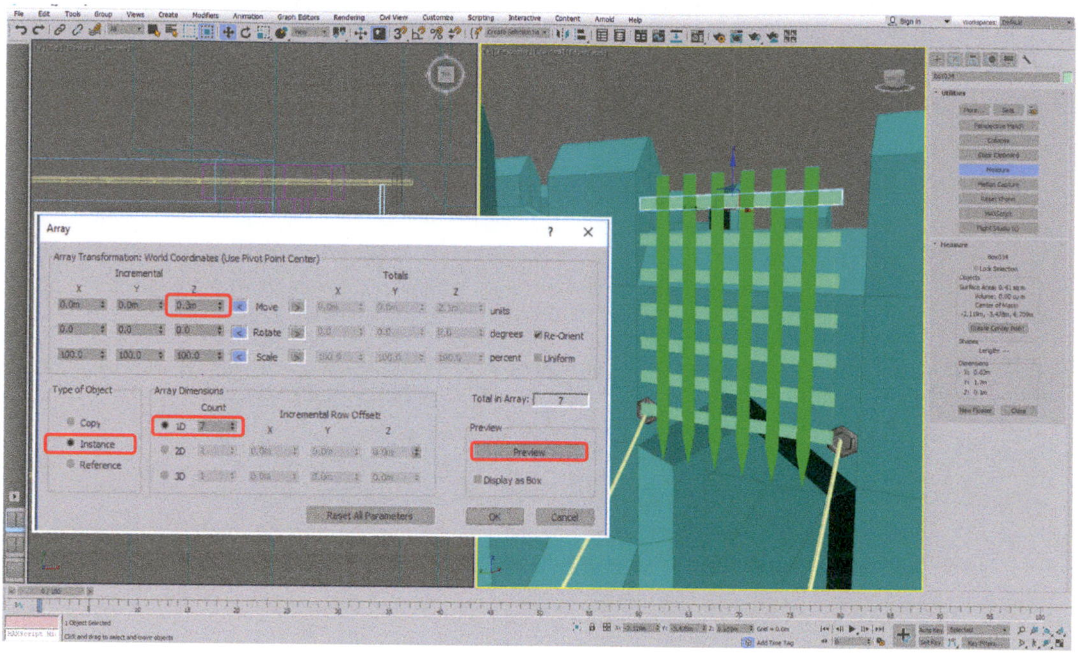

IMAGE 5.101

Select all the horizontal and vertical bars we just created. In the top Tool Bar, select the Group tab and then select Group from the list.

Group

The Group tool allows you to group two or more objects together without needing to weld them. The group will act as one object with a new pivot point at the center of mass for the grouped objects. The "Open" menu item allows you to select individual objects within the group without breaking the grouping. Changes can be made to the individual objects. When finished with the individual object, select the "Close" option to return to the normal group state. A group can be modified with transforms and be animated. A group can be part of another group.

Name the group "portcullis."

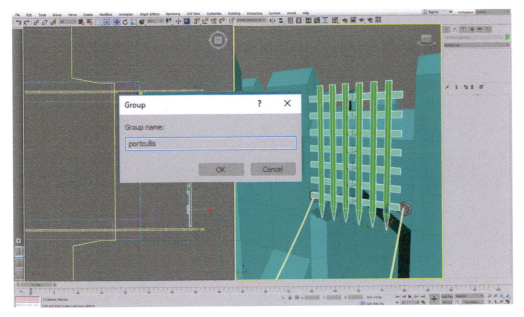

IMAGE 5.102 (Save 5-36)

Position the portcullis in the entrance way, in the flat section of the doorway in the "up" position, the bottom points exposed in the doorway as shown.

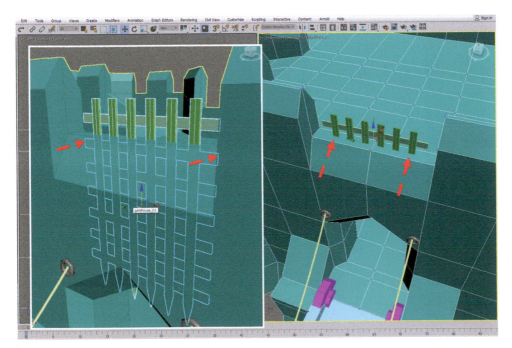

IMAGE 5.103

The embrasure between the two merlons is too short to hide the top of the portcullis gate. Select the six vertices of the embrasure above the portcullis as shown, and change the Z-coordinate Display value to 7.0, covering the portcullis gate.

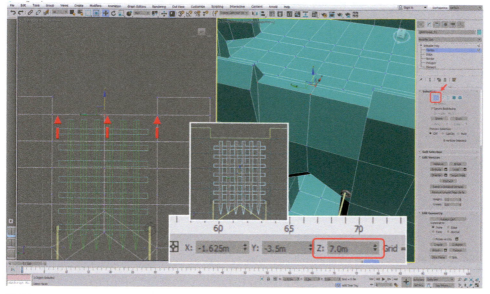

IMAGE 5.104

Move the Time Slider to zero, and turn on the Auto Key for Animation Mode.

Click on the Set Key(s) button to the left of the Auto Key to create a keyframe at zero. Next, move the Time Slider to 30. Move the portcullis down to a closed position, the points slightly penetrating the Gate House mesh. Play the animation. The gate should close before being visibly blocked by the raised drawbridge.

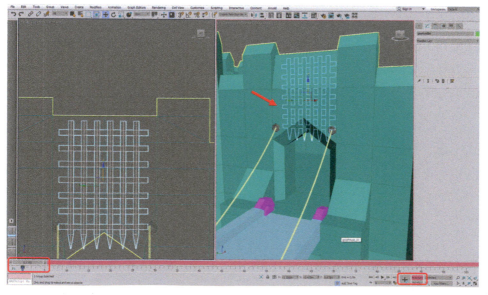

IMAGE 5.105

There is just one last thing to do to finish the modeling part of the Gate House. Select the Gate House mesh. In the modifier Stack, right-mouse click and select Collapse-All to collapse the Stack. We won't be making anymore modeling changes to the quarter section: no need for the Symmetry modifiers. With the gatehouse mesh in Vertex mode, select the bottom row of vertices. Using the Scale and Move tool, flair the vertices out, away from the center to create a batter at the bottom of the wall. We could not do this to the quarter section earlier as the vertices around the front would have gone in undesirable directions.

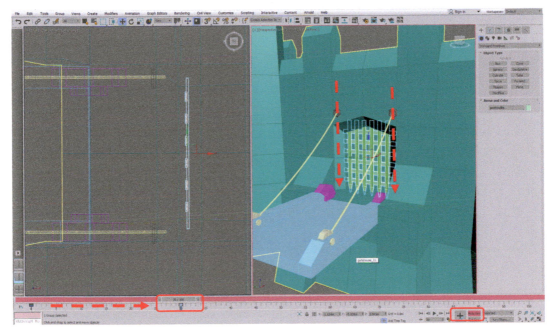

IMAGE 5.106

The inside batters on the front and back sides of the two towers are angled the opposite of way than they should be. They should angle toward the center of the mesh. Select the eight vertices shown in the bottom row on the front and back sides of the Gate House mesh as shown, and with the Select and Scale tool, bring them toward the center so that the segments above them are vertical.

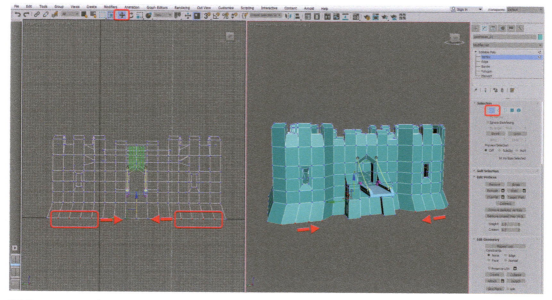

IMAGE 5.107

Then, select just the two vertices at the bottom of the inside bevel on the front and back sides of the towers and shown. Move them toward the center of the mesh so that they are symmetrical with the outside batter bevels.

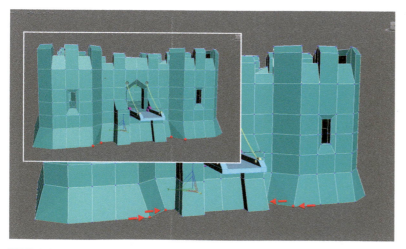

IMAGE 5.108

That does it! You've completed a very complex module and added some important new tools to your skills repertoire.

Next, we will make the Corner Turret.

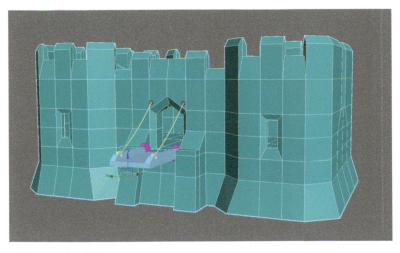

IMAGE 5.109 (Save 5-37)

Chapter 5 Exercise: Wine Barrel

IMAGE 5.110

Model a big wine barrel. For this model, you can use multiple meshes to create the finished model. The design can be of your choice or you can follow the example I made. Be sure to do some research to define your design. Using a cylinder for the barrel shape, I used the Select and Scale tool to create the shape, widening the vertices in the Y-axis, and then the X-axis. The rings around the barrel are cylinders, shaped the same way as the barrel. The spout is a cylinder and two cones. The base is a modified box. When you complete Chapter 7, Unwrapping the Model, you can return to the finished wine barrel model and complete the unwrapping and texturing of your model.

In the companion folder online, you will find the 3ds Max file iterations saves from when I modeled the wine barrel and the texture file, "accessory_textures.png" for your use.

IMAGE 5.111

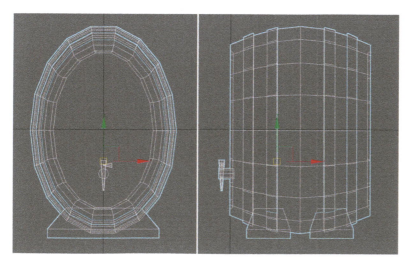

IMAGE 5.112

Modeling the Turrets

Concepts/Skills/Tools Introduced in This Chapter

- Lathe Modifier
- Material Editor
  - Compact Editor
  - Creating a Material
  - Applying a Material
  - Material/Map Browser
  - Assign Material to Selection
- Stairs
  - Spiral Staircase
- Tube
- Angle Snaps
- Attach
- Import
  - Merge
- Array Tool
- Detach Taper Modifier
- Image Template

We will create two turret models using two different approaches. To make the first, the Corner Turret, we will use the Lathe tool to get started. The second, the Mid-Wall Turret, will be done using a primitive, the tube. The Corner Turret module will connect to two Curtain Wall modules at the corner of the perimeter wall. The Mid-Wall Turret will be used to extend the wall between other modules, with a Curtain Wall module on either side, aligned in 180 degrees. As with previous modules, I have done the preliminary research and developed a sketch to work from.

From the GDD, I also noted some parameters that needed be taken into consideration.

> Corner Module:
> Overall Height from ground level: up to 11 meters
> Doorways: 1 at ground level inside the wall, 2 at 4.5-meter height to allow Curtain Wall access by player, and 90 degrees to each other
> Module diameter: up to 11 meters
> Needs to have a "batter" at the bottom
> Interior circular staircase useable by player
> Hand-painted, shader-textured sides
> Polygon count: under 1,800
> Mid-Wall Turret Module:
> Overall Height from ground level: up to 10 meters
> Doorways: 2 at 4.5-meter height to allow Curtain Wall access by player, and 180 degrees to each other
> Module diameter: up to 7 meters
> Needs to have a "batter" at the bottom
> Player passes through turret, no ground access
> Hand-painted, shader-textured sides
> Polygon count: under 900

Note: The characters in the game will be scaled to 1.15 meter; short, stocky, fantasy dwarf styling. The structures in the environment should be scaled accordingly.

Below are three of the images that I used for reference when designing the Turrets and the final sketch we will work from.

IMAGE 6.1

IMAGE 6.2

IMAGE 6.3

IMAGE 6.4

Open a new project in 3ds Max, and save it as "lastname_turrets_01." In the Scene Explorer, create two new layers: one called "Placeholder" and the other called "Corner Turret." Click on the Placeholder layer to make sure it is the active layer.

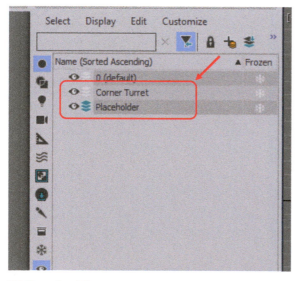

IMAGE 6.5 (Save 6-1)

First, we will model a placeholder for the Corner Turret. In the Top Viewport, create a cylinder with parameters as shown in the image below.

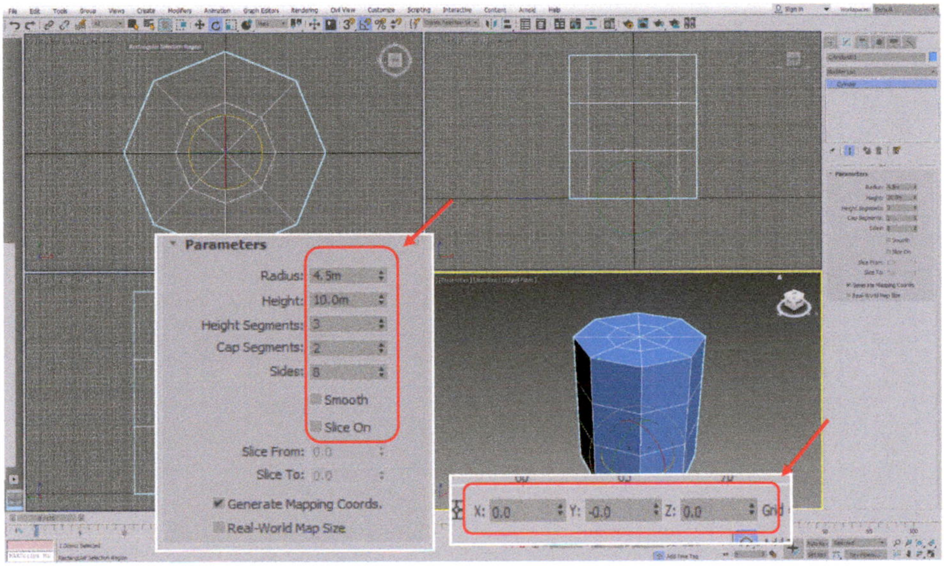

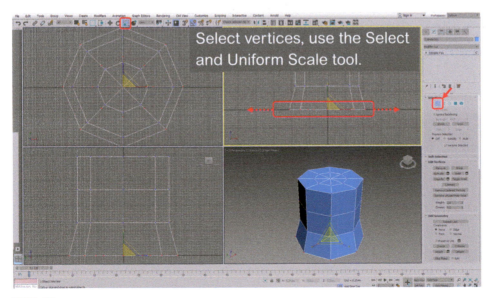

IMAGE 6.6

Center the mesh at 0, 0, 0 on the X-, Y-, Z-axes in the Coordinate Display area of the user interface (UI).

Toggle the Scene Explorer closed using the Scene Explorer button icon on the Main Tool bar to maximize the available work space for modeling.

Convert the cylinder to an Editable Poly. In vertex mode, select the bottom row, and as we have done on previous models, flair out the base to create the batter using the Select and Uniform Scale tool.

IMAGE 6.7

Select the vertices in the second row from the bottom, and in the Coordinate Display boxes, change the Z-value to 1.5. This will align them with the top of the batter that we created in the other models.

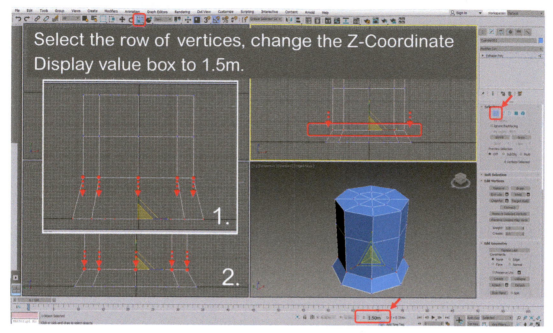

IMAGE 6.8

Next, select the second row from the top and change their Z-coordinate to 8.0 meters.

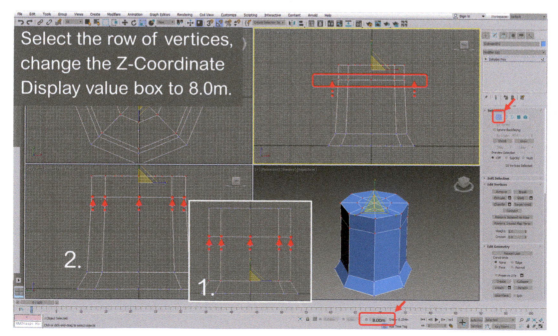

IMAGE 6.9

Select the top two rows of vertices, and scale them slightly toward the center of the mesh to create a taper on the middle vertical wall section. Now, select just the top row and flair the vertices out to create an angle at the top.

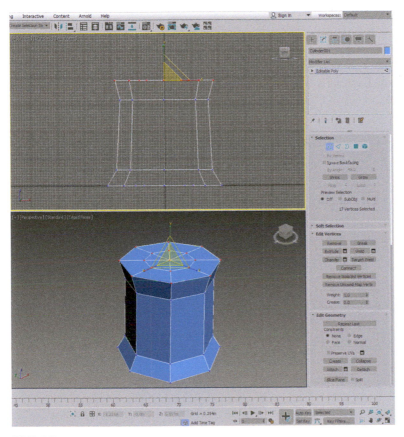

IMAGE 6.10

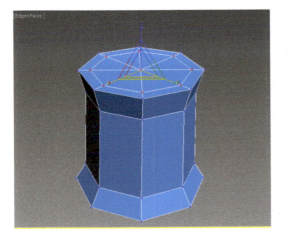

IMAGE 6.11 (Save 6-2)

Switch to Polygon mode, and select the narrow ring of polygons we just created and extrude them 1.0 meter.

Loop Tool

To select multiple vertices, edges or polygons along a row, select the first vertex, edge or polygon, then hold down the Shift-key and select an adjacent one. The program will automatically select the entire continuous row of vertices, edges or polygons. This saves you from hand picking each one individually. There is also a Loop tool on the Ribbon that will do this procedure.

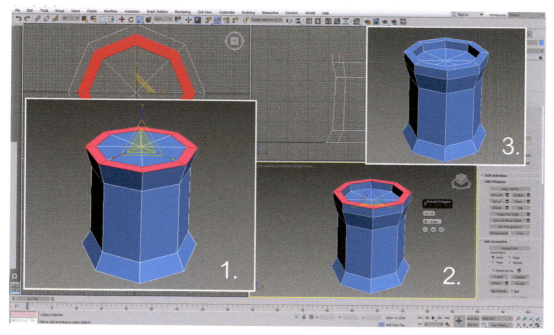

IMAGE 6.12 (Save 6-3)

That completes the placeholder. Rename the cylinder "corner_turret_placeholder." Save the file, and in the Scene Editor, turn off the Placeholder layer and turn on the Corner Turret layer.

The Corner Turret Module

We will use a new tool, the Lathe modifier to create the base mesh for the Corner Turret. The cylindrical shape lends itself to that tool.

The Lathe Modifier

When applied to a shape, like a line, the lathe modifier generates a new object using a sweep of the shape around an axis. A number of variables are available to modify the lathe results such as the number of sides, axis alignment, and degrees of the sweep.

We will create a line for the Lathe modifier to sweep around an axis to generate the turret shape. To create a line correctly, we will use a template to "trace" our line vertex placement. From the resource files, download the .png image file, "c-7-turret_1_template."

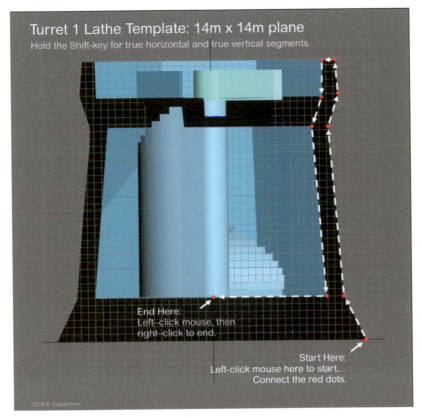

IMAGE 6.13

From the Geometry tab of the Command Panel, create a Plane in the Front viewport with parameters as shown in the image below.

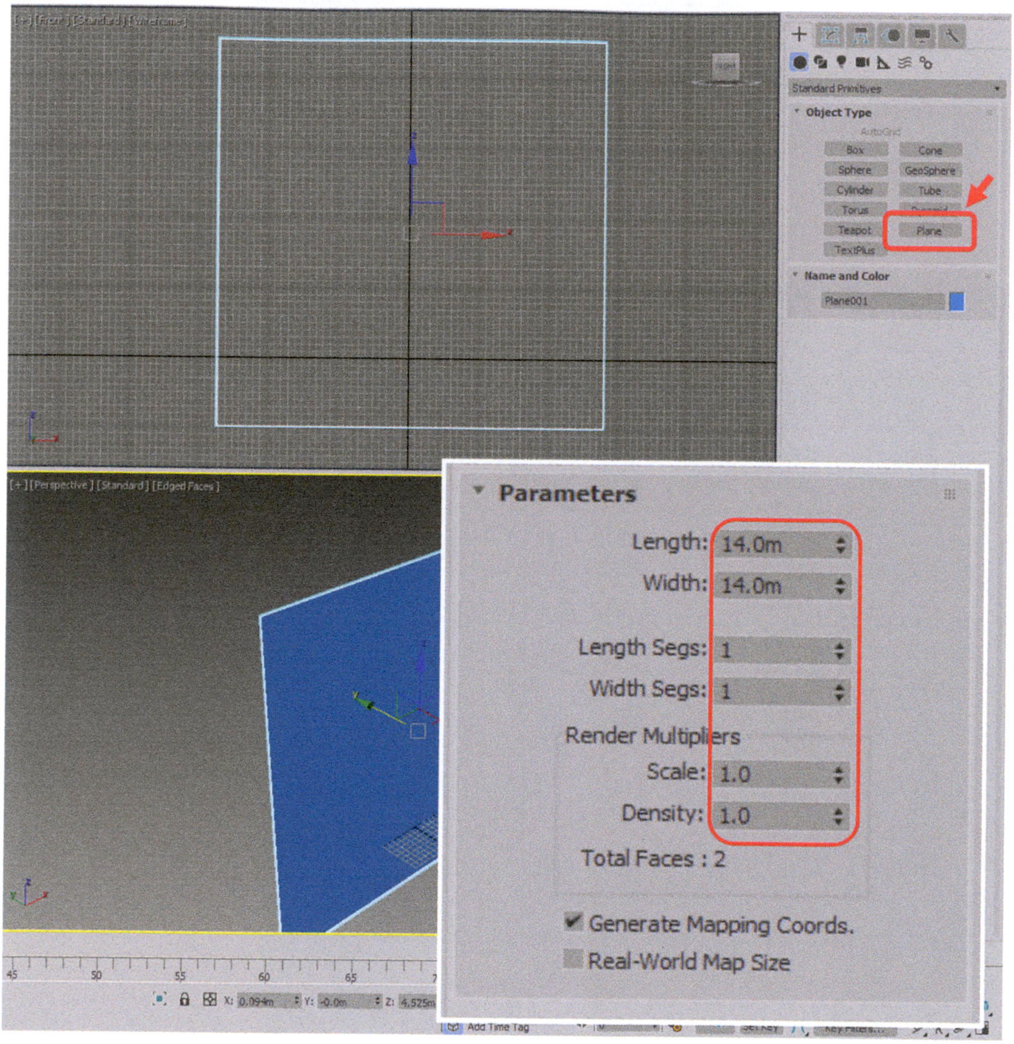

IMAGE 6.14

We will apply a texture, the .png image you just downloaded, to this plane. To do this will require several steps using the Material Editor. You will be using the Material Editor frequently in your work with 3ds Max. Although the steps will seem cumbersome at first, through much repetition, you will become very accustom to clicking through the steps without giving it a second thought. Trust me, you'll get used to doing the steps by memory in a short time.

The Material Editor

Materials play a very important role in a game. From toon to realistic, textures can make or break a game. Applying a texture to an object requires that the object has mapping coordinates and that there are lights in the scene, added or default. The texture has defined properties that will determine how the lights in the scene will be reflected off it, defining how it will be seen by the viewer. Today, most textures are shaders, a group of texture maps combined into one to yield dynamic imagery in the game with reflections, refractions, surface textures and more. We will use simple textures to get started.

Compact Editor

We use the Material Editor to build the texture with properties we define and to apply the texture to the object. There are two Material Editor versions. The original one to 3ds Max is the Compact Editor. It is the simpler, smaller Editor of the two. It is the better choice for quick applications of existing textures that won't require much in terms of development.

Slate Editor

Introduced in 3ds Max 2011, the Slate Editor is a node-based editor using wires to connect images with attributes and modifiers. If you are creating new textures, the Slate Editor is the choice to use as it features especially suited for this task.

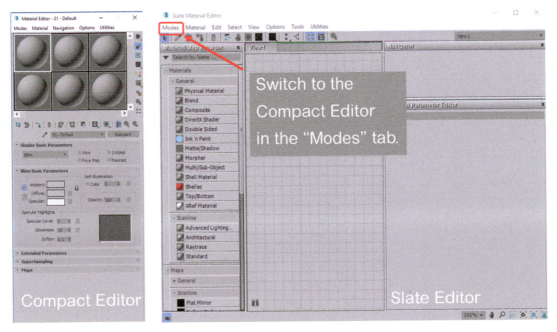

Switch to the Compact Editor in the "Modes" tab.

IMAGE 6.15

As we have our material image already prepared, we will use the Compact Editor. Click on the Material Editor icon button on the Main Tool bar. If the Slate Editor opens, switch to the compact editor by either holding down the Material Editor icon on the Main Tool bar to open the flyout and select the second icon, the Compact Editor, or click on the Modes tab at the top of the Slate Editor window and switch to the Compact Editor. They are interchangeable at any time, nothing will be added or lost by switching.

In the Compact Editor, you MUST do the following procedures in the order given if you want the material to work properly:

1. With the mesh you are texturing selected, click on the "Get Material" icon button. This will open the Material/Map Browser window.
2. In the Material/Map Browser, browse to Materials > General > Standard (select "Standard" by double clicking it). This will define the type of map you are using for this texture.

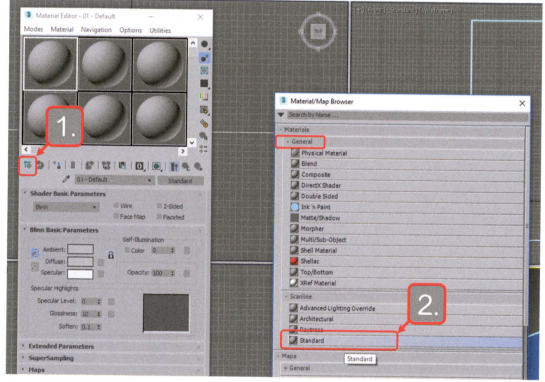

IMAGE 6.16

3. At the bottom of the editor, click on the "Maps" rollout to open it.
4. The second attribute is Diffuse Color. Click on the "Map" box for Diffuse Color (it currently reads "No Map").
5. In the pop-up window, navigate to Maps > and expand the "+General" menu.

6. Double click on the "Bitmap" type of map.

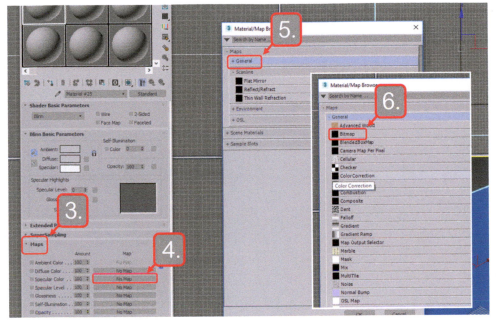

IMAGE 6.17

7. In the Select Bitmap Image File window, navigate to wherever you downloaded the image file earlier to and select it. If you have done the preceding steps correctly, the image will fill the sphere in the first material slot. If the image is present, but is a square, you did not do the process correctly. That texture will not work correctly. If you need to repeat the process, click on the material slot to the right of the first one and give it another try.

IMAGE 6.18

8. Apply the texture to the mesh by either dragging the selected mesh or clicking on the "Assign Material to Scene" icon button.

9. The assigned material will turn the mesh gray. Click on the "Show Shaded Material in Viewport" icon button, and the image will appear on the plane in the perspective viewport. Close the Material Editor.

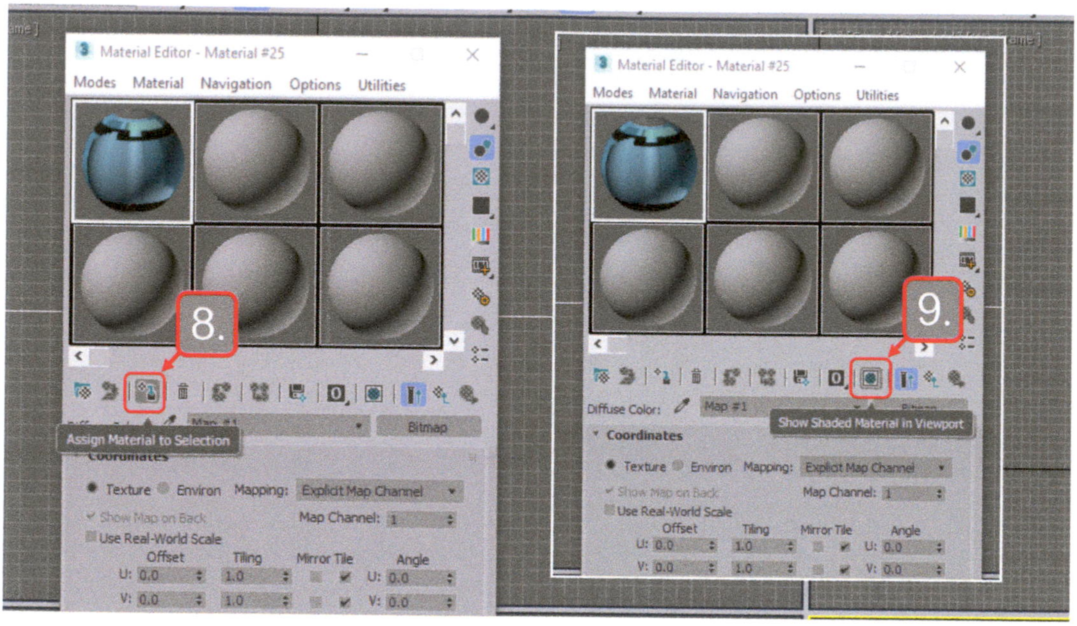

IMAGE 6.19 (Save 6-4)

Those are the steps you will repeat to apply textures to an object. Now, we can begin the modeling.

In the Front Viewport, change the Wireframe setting in the upper left corner to Default Shading. Then, change the "Standard" quality setting to "High Quality" to bring the image into better focus. Next, maximize the Front viewport with the toggle icon in the lower right corner of the UI. Using the Select and Move tool, move the plane so that the X- and Y-axes in the image closely align with the viewport axis.

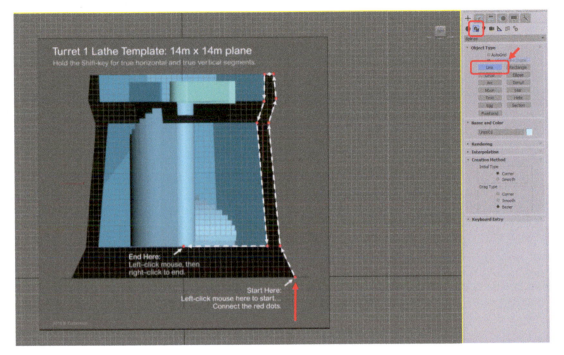

IMAGE 6.20

We're ready for the Line tool. Select the Shapes tab icon in the Create Panel of the Command Panel. In the Splines category, select the first button, "Line." In the Front viewport, left-mouse click on the first red dot (Start Here) and continue to connect the dots to the last one along the path. After you click on the last red dot, right-mouse click to end the line creation. When you want the line to be a true vertical or horizontal, hold down the Shift-key to lock on the X- or Y-axis. If the line is not as you like, simply delete it and redo the line from the start. In a later chapter, we will use the line tool again and will be using the different sub-tools for modifying the line. For now, the simple point-to-point clicks will do.

Open the Scene Explorer and in the Corner Turret layer, turn off the Plane001. The spline you created will be clearly visible. Adjust the spline's position if necessary so that the two end points intersect the X- and Y-axes.

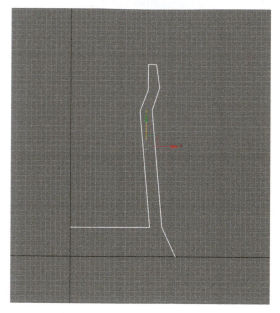

IMAGE 6.21 (Save 6-5)

Switch from the Create Panel to the Modify Panel in the Command Panel. Add a Lathe modifier from the Modifier List. Chances are, an oddly shaped mesh will appear in the viewport. We need to select the correct Direction and Align parameters in the Command Panel to create the proper shape. For mine, the "Y-axis" and the "Min" align buttons created the correct shape. Change the parameters to the ones shown here.

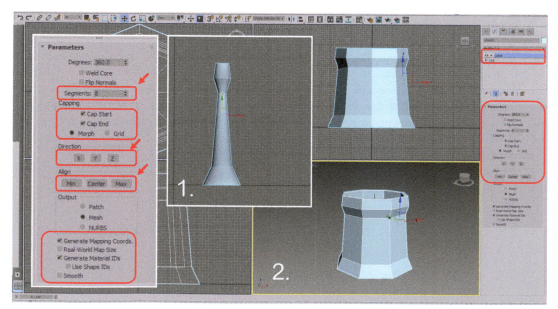

IMAGE 6.22

The pivot point for the mesh is still over to the side of the mesh where the line we lathed was. Switch to the Hierarchy panel to select the "Affect Pivot Only" button. Enter zeros in the Coordinate Display value boxes to move the pivot over to the center of the mesh. Remember to click the "Affect Pivot Only" button to turn it off before proceeding.

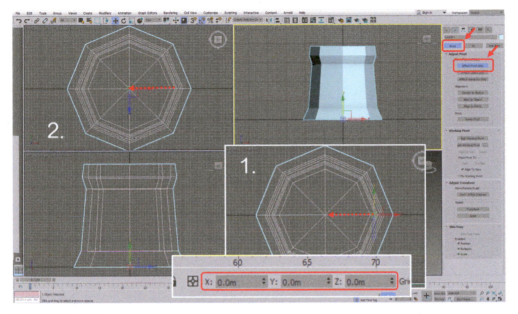

IMAGE 6.23 (Save 6-6)

Next, right-mouse click on the Angle Snaps Toggle icon on the Main Menu bar. In the pop-up window, change the Angle value box to 22.5 degrees and close the window.

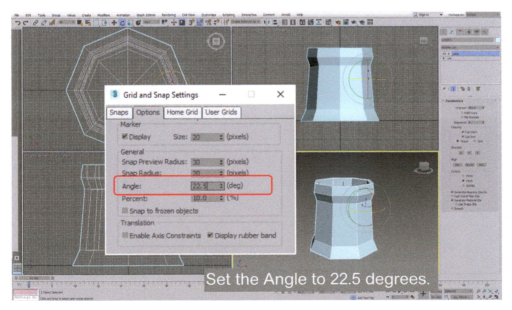

IMAGE 6.24

Turn on the Toggle Angle Snaps icon button. Using the Select and Rotate tool, in the Top Viewport, drag the outer gray circle of the gizmo one "snap click" so that four sides of the mesh are tangent to the X- and Y-axes as shown. This will make it easier to work on these sides for extruding and other operations coming up.

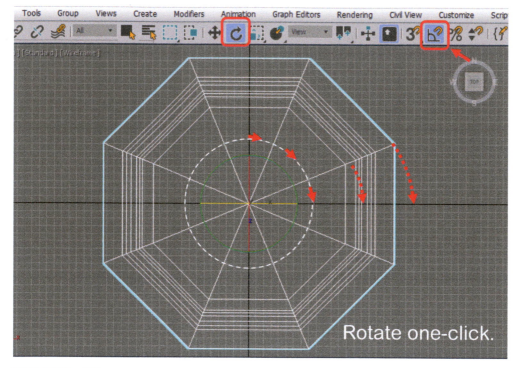

IMAGE 6.25 (Save 6-7)

194

Right-click on the mesh, and convert it to an Editable Poly. Also, let's rename it "corner_turret." In vertex mode, select the bottom row of vertices and enter zeros in the Coordinate Display. That will move the bottom of the mesh to the origin axis.

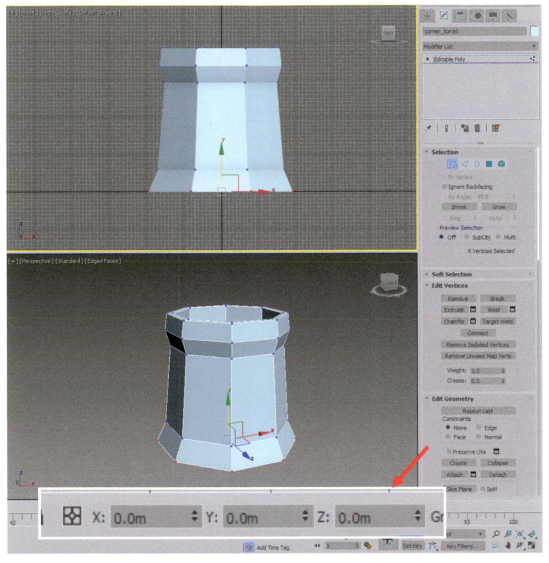

IMAGE 6.26

The inside floor vertices are on approximately the same plane as the outer second row. With both rows selected, right-click in the Top Viewport (perpendicular to the front viewport) and click on the View Align button in the Command Panel to get them aligned. Select the second row of vertices from the bottom, and change the Z-axis values in the Coordinate Display to 1.5 meter.

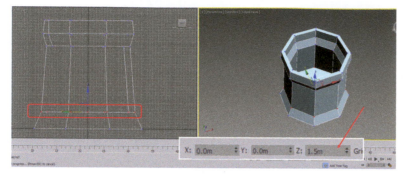

IMAGE 6.27 (Save 6-8)

Select the next row up of vertices. Align the inside and outside rows using the View Align tool again as in the previous step. Enter values in the Z-Coordinate Display of 7.5 meters.

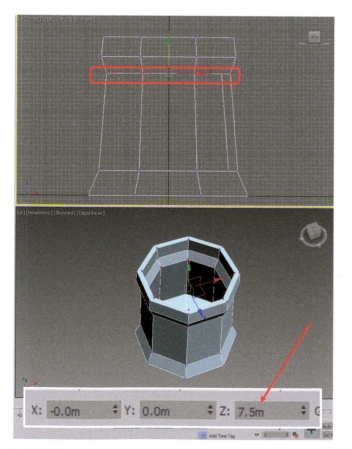

IMAGE 6.28

Select the second from the top row of vertices and repeat the View Align, and in the Z-Coordinate Display, enter 8.5 meters.

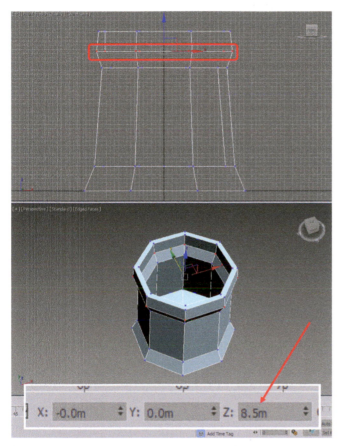

IMAGE 6.29

Finally select the Top Viewport, View Align the vertices to align them and change the Z-Coordinate Display to 9.5 meters.

Normally, I am not so detail oriented with the Coordinate Display entries, going more by the eye. However, I am here with the intent of limiting variations that can lead to problems for learners.

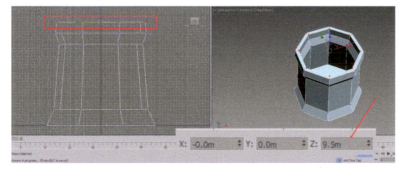

IMAGE 6.30 (Save 6-9)

The turret shape is good, but we won't be able to easily create the merlons at the wall top because there are not enough segments divisions on top to extrude "every other one" as we have done with previous modules. To quickly add the needed segments, we'll use the Slice Plane in Vertex mode.

Select the Slice Plane to activate it in the scene. Click on the "Reset Plane" button to the right of the Slice button. The yellow slice plane should reorient on the Z-axis, aligned to a row of vertices if it already wasn't on one. Right-mouse click on the Angle Snaps icon toggle button on the Main Tool bar to open the Angle Snaps window. In the window, set the angle to 15 degrees and close the window. Each section is 45 degrees. We want to divide them into thirds, hence, 15 degrees.

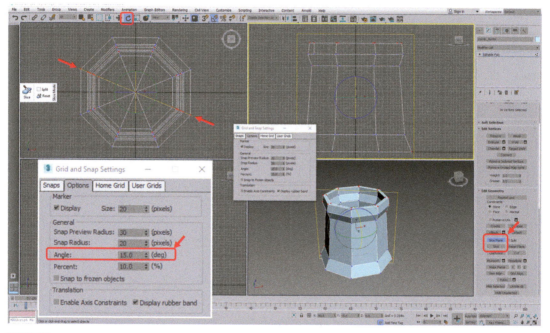

IMAGE 6.31

With the Angle Snaps button "on," use the Select and Rotate tool to rotate the Slice Plane. In the Top Viewport, rotate the gray outer ring of the gizmo "one-click" in either direction.

Next, click on the "Slice" button to create new vertices. Rotate the slice plane again, "one-click," and then click on the Slice button. Continue repeating the process seven more times to complete the addition all the way around the Turret.

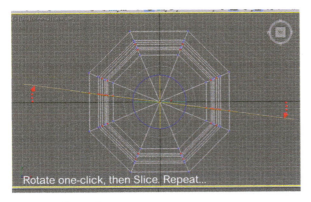

Rotate one-click, then Slice. Repeat...

IMAGE 6.32 (Save 6-10)

The GDD calls for players to be able to access the Corner Turret on two sides from the Curtain Wall and from the ground level inside the castle walls. We need to add doorways with threshold levels of 4.5 meters, the walkway height of the Curtain Wall (good thing we are using coordinates!). In Vertex mode, turn on the Slice Plane tool again. Change the angle in the Angle Snaps window to 22.5 degrees. Using the Angle Snaps to control the rotation, position the Slice Plane so that it is horizontal, parallel to the vertex rows on the X-axis. First, rotate it so that it aligns with the X-axis, and then rotate in the Y-axis direction. Set the Z-coordinate to 4.5 to move the Slice Plane to the height of the Curtain Wall walkway, and then click on the "Slice" button to create the row of vertices. We will use this row of vertices to also create the windows. They are our next target. Turn off the Slice Plane.

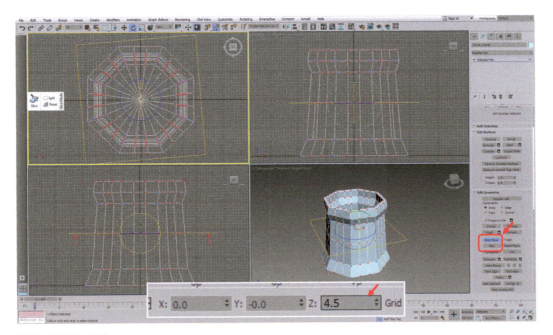

IMAGE 6.33 (Save 6-11)

To start the making of the Turret windows, select the polygon on the outside of the Turret as shown. Next, select the Inset tool in the Edit Polygons section of the Modify Panel. Set the size of the inset to approximately what is shown in the image, a very narrow slit. Then, using the Select and Scale tool, widen the inset as shown. By doing the scaling as we did, we avoided any "bending" of polygons due to the tapered walls.

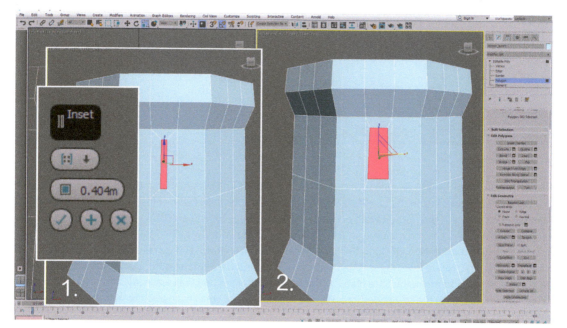

IMAGE 6.34

Now, use the Inset tool again and create a narrow window frame border as shown.

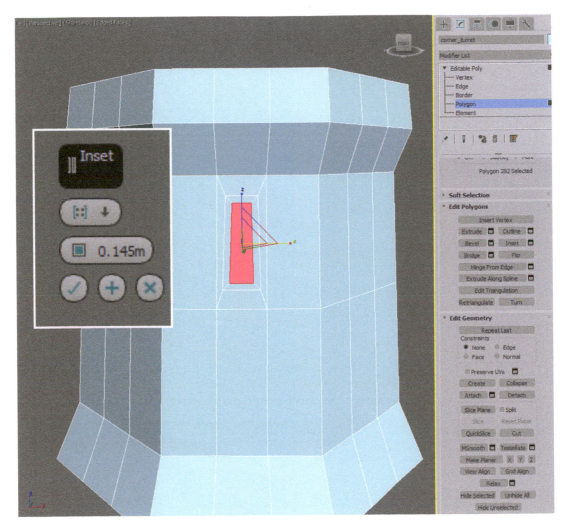

IMAGE 6.35

Using the Select and Move tool, move the polygon toward the center of the turret slightly to create the bevel of the window frame as shown. Then, extrude the polygon −0.125 meter to create the flat sides of the window frame.

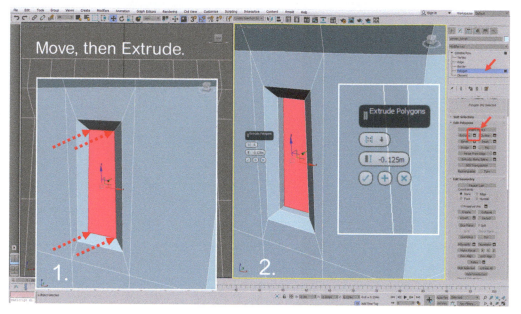

IMAGE **6.36** (Save 6-12)

Delete the polygon to open the window hole, and delete the polygon on the inside wall behind it. Like with the windows we made for the Gate House, use the Border tool in Borders sub-object level mode to select the borders of the inside hole and the outside hole, and then use the Bridge tool to connect them.

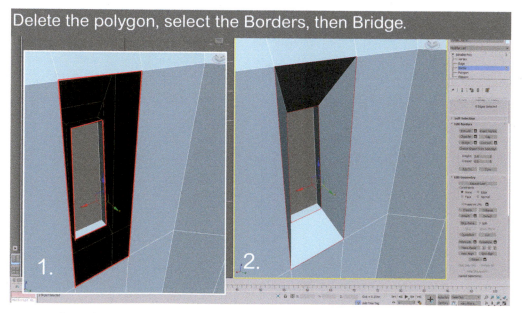

IMAGE **6.37** (Save 6-13)

We could repeat the same steps we did on this window to the other seven sides to create all the windows, time consuming. A faster way would be to clone this window seven times. Select the polygons in the same row of the other seven sides on the outside of the mesh and the polygons on the inside of the mesh. Delete the selected polygons, leaving the side with the window as shown. Next, select the polygons that make up the window panel. In the Modify Panel, select the Detach button. This will make this polygon group a separate mesh from the turret. When the Detach pop-up window opens, rename the mesh "window," a temporary name.

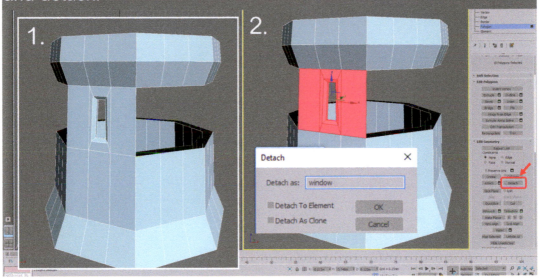

IMAGE 6.38 (Save 6-14)

I changed the color of the window mesh to green, so you can see it as a separate mesh. We can now clone it to the other sides. The pivot point is in the same place as the Turret mesh, so we can rotate it and expect perfect alignment. In the perspective viewport, select the window element. Go up to the Tools drop-down menu on the top tool bar, and select the Array tool from the list to open the Array window. Set the Z-value box in the Rotate row to 45 degrees. Change the count to eight. Click on the preview button to see if the array is correct. When it is, click OK.

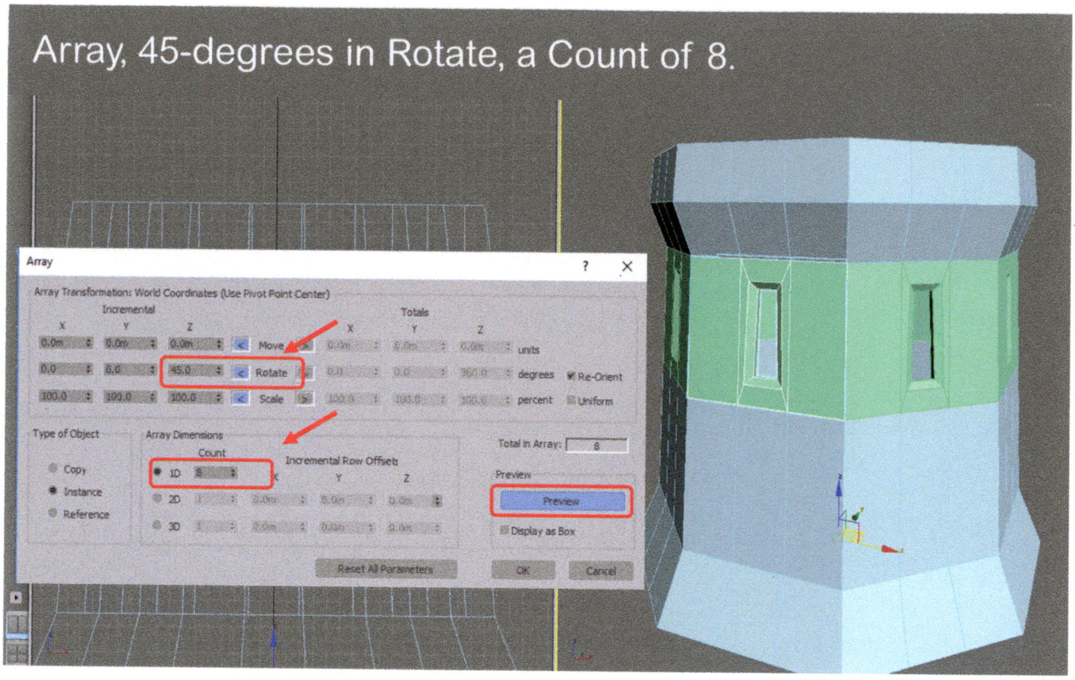

IMAGE 6.39

In the next step, we will attach everything back together. Select the Turret mesh. Click on Editable Poly in the Modifier Stack. Scroll down to the Edit Geometry section, and select the Attach caddy. In the pop-up window that will open, select all the window elements and then click the Attach button.

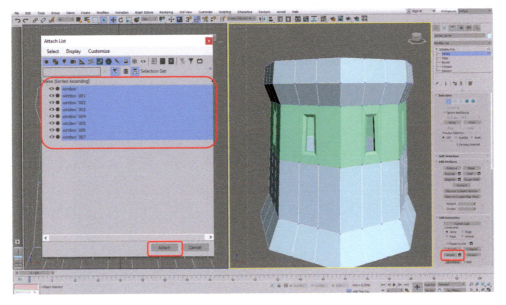

IMAGE 6.40 (Save 6-15)

We need to weld the vertices at the tops and bottoms of the window panels. The Array tool does not weld vertices. In the front viewport, select the vertices at the top of the windows and then open the Weld caddy. Weld the vertices (remember, increase the number in the area of influence value box until the After number is lower than the Before number without distorting the model). Repeat the operation on the window bottom vertices.

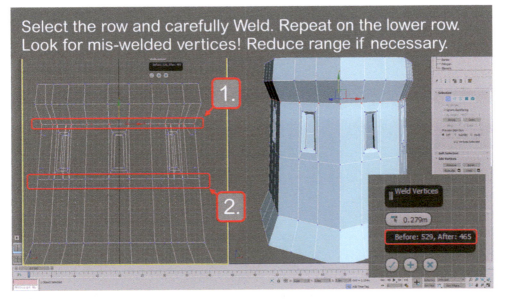

IMAGE 6.41

We'll create the three doorways now. Let's bring the Curtain Wall module into this scene to help align the doorway with the Curtain Wall walkway.

From the File tab on the top menu, select Import > Merge. In the pop-up window, select the curtain_wall and position it as shown in the scene. Our door will be where the window is at the end of the Curtain Wall walkway.

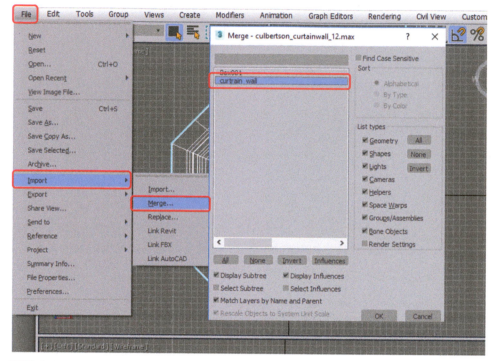

IMAGE 6.42

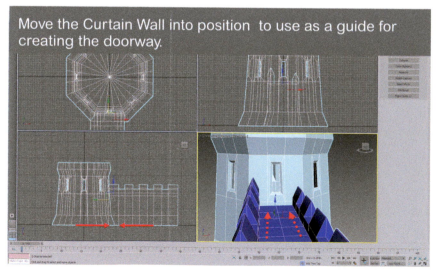

IMAGE 6.43

Rather than wrestle with the current window polygons to make a doorway, let's just delete the window, inside the turret and outside the turret as shown.

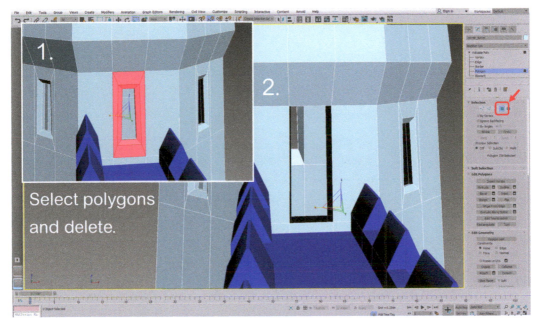

IMAGE 6.44 (Save 6-16)

Use the Border sub-object level mode to select the border of the outside opening. Next, select the Cap tool to close the opening with a polygon. Select the Inset tool again, and create a doorframe.

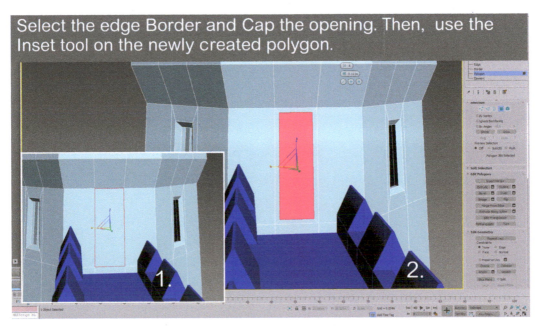

IMAGE 6.45

Like with the windows, use the Select and Move tool to move the polygon toward the Turret center, creating a beveled doorframe.

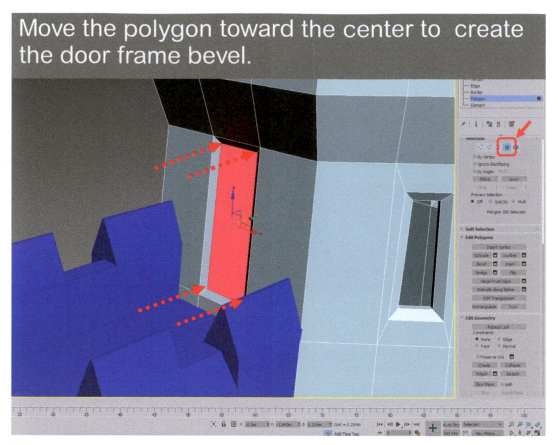

IMAGE 6.46

Delete the inset polygon to create an opening. Use the Border tool to select the borders of the two openings, and then use the Bridge tool to connect them, creating the walk-thru for the doorway. Use the Select and Scale tool to adjust the vertices of the doorway to widen the base of the door as shown and the top of the door slightly.

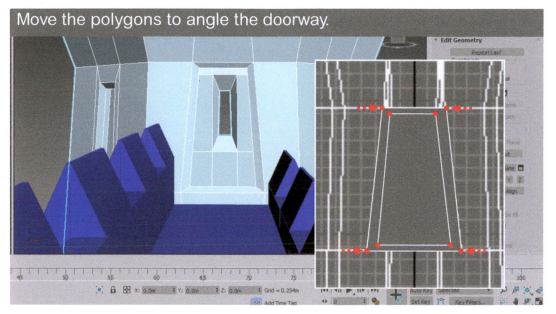

IMAGE 6.47

IMAGE 6.48 (Save 6-17)

Hide the Curtain Wall in the Scene Explorer, because we won't be needing it now.

The GDD calls for a second door, 90 degrees from this door, which would be two panels to the right. We could model another one or use the Array tool again. Using the same steps as we did with the windows, we'll need to detach the door panel. Select the polygons as shown, inside the turret and on the outside.

Select the Detach button, and in the Detach window, temporarily name it "Door."

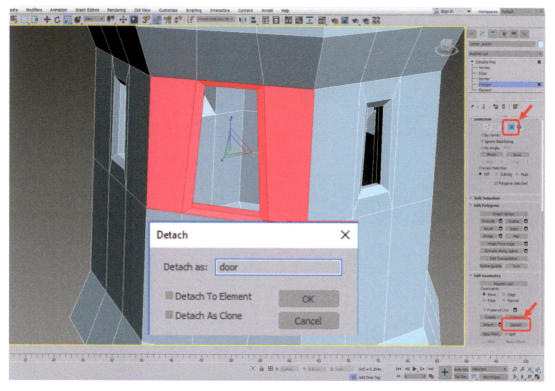

IMAGE 6.49 (Save 6-18)

Rotate around the turret, two panels counterclockwise from the Detached Door, and delete the window panel. To create an opening for the Detached Door to be copied into.

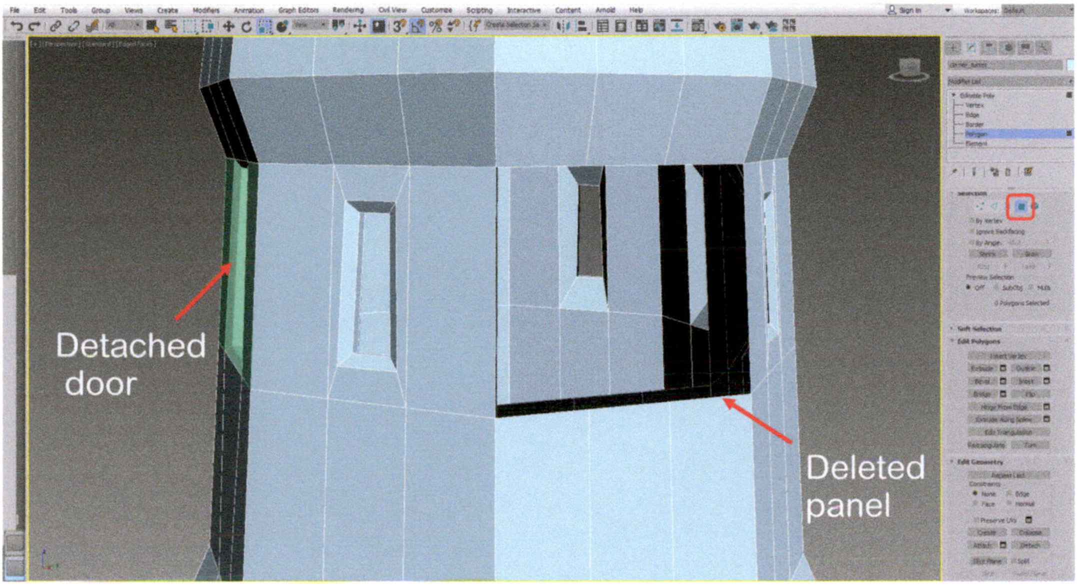

IMAGE 6.50

Open the Array tool in the Tools tab of the top tool bar. Set the rotation value in the Z box to 90 degrees, and change the 1D Count box value to 2. Look at the preview to see if it is correctly filling the new space.

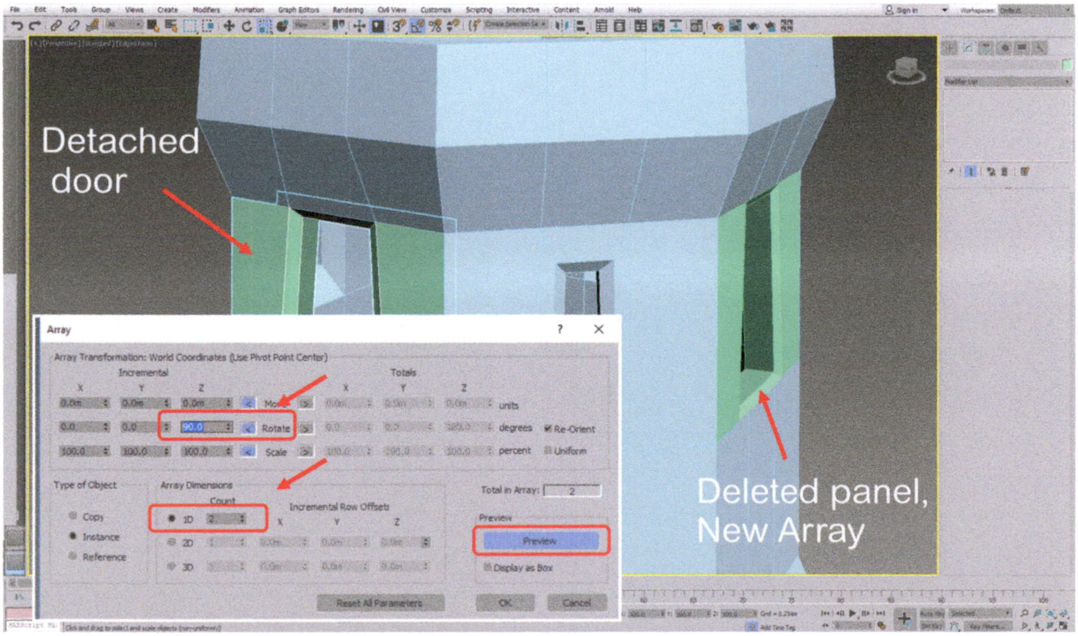

IMAGE 6.51

Like with the window panels, we need to "attach" the door panels to the Turret to make them one mesh and then weld the top and bottom rows of vertices. Go ahead, and perform those operations.

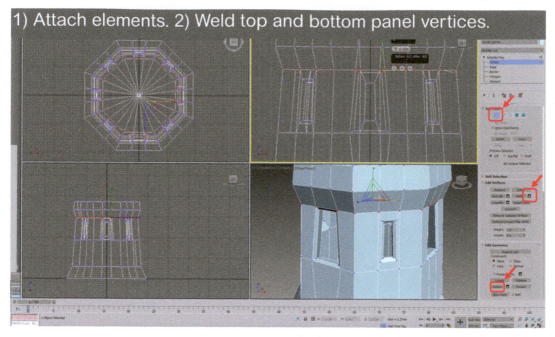

IMAGE 6.52 (Save 6-19)

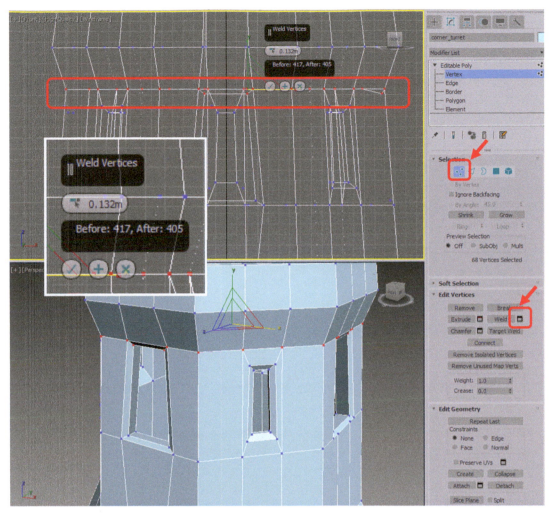

IMAGE 6.53 (Save 6-20)

Next, we will make the ground-level doorway. Select the Turret as shown, and then using the Angle Snaps, rotate the turret so that the selected polygon is parallel to the X-axis line. This will make it easier to work with, keeping everything "square" for extrusions and scaling while making the doorway.

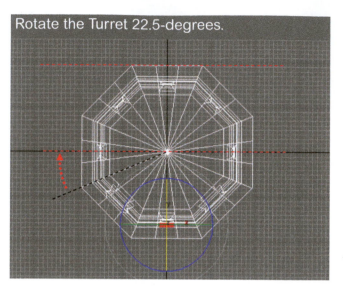

Rotate the Turret 22.5-degrees.

IMAGE 6.54

Using the Select and Move tool, move the polygon toward the center of the mesh on the Y-axis to create the door bevel.

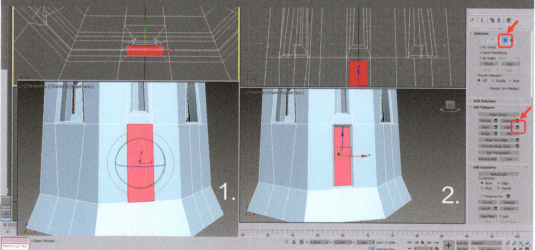

Select the panel as shown for the lower door. Inset the panel, then move inward as with the precious door to create the doorframe.

IMAGE 6.55

Delete the polygon to create an opening, and delete the polygon behind it on the inside of the turret. As with the previous doors and windows, select the borders of the openings and use the Bridge tool to connect them.

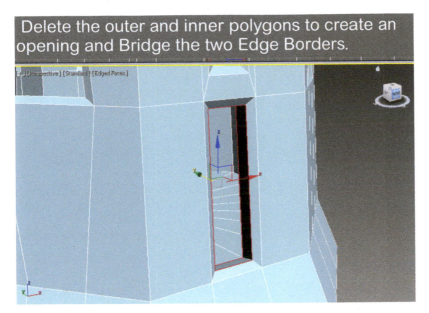

Delete the outer and inner polygons to create an opening and Bridge the two Edge Borders.

IMAGE 6.56

Use the Select and Scale tool to widen the base of the doorway.

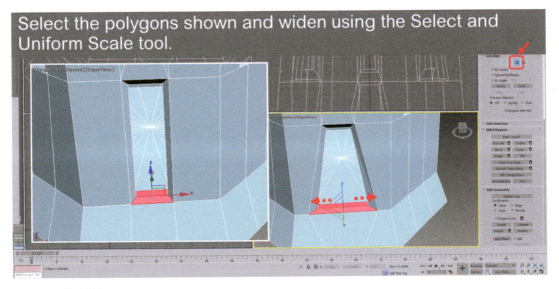

Select the polygons shown and widen using the Select and Uniform Scale tool.

IMAGE 6.57 (Save 6-21)

Looking over at the second upstairs door, there are two vertices that need welding. Target Weld the two floating vertices to the window frame as shown. Weld the two similar vertices on the inside of the turret under the same doorway.

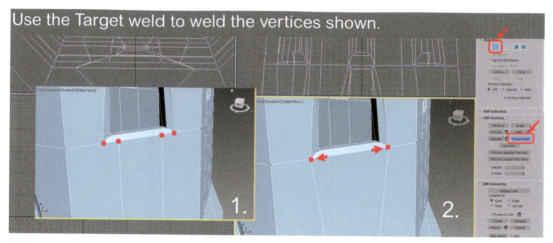

IMAGE 6.58

The majority of the modeling for this model is behind us at this point. We still need to add a staircase, the interior first floor and second floor and the Merlons on the top wall. To add the staircase, we could create the bottom setup and use the Array tool to clone the step vertically and rotated, multiple times to make a spiral staircase. A lengthy process. Or, we could use the stair tool!

In the Geometry tab of the Create Panel, click on the drop-down menu with Standard Primitives is selected. Change the selection to "Stairs."

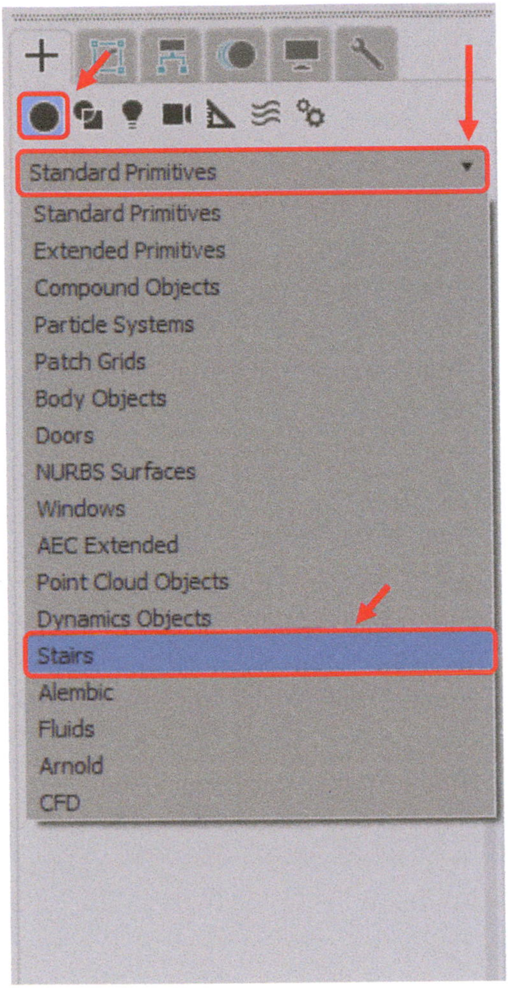

IMAGE 6.59

Select the "Spiral Stair" option, and then in the Top Viewport, click and drag the mouse to create the pre-made staircase radius, release the mouse and drag it toward the top of the UI to create the height. Once it is created, change the parameters in the Modifier Panel as shown. Change the Coordinate Display values to X: 0 meter, Y: 0 meter and Z: 1.5 meter to raise the staircase up to the interior first floor and orient as shown. If you want to, try different variations of the parameters to see the stair tool capabilities, and then return them to our settings.

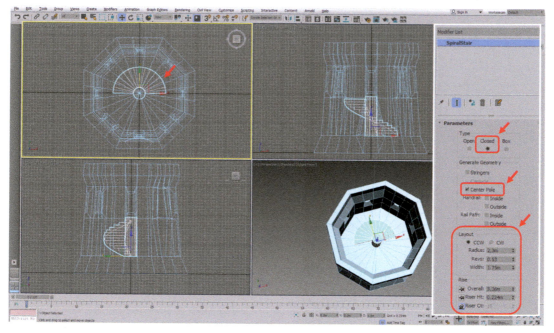

IMAGE 6.60 (Save 6-22)

Next, let's make the floor at the top of the stairs. Create a tube with the parameters as shown in the image below.

Rename the tube, "floor_closed."

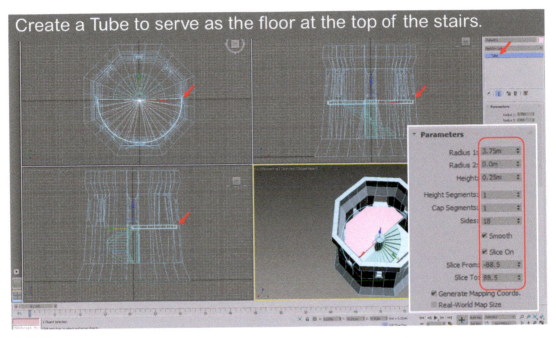

IMAGE 6.61

Next, with the tube still selected, mirror the tube with the Mirror tool on the Main Tool bar, changing the "Radius 2" value of its parameters to 2.3 meters. This will create an opening for the player to run up the stairs. Rename the tube, "floor_open."

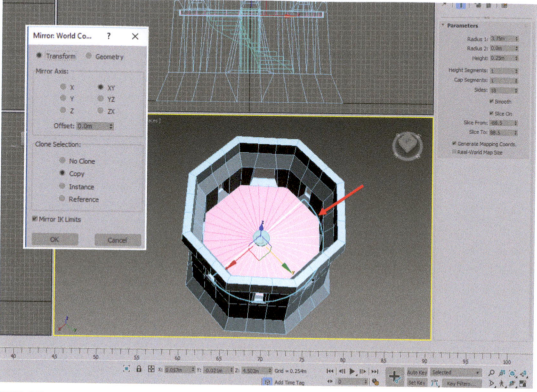

IMAGE 6.62

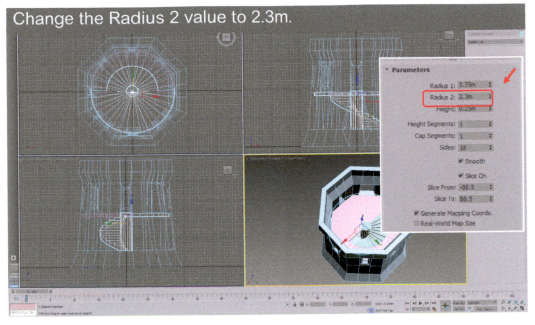

IMAGE 6.63

Open the Scene Explorer, and turn off the corner_turret layer. Select the spiral staircase and the two floor sections we just made. Open the Array tool to quickly clone the group into place for the second floor. Create a copy (not an instance) by using the settings in this image.

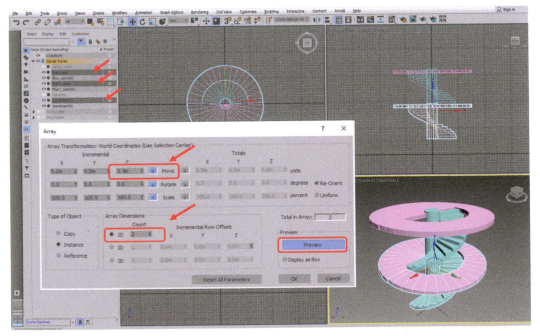

IMAGE 6.64 (Save 6-23)

Turn the corner_turret layer back on. Select the two top floors, and change the Z-Coordinate Display values to 8.7 meters. You might need to do one at a time. Then, select the upper staircase and change the overall value in the "Rise" section of the Modifier Panel to 4.2 meters to bring the staircase up to the floor level. At this height, the player should be able to look out the embrasures between the merlons.

This completes the modeling of the Spiral Stairs. They were carefully modeled to insure there was space for the character height (which will be 1.75 meter) when the player moves up and down the stairs.

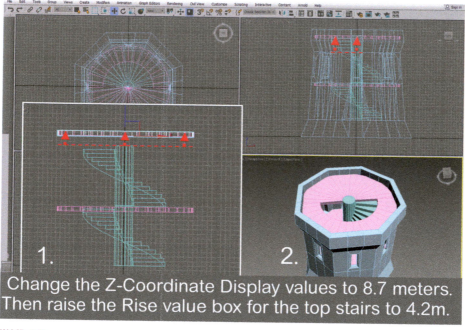

Change the Z-Coordinate Display values to 8.7 meters. Then raise the Rise value box for the top stairs to 4.2m.

IMAGE 6.65

Lastly, we'll finish the top of the wall with merlons as on the precious modules.

Select the top polygons as shown. Then, open the Ribbon and select the Insert tool in the Loops section to divide the polygons.

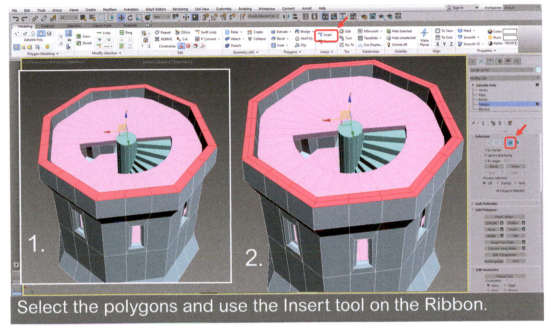

Select the polygons and use the Insert tool on the Ribbon.

IMAGE 6.66

Deselect the polygons shown, leaving the red ones in the image selected. Next, extrude the polygons 0.5 meter.

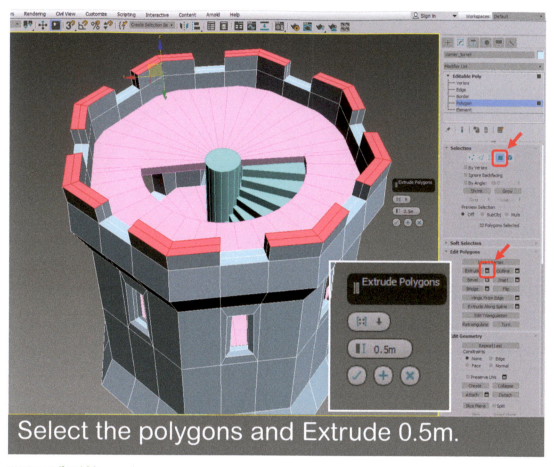

IMAGE 6.67 (Save 6-24)

Use the Target Weld tool to weld the vertices as shown, around the top of the entire turret. Weld from the upper vertices to the lower vertices.

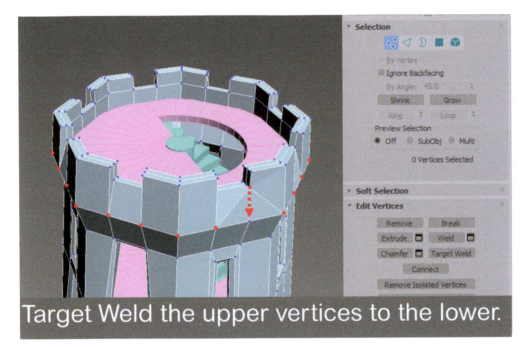

Target Weld the upper vertices to the lower.

IMAGE 6.68

After welding the vertices, select the edges in the middle of the top of the merlons, and with the Select and Move tool, raise them slightly to create a short peak. The merlons now have the same "family" look as the merlons on the other modules we made earlier. This finishes the modeling of the Corner Turret. The polygon count is 1,519. Within the set limit.

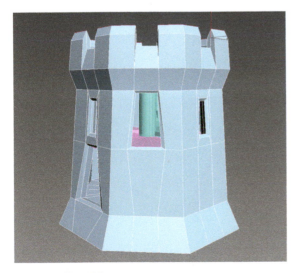

IMAGE 6.69 (Save 6-25)

The Mid-Wall Turret

The Mid-Wall Turret is a lot simpler model than the Corner Turret. First, we'll make the placeholder model. In the Scene Explorer, change the active layer to the Placeholder, and then turn off the corner_turret_ placeholder sub-layer.

Create a box in the Top Viewport, and set the Coordinate Display values to 0, 0, 0. Change the Parameter settings in the Modify window as shown. Rename the box "midwall_turret_placeholder." Convert the box to an Editable Poly.

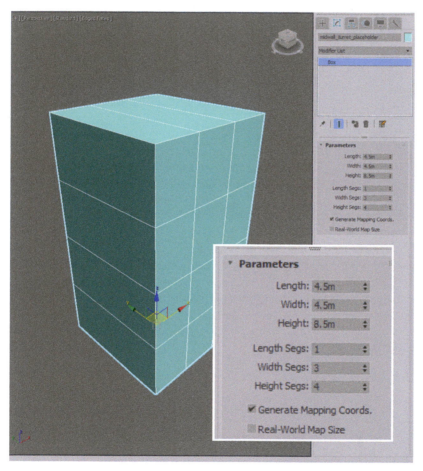

IMAGE 6.70 (Save 6-26)

In Vertex sub-object level mode, select the row of vertices that are second from the bottom row and enter a Z-value of 1.5 meter in the Coordinate Display for the top of the batter.

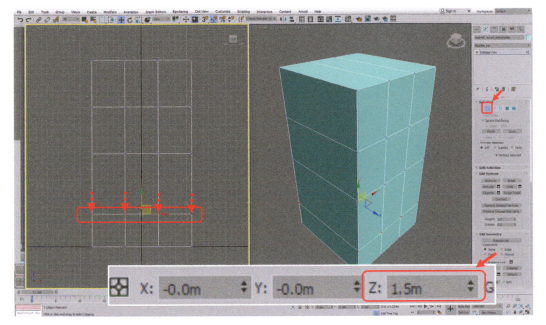

IMAGE 6.71

Next, flair out the bottom row of vertices to create the batter. Select the second from the top row of vertices, and enter a Z-value of 7.0 in the Coordinate Display.

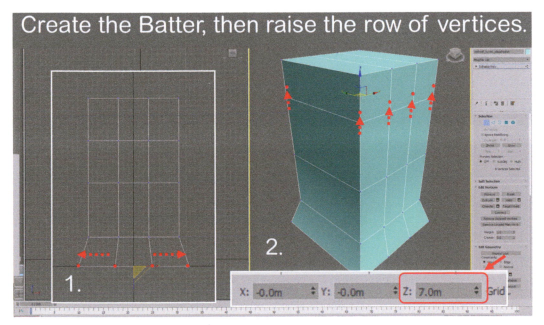

IMAGE 6.72

In Polygon sub-object level mode, select the polygon shown as well as the corresponding one on the opposite side of the mesh. Extrude these two polygons –1.5 meter to represent the walk-through. That completes this placeholder.

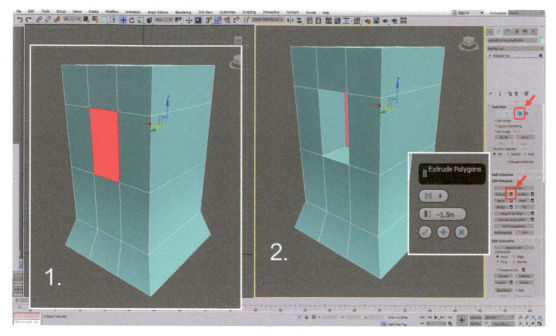

IMAGE 6.73 (Save 6-27)

Now let's make the model. In the Scene Explorer, create a new layer, "Mid-Wall Turret." Create a tube in the Top Viewport with the parameters as shown, and rotate it so that the sides are parallel with the X-/Y-axis. Rename the tube "midwall_turret."

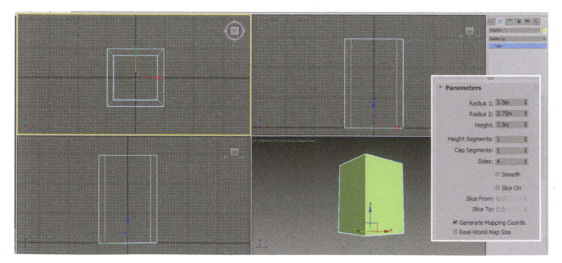

IMAGE 6.74 (Save 6-28)

Convert the tube to an Editable Poly. In Vertex sub-object level mode, turn on the Slice Plane tool. Use the Angle Snaps to position the Slice Plane so that it is horizontal, parallel to the X-axis. In the Coordinate Display, set the Z-value to 1.5 meter, the height of the batter. Click the "Slice" button.

Next, enter a Z-value of 4.5 meters in the Coordinate Display, the height of the Curtain Wall walkway to move the Slice Plane and then click the "Slice" button. One more row to go, move the Slice Plane up the tube again, entering 7.0 in the Z-value of the Coordinate Display and click the "Slice" button to create vertices.

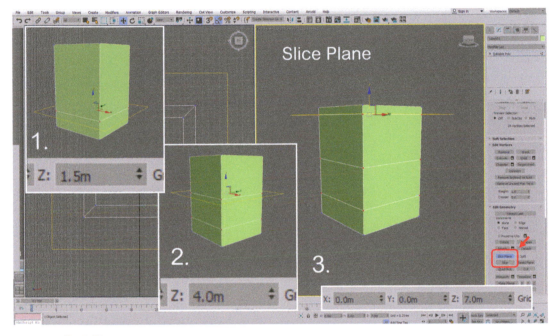

IMAGE 6.75 (Save 6-29)

Next, rotate the slice plane, with the Angle Snaps on, to vertical and intersecting the tube from corner-to-corner in the Top Viewport. Change the Angle Snaps' angle to 30 degrees. Rotate the Slice plane 30 degrees, and click the "Slice" button. Repeat the procedure again and continue around the tube so that all sides are subdivided as shown.

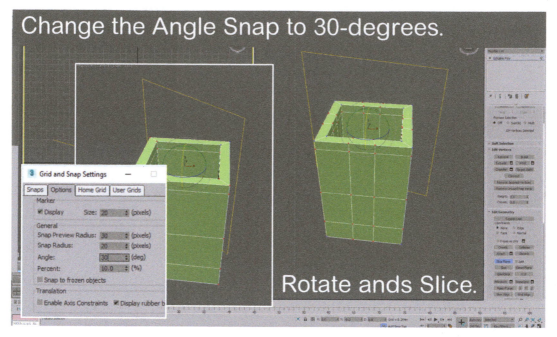

IMAGE 6.76 (Save 6-30)

Close the Slice Plane. In Vertex sub-object level mode, flair the bottom row of vertices to create the batter. Next, open the Scene Explorer and turn on the Curtain Wall layer. If necessary, position the Curtain Wall as shown to align with the turret. Next, use the Select and Scale tool to widen the selected rows of vertices for the walk-through doorways. Turn off the Curtain Wall layer when completed.

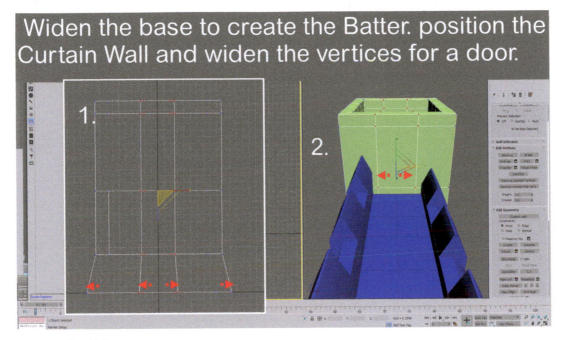

IMAGE 6.77 (Save 6-31)

Select the polygons where the doors will be on opposite sides of the turret, including the ones inside the turret. Delete all four polygons.

Can you guess our next move? Bridge the gaps between the openings to create the walk-through space. In Border sub-object level mode, select the two borders of the two doors and bridge them first.

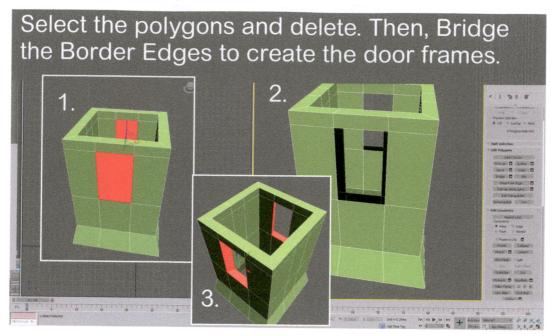

IMAGE 6.78 (Save 6-32)

We can't bridge the two openings as they are closed meshes, not open. The polygons inside the turret are not necessary, and the player will only have access to the walk-through. So, we can delete the polygons inside the turret, which will create an open mesh to help our bridge of the two doorways. Hold the Shift-key and select the polygons inside the turret and on the bottom, and then delete them.

Switch back to the Border sub-object level mode and select the two doorway borders and click the Bridge button to connect them.

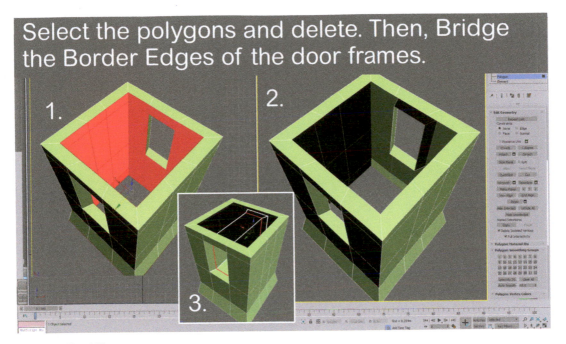

IMAGE 6.79 (Save 6-33)

Select the polygons on the top of the turret, and use the Ribbon Inset tool to divide them as we did with the Corner Turret. Deselect the polygons in the center of each wall as shown, and extrude the remaining polygons 0.75 meter to create the merlons. As we did with the Corner Turret, Target Weld the vertices vertically to create the merlon angles (Save 6-21).

Next, select the top center edges of the merlons and use the Select and Move tool to raise them slightly to create a peak as shown.

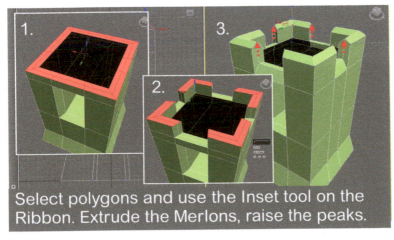

IMAGE 6.80

The last modeling step will be to apply a taper modifier to the turret. Click on Editable Poly at the top of the Modifier Stack to get out of the sub-object level mode. Next, add a Taper modifier to the Stack. Adjust the "Amount" value box in the Taper Parameters to −0.2 to add a slight taper. If you want, try changing the other values to see what the taper modifier can do. Then, change the value back to our setting.

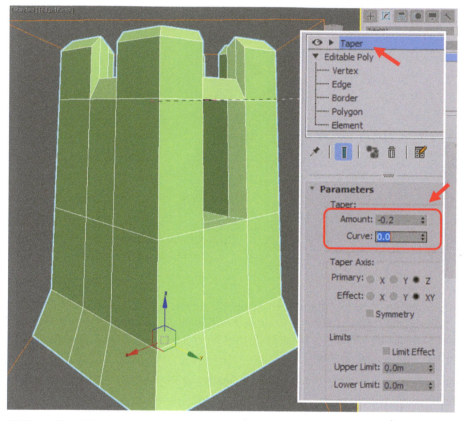

IMAGE 6.81 (Save 6-34)

Right-mouse click in the modifier stack, and collapse the Stack. This completes the modeling of the two turrets.

Next, we will test your newly honed skills in creating the center of the castle, the Keep.

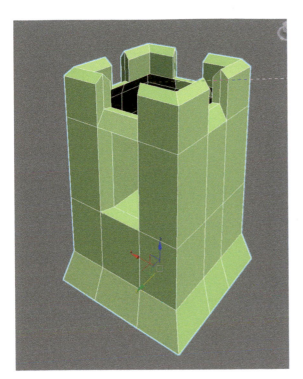

IMAGE 6.82

Chapter 6 Exercise: Cannon

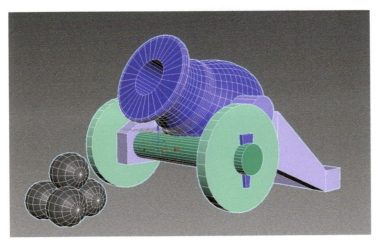

IMAGE 6.83

Model a medieval cannon. For this model, you can use multiple meshes to create the finished model. The design can be of your choice or you can follow the example I made. Be sure to do some research to define your design. Using a line to define the shape, I used the Lathe tool to create the cannon barrel shape. The other parts are modified primitives. When you complete Chapter 7, Unwrapping the Model, you can return to the finished cannon model and complete the unwrapping and texturing of your model.

In the companion folder online, you will find the 3ds Max file iterations saves from when I modeled the cannon and the texture file, "accessory_textures.png" for your use.

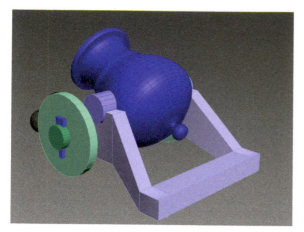

IMAGE 6.84

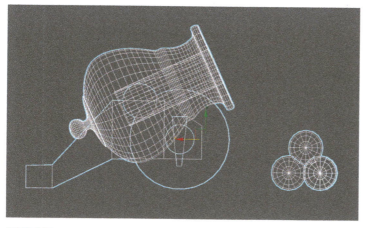

IMAGE 6.85

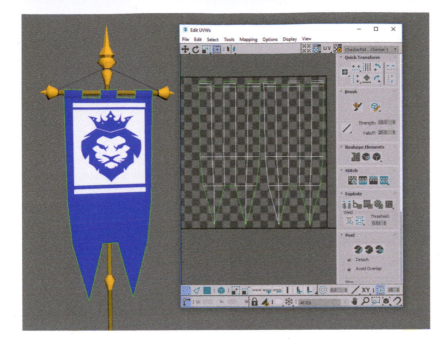

Unwrapping the Model

Concepts/Skills/Tools Introduced in This Chapter

- UVW Map
- Unwrap UVW
- Edit UVWs Editor
  - Transforms
    - Move Selected Sub-Objects
    - Rotate Selected Sub-Objects
    - Scale Selected Sub-Objects
  - Explode > Break
  - Stitch
- Quick Map Planar
- Render Template
- Checkerboard Utility Texture
- Normal Mapping
  - Named Selection set
  - Box Mapping
  - Best Align

- Render Setup
- Environment (Background)
- Render Output
  - Power of Two
- MJPEG Compression
- Adobe Photoshop
- Pyramid

We now have a nice collection of castle modules. The modules look medieval and look like they were constructed for the same castle. Only problem is, they don't have any textures. Texturing was purposely held off until this point to make sure that you could concentrate on developing your modeling basics and have an opportunity to reinforce them through repetition. Before you apply a texture to a mesh, its polygons need to have mapping coordinates.

Mapping coordinates, or UVW coordinates, identify the placement, orientation and scale of a 2D image on a textured mesh. Most primitive geometric objects received mapping coordinates when created by default (the "Generate Coordinates" tick box is checked in the objects parameters). Typically, editable polys and editable meshes do not have mapping coordinates. To add them to the object, there are several paths we can take to apply them.

UVW Map

The simplest manner of adding mapping coordinates is to add a UVW Map modifier to the object. When added to the mesh, the UVW Map modifier provides mapping coordinates that can accept the projection of a 2D, flat image. In most cases, the mapping coordinates will require adjusting to get the best available image placement, orientation and scale.

Let's model a simple object to use the UVW Map modifier so that you can see its range of mapping options. We'll make a banner-flag for the Gate House module as an accessory.

Open a new project in 3ds Max. Name it "lastname_banners.max." In the Scene Explorer window, create two layers, Banner 01 and Banner 02. Make the Banner 01 layer active, and close the Scene Explorer.

In the Left Viewport, create a plane (in the Geometry tab of the Command Panel) with the parameters shown in the image below.

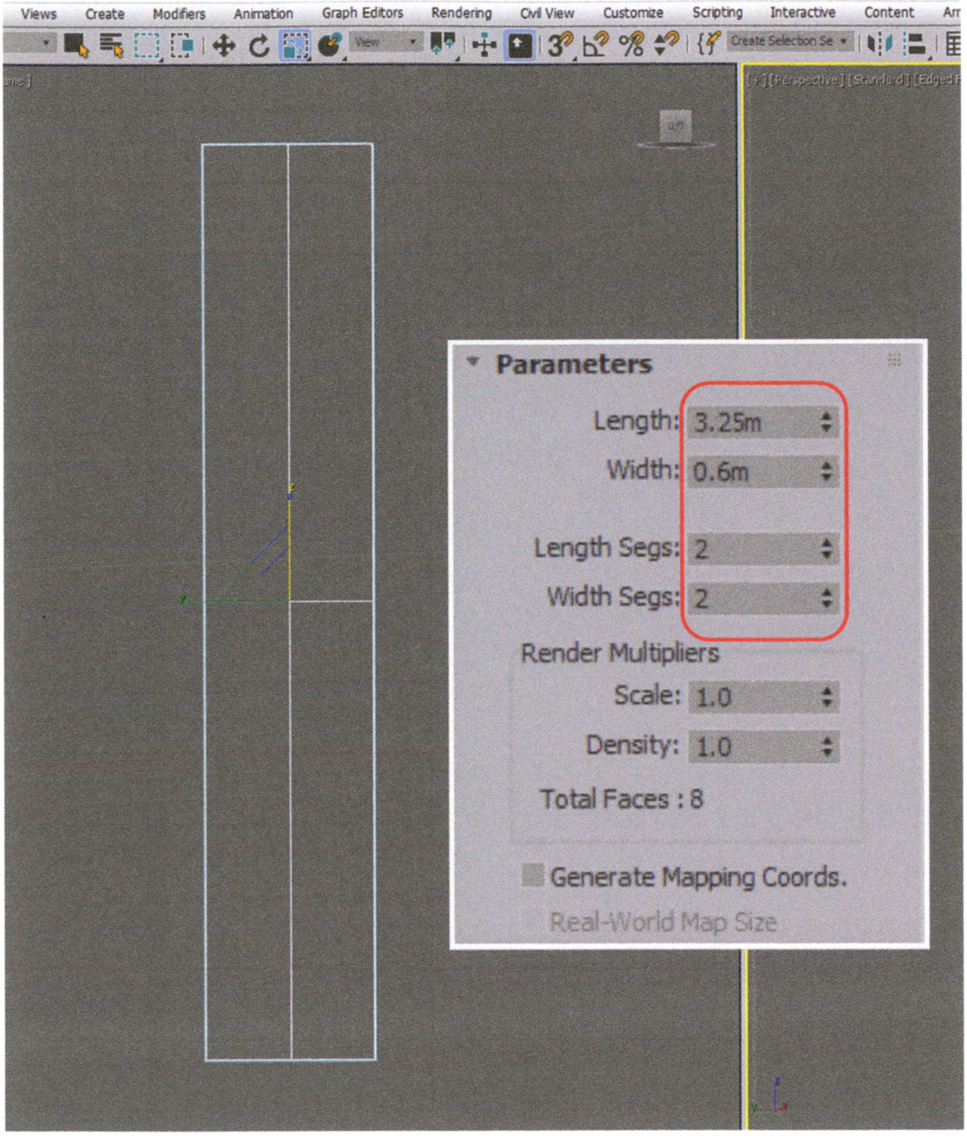

IMAGE 7.1 (Save 7-1)

Convert the plane to an Editable Poly, then select the middle row of vertices and change the Z-Coordinate Display to 2.0 meters. (Save 7-1)

Switch to the Select and Uniform Scale tool, and scale the row of vertices toward the center of the banner until the X-Coordinate Display value changes to 80. Next, select the middle vertex of the bottom row and change its Z-Coordinate Display value to −6.5 meters. This will make our banner a more interesting shape.

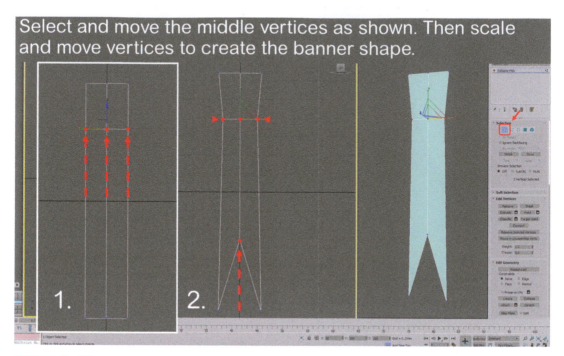

IMAGE 7.2 (Save 7-2)

Assigning the Banner Texture

Open the Material Editor from the Main Tool Bar. Download the Banner_01.png image from the files folder to a location of your choice on the computer. Since we are using an existing texture map image, not needing to create or add any other textures to the map, we can use the Compact editor (switch from the Slate Editor if necessary: Mode > Compact Material Editor). Repeat the steps we used to apply the texture to the plane in Chapter 6:

1. With the mesh you are texturing selected, click on the "Get Material" icon button. This will open the Material/Map Browser window.

2. In the Material/Map Browser, browse to Materials > General > Standard (select "Standard" by double clicking it). This will define the type of map you are using for this texture.

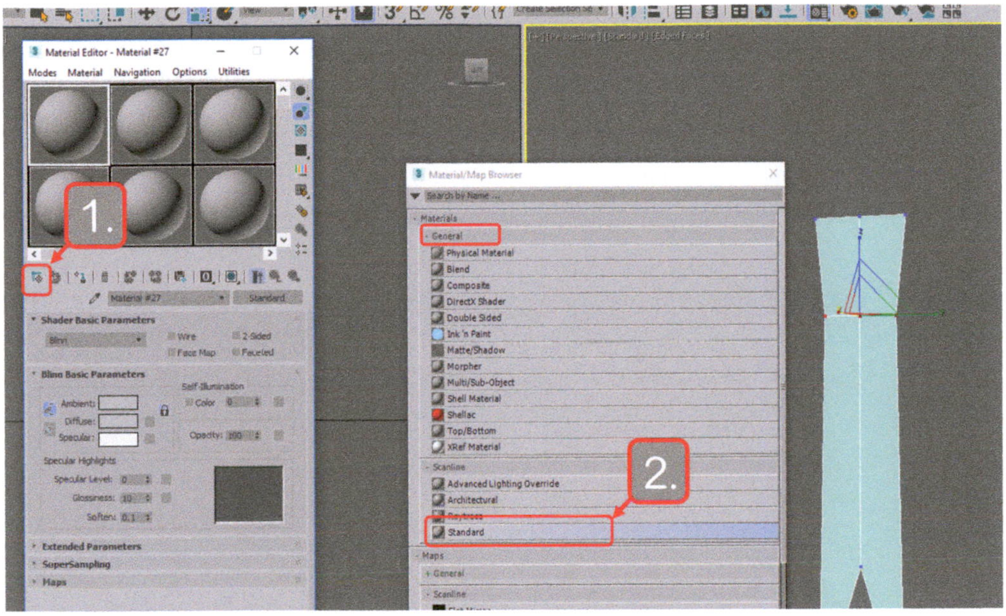

IMAGE 7.3

IMAGE 7.3

3. At the bottom of the Editor, click on the Maps rollout to open it.
4. The second attribute is Diffuse Color. Click on the "Map" box for Diffuse Color (it currently reads "No Map").
5. In the pop-up window, navigate to Maps > and expand the "+General" menu.
6. Double click on the "Bitmap" type of map.

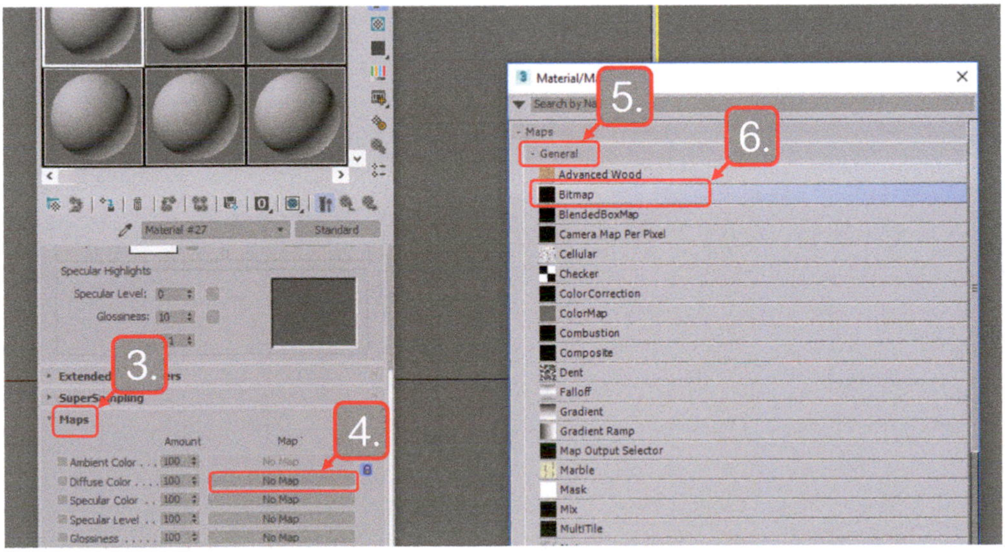

IMAGE 7.4

7. In the Select Bitmap Image File window, navigate to wherever you downloaded the image file earlier to and select it. If you have done the preceding steps correctly, the image will fill the sphere in the first material slot. If the image is present, but is a square, you did not do the process correctly. That texture will not work correctly. If you need to repeat the process, click on the material slot to the right of the first one and give it another try.

8. Apply the texture to the mesh by either dragging the selected mesh or clicking on the "Assign Material to Scene" icon button.

9. The assigned material will be gray. Click on the "Show Shaded Material in Viewport" icon button, and the image normally would appear on the plane in the perspective viewport. However, our banner does not have any mapping coordinates, so the image cannot be projected on it correctly.

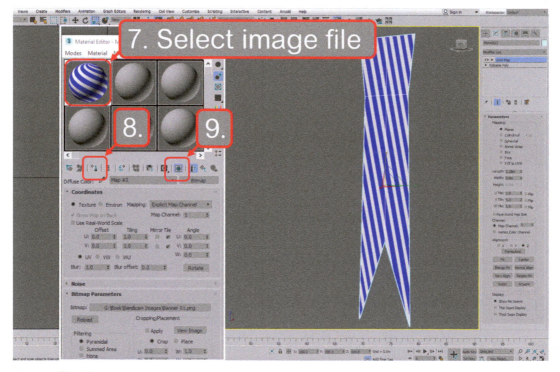

IMAGE 7.5 (Save 7-3)

In the modify panel, open the Modifier List and apply a UVW Map modifier by selecting it. The material we created will appear on the mesh. By default, the Planar projection option is selected. The material map is being projected across the mesh as a plane. Why is it called "UVW" you might ask? It is the equivalent of "XYZ" for the axis orientations. U, V and W are used so as to not get the mapping coordinates confused with the geometry coordinates. UVW corresponds with XYZ.

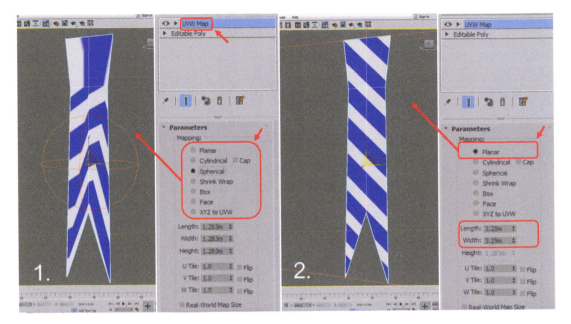

IMAGE 7.6 (Save 7-4)

Click on the other options (cylindrical, spherical and the others to see what they would look like). Planar appears to be the best option, switch back to it as the selection.

To get the truest fit, change the size of the plane in the Length to 3.25 meters, the height of the banner and the Width to 3.25 meters to make the mapping plane square, matching the map image size ratio. The image projection on the banner mesh now matches the texture image.

Unwrap UVW Modifier

The results from our mapping are fine using the UVW Mapping method if the image can be projected with desired results, tiled or scaled to fit the mesh. On most occasions, you are probably looking for more control over the placement of the image projection on the model. Texture map images typically are several images combined into one, covering different parts of a mesh or used for two or more different meshes. The image below has textures for two short and two long banner-flags to hang from the Gate House module. The images have more detail than the previous banner we made, requiring exact location and scaling of the map on the mesh. To achieve mapping that is more accurate, we will use the Unwrap UVW modifier. Think of it this way: the UVW Map is better than no map at all, and the Unwrap UVW modifier is better than the UVW Map Modifier. Although it requires more work to apply to the mesh, it yields the best results.

Let's replace the current UVW Map modifier on our banner with the Unwrap UVW modifier. In the Modifier Stack, click on the UVW Map, and then either click on the Trash Can icon below the Stack or right-mouse click in the stack to open a menu and select "Delete" to remove the modifier. The image will disappear from the mesh.

Next, add the Unwrap UVW modifier to the Editable Poly. The image will reappear, the modifier using the previous mapping coordinates from the UVW Map we applied.

Warning: Do not apply the Unwrap UVW modifier while you are still in a sub-object level! The modifier will not work. Click on "Editable Poly" first to go up to the object level. If you see any sub-object level highlighted, you are still in sub-object level. If you are having issues working with the modifier, you could try deleting the modifier (you will be automatically put into a sub-object level mode when you delete the modifier). Get out of the sub-object level mode and reapply the modifier.

This warning applies to most modifiers—do not apply when in sub-object level mode. An exception is the Symmetry Modifier, which work better when in Edge sub-object level.

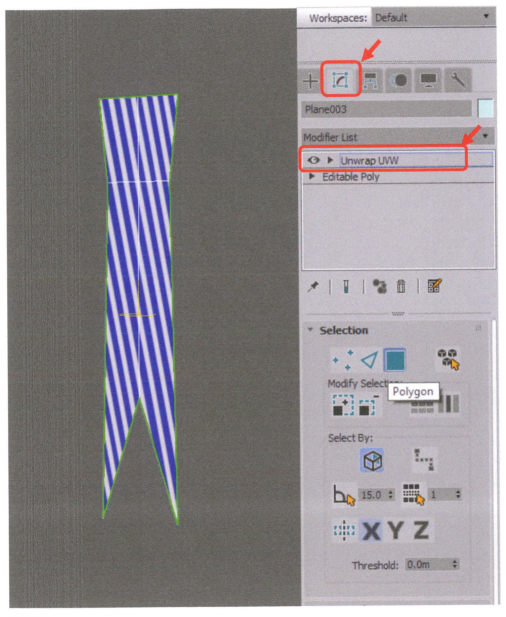

In the Modifier Stack, expand the Unwrap UVW modifier to show the sub-object levels. Select the Polygon level in the UVW modifier (not the Editable Poly!). You can also select the level by using the icon buttons in the Selection section below the Stack. Using your mouse, drag a selection box to include all the mesh polygons.

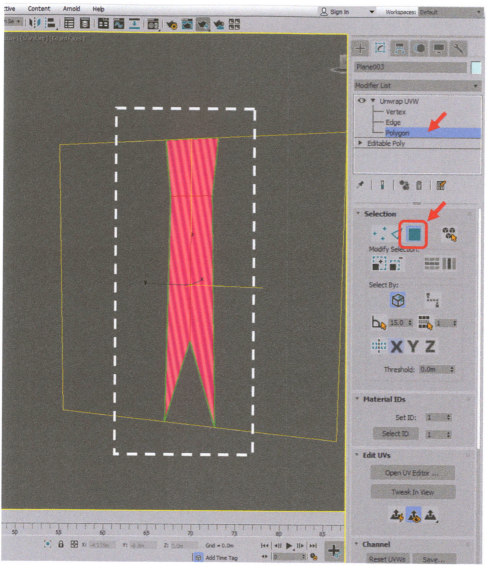

IMAGE 7.9

The next step is to click on the "Open UV Editor…" button to open the editor. The Editor opens as a pop-up window.

At first, it might look a bit intimidating. We will start out using just a few of the tools to ease into its use. At the top of the window is a Tool Menu bar. On the left, below the Tool Bar are some transform tools used to move, rotate and scale sub-objects in the UV Editor window, use these tools. The transform tools on the Main Tool bar do not work in this window.

The UV Editor window displays how the UVW coordinates will project the 2D image on the mesh. The heavier grid lines creating a box show the boundaries of a texture map. Your goal in mapping a mesh is to "pack" all of the mesh into this square. Any mesh parts that are not within the square will not be mapped correctly. The odd thing to understand is, the texture map square does not have any dimensions relating to the size of the mesh. The size is related to the image projection. In the lower left corner, the coordinates are (0, 0). In the upper right corner, they are (1, 1). Once the mesh is all packed within the texture map square, you will generate a template specifying a size for the texture map, which can be any power of 2's size you want.

Power of Two

In video games, textures used for mapping objects should be created so that their dimensions are a "power of two." What is power of two for textures? The progression numbers used for the width and height of the image are numbers can be either be divided evenly by the number 8 or can be doubled or divided evenly by 2 (2, 4, 8, 16, 32, 64, 128, 256, 512, 1024, 2048…). Images using these numbers for their dimensions are processed much more easily and quickly by the computer processor due to the manner of data handling in processing the information in "data chunks." All texture images should be created using these numbers for the image width and height. If the images are not in the Power of Two format, the processor will need to modify the data to get them, so they will function correctly, robbing computing resources needed for running the game. For 2D sprite images, the power of two sizing does not apply. The images are processed differently.

When packing your objects into the UVW Editor texture map square, consider which mesh parts are the most visually important for the player to see. If something needs to be more detailed than the rest of the object, make that part larger in the texture map so that part of the image, being larger, will display more detail with a higher level of sharpness. It is kind of confusing, but, as we go along, you hopefully will get a better understanding.

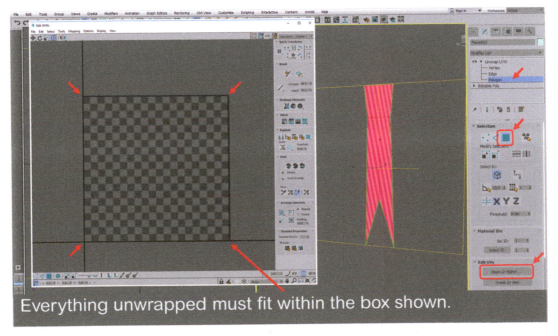

Everything unwrapped must fit within the box shown.

IMAGE 7.10

Our banner polygons are filling the texture map square in the UV Editor. Obviously, they are not scaled to the proportions like the banner.

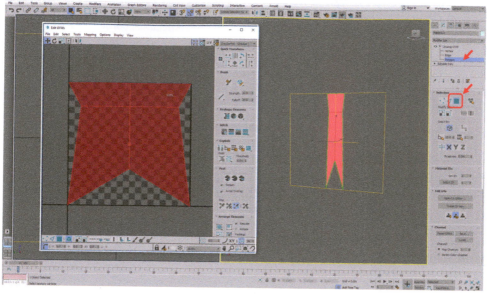

IMAGE 7.11

We could correct this using several different methods. We could manually scale it using the Editor's "Scale Selected Sub-objects" tool, but it wouldn't be accurate. Another method would be to select the "Quick Planar Map" button in the Edit UV's section of the Modify Panel. Since our mesh is a simple plane, the Quick Planar Map is a good choice. Select that button. The polygons will take the correct proportions, as large as they can, and all still fit in the Texture Map square.

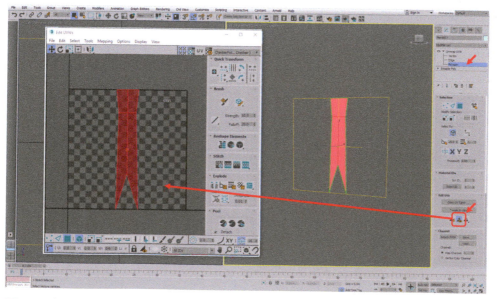

IMAGE 7.12 (Save 7-5)

Changing the UV Edit Window Background

We need to utilize the space allotted in the UV Editor so that every polygon in the mesh gets mapped. In this case, with the Banner, we already have a texture image to use. If we bring that image into the UV editor as a background image within the allotted square space, we could move the mesh directly over the part of the image that it needs to be mapped to. Download the Banner_02.png image to your computer from the book files, and save it to a location you can easily access. Next, in the UV Edit window, click on the drop-down menu in the upper right corner of the menu bar. Select the "Pick Texture" option. In the pop-up window, navigate to where you saved the Banner_2.png image and select it. The image will now appear in the Edit UV's window, within the boundary lines.

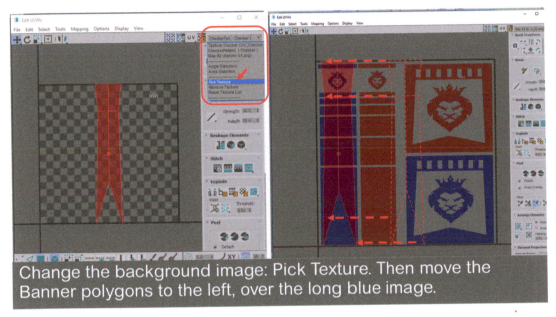

Change the background image: Pick Texture. Then move the Banner polygons to the left, over the long blue image.

IMAGE 7.13

Using the "Move Selected Sub-object" transform tool in the upper left corner, move the banner mesh polygons to the left over top of the long blue banner image.

The polygons are taller than the image. Use the "Scale Selected Sub-object" tool to reduce the overall size of the mesh. Adjust the size and position of the mesh to fit the image as shown.

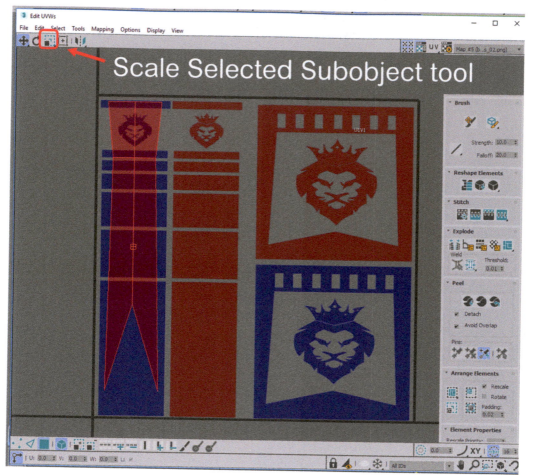

IMAGE 7.14

We need to change our texture in the Material Editor from the blue stripes texture we originally used. Open the Material Editor from the Main Tool bar. If the Material Editor is open to the top level of the Maps rollout, click on the map name in the Diffuse Color box.

In the Bitmap Parameters section, click on the "Bitmap" box (it currently shows the path to the Banner_1.png map on your computer. The image below shows the path on my computer, your computer's path will be different). When you click on the Bitmap box, a selection window will open to identify an image. Navigate to the Banner_2.png image, and select it.

You might need to click the "Assign Material to Selection" button in the Material Editor for the image to appear on the banner mesh. Once it is applied, do you notice how the projection fits accurately and also how it is a more complex image to fit to the mesh than the blue stripes were.

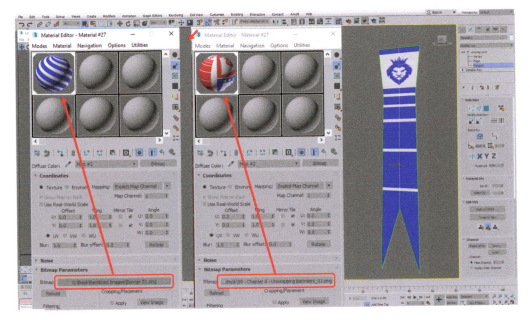

IMAGE 7.15 (Save 7-6)

We can use the same texture map to apply onto another mesh, creating a red banner. Select the blue banner mesh in one of the main viewports. Hold the Shift-key down, and with the Select and Move tool, drag the mesh to the right. A cloned mesh will appear along with the clone pop-up window. We want a "copy," so we can texture it independently for the original mesh. It will utilize the same texture map, but we will change the mapping location on the image in the Edit UVW's window.

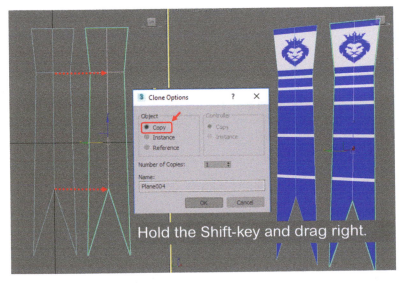

IMAGE 7.16

Open the Unwrap UVW modifier of the cloned banner in the Modifier Panel. Select the Polygon level, and then select the polygons on the mesh as shown. Open the UV Editor window if it is not open. Using the Move Selected Sub-objects tool in the UV Editor, drag the selected polygons to the right, locating them over top of the long red banner image.

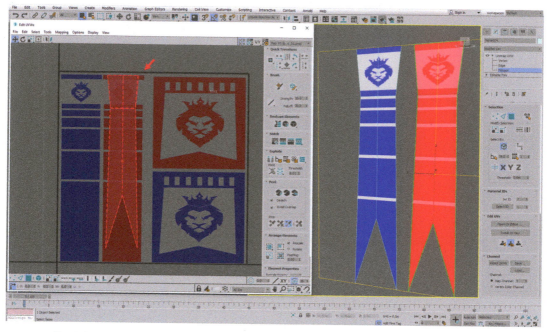

IMAGE 7.17 (Save 7-7)

The images on the meshes we see in the in the perspective viewport is not that great. That is because the viewport renderer, although it has a higher-resolution setting, in 3ds Max is not a high-resolution renderer by design. To see how the texture maps will appear in the game, we can render an image using the output renderer at a higher quality.

On the Main Tool bar, click on the Render Setup icon button (F10). The Render Setup window will open. In the Output Size area of the Common Properties section, select the 800 × 700 option ("Custom" option in the dropdown menu). Next, you can select the Render button at the top of the window, and the image will be rendered, though the image will not be saved. To save the image, if you choose to, scroll down the window to the Render Output box. To the right, click on the "File" button and navigate to where you want to save the image and name it. You will also need to specify what kind of file type you want. If it is a still image, you will likely choose a .jpg, .png or .tga format.

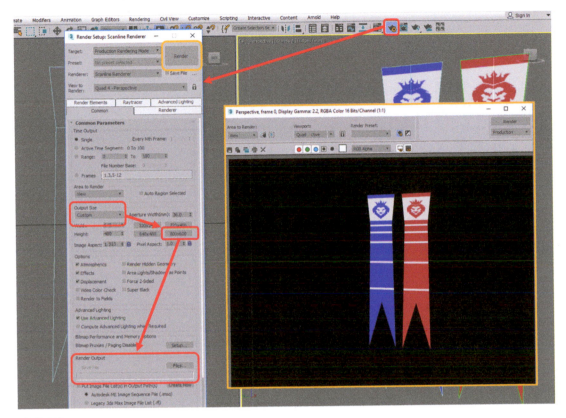

IMAGE 7.18

Render Output

3ds Max can output many image formats. When rendering a single image, click on the "Single" radio button at the top of the Common Properties section of the Render Setup window. If it is to be an animation, select the Active Time Segment radio button or specify a start and end frame in the Range section. When you scroll down to the Render Output area, click on the Find button to open the save window. After naming the file and selecting a location to save, choose an AVI file for the Type, and in the setup window that pops up, chose the MJPEG Compressor. The rendering will be an animation.

Let's make another, shorter banner using the same steps we used in modeling and unwrapping the long banner. Open the scene explorer and turn off the Banner 01 layer and turn on the Banner 02 layer and make it active. Create a plane, with the parameters as shown below, in the Left viewport.

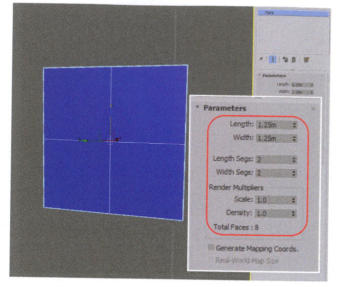

IMAGE 7.19 (Save 7-8)

Center it at the origin point 0, 0, 0, and convert it to an Editable Poly. Move the center row of vertices up, changing the Z-Coordinate Display value to 0.4 meter. Scale the two outside vertices toward the center to create the narrow neck of the banner. To finish the new banner, select the center vertex on the bottom row and change the Z-Coordinate Display box value to −0.4 meter to create the triangular bottom edge.

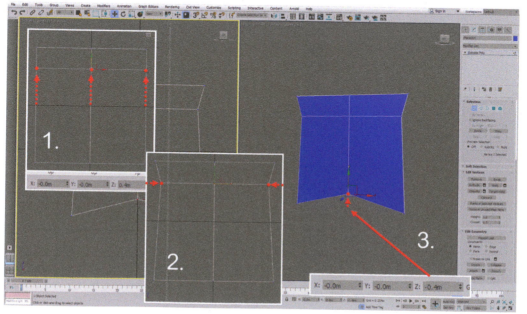

IMAGE 7.20

Click on Editable Poly at the top of the Modifier Stack to get out of the sub-object level up into the top, object level. Now, apply an Unwrap UVW modifier and select the Polygon sub-object level in the modifier. Select the Polygon Sub-object level in the modifier (not the Editable Poly!), and select the polygons of the mesh as shown.

Unwrapping a 2D Object

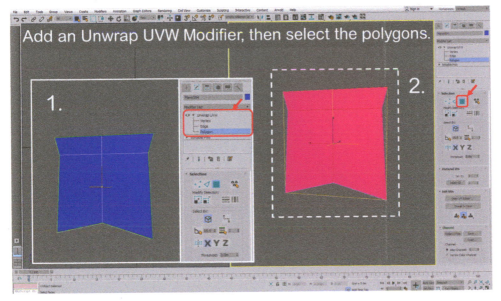

IMAGE 7.21

This time, we will use the tools in the Projection section, instead of the Quick Planar Map. Select the "Planar Map" icon from the map shape row, and then select the "Best Align" icon button in the row below. We get the same results as we did before when we used the Quick Planar Map.

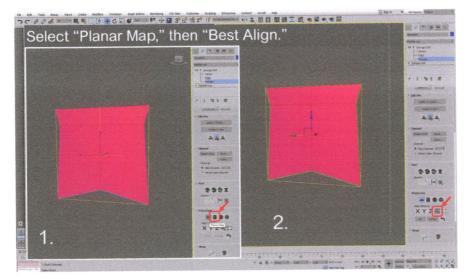

IMAGE 7.22

As before, use the move and scale tools to scale the polygons to scale to a smaller size and move to the image location of the blue short banner as shown. Assign the material in the Material Editor to the new banner. The texture should appear on the mesh.

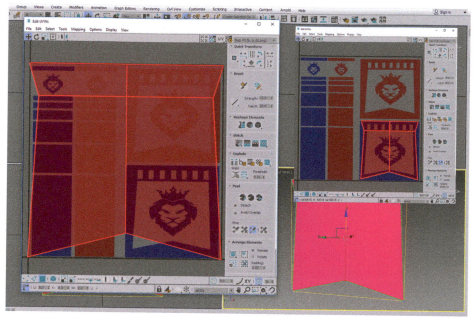

IMAGE 7.23

On your own, clone the new banner to create a second one, a copy. Then, open the Unwrap UVW modifier in the Modify Panel and get into Polygon sub-object level mode. Move the polygons for this mesh in the UV Editor window so that they cover the red short banner image as shown. Rename the meshes, "banner_02_red" and "banner_02_blue."

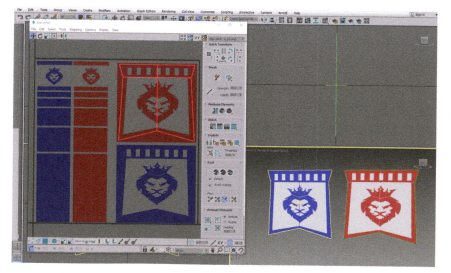

IMAGE 7.24 (Save 7-9)

256

Note how we used one texture map image to texture four separate objects. On the texture map image, the short banners (banner_02) actually take up more area in the Edit UVW's window than the tall banners (banner_01). That is because, in the game, the short banners will be closer to the player, hanging over the front entrance, we want them to be sharp and detailed. The long banners will be higher up the wall, away from the player. They don't need to be as detailed. In a video game, the texture maps can add a sizable amount of data to the game file. Using texture maps efficiently will help to keep the overall file size for the game down. Notice also that the images are larger than the polygons that overlay them. This allows a buffer area, a margin of error, to ensure that the polygons are completely mapped with texture around the borders.

We started out on our unwrapping adventure with a 2D object, a plane, to try to keep things simple so you might get the overall concept of unwrapping a mesh in the UV Editor and applying a texture. If you get the basic concept, that's a win! If it still seems a bit nebulous, maybe it will make sense after the next unwrapping exercise.

In 3ds Max, save the Banners project. Add a new layer to the Scene Explorer, called "Hitching Post" and turn off the Banners layers. This will be a quick exercise, moving now to unwrapping a full 3D object. In the Top viewport, create a pyramid and center it at the origin, (0, 0, 0) as shown in the image parameters below.

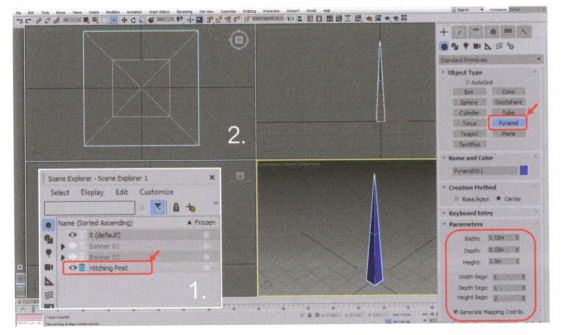

IMAGE 7.25

Convert the pyramid to an Editable Poly, and move the middle row of vertices by changing the Z-Coordinate Display box value to 1.45 meter. That makes the post, now we'll make the ring to tie the horse's reins to.

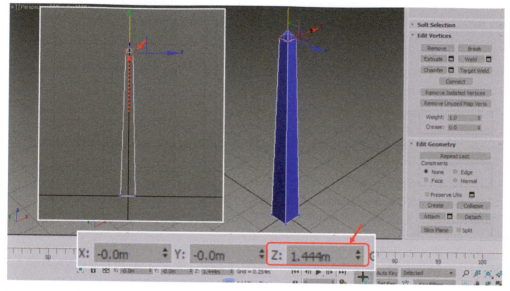

IMAGE 7.26 (Save 7-10)

In the Front viewport, create a Torus with the parameters shown below. Locate the torus at a Z-Coordinate Display box value of 1.2 meter, and move it to the front side of the post so that the back side is touching (angled) the post as shown.

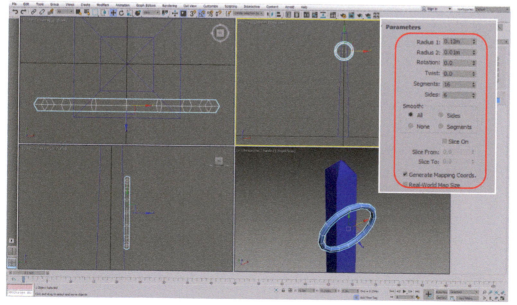

IMAGE 7.27

The ring needs to be attached to the post at the top. Create a three-sided cylinder in the Left viewport as shown, positioned to look like it is holding the ring. The cylinder's parameters are as shown.

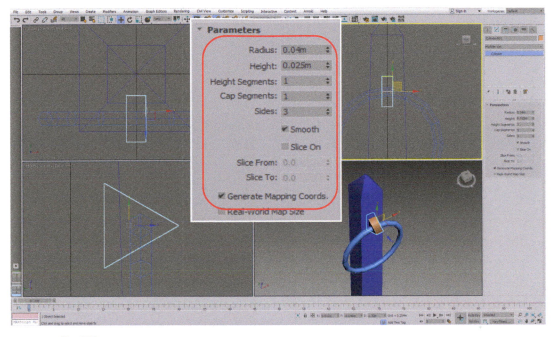

IMAGE 7.28 (Save 7-11)

We are ready to unwrap the hitching post. Download the "CurtainWallTexture_01.png" image to your computer to a location of your choice that you can easily access.

Unwrapping a 3D Object

Select the ring, and convert it to an Editable Poly. Add an Unwrap UVW modifier to the mesh in the Modifier Panel. Select the Polygon sub-object level of the modifier (not the Editable Poly!). Notice that the mesh has a green line around the perimeter. This is the "seam" line. Using planar mapping by default, 3ds Max has determined that this collection of edges is where a seam should be. With unwrapping, we need to imagine the 3D object being unfolded into a flat 2D shape. Imagine a cardboard box, which started out as a flat object, being unfolded back into its original flat shape. With it flat, it could go through a printer to get decorated. Likewise, if we can get our mesh into a "flat" state, we can print or project our 2D texture map image on the sides. Basically, that is what we are doing.

While still in Polygon Sub-object level of the unwrap UVW, drag a selection box over the ring in the Front viewport, selecting the whole object. If you look at the top viewport, you might notice that only the front half of the mesh polygons were selected.

By default, 3ds Max has the "Ignore Backfacing" button active. With it on, you can only select polygons with their normals facing toward you in the viewport. Click the Ignore Backfacing button to turn it off, and reselect the ring polygons. All the polygons, including the backside should now be selected.

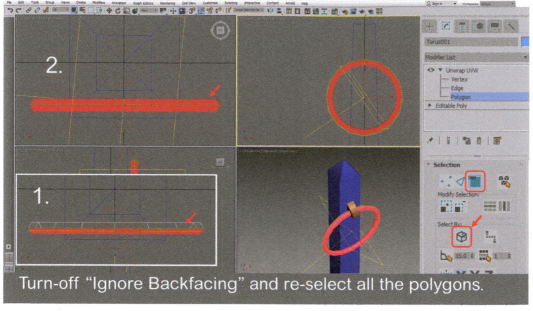

Turn-off "Ignore Backfacing" and re-select all the polygons.

IMAGE 7.29

Open the UV Editor. The selected polygons fill the Edit UVW's window.

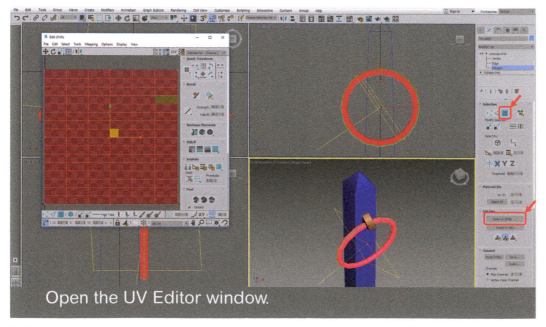

Open the UV Editor window.

IMAGE 7.30

The ring will be assigned one texture image. Scroll down the Modify Panel to the Projection section. Click on the Planar Map to select the type of map, and then in the "Align Options" below the Map types, select "Y." The Edit UV's window will show the ring polygons in a circular orientation. Note that this is both the front and the back sides of the mesh polygons stacked together.

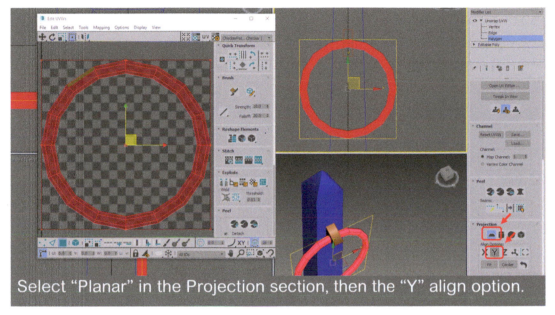

Select "Planar" in the Projection section, then the "Y" align option.

IMAGE 7.31

Change the background image in the UV editor to the CurtainWallTexture_01.png image using the Pick Texture option in the upper right corner drop-down menu.

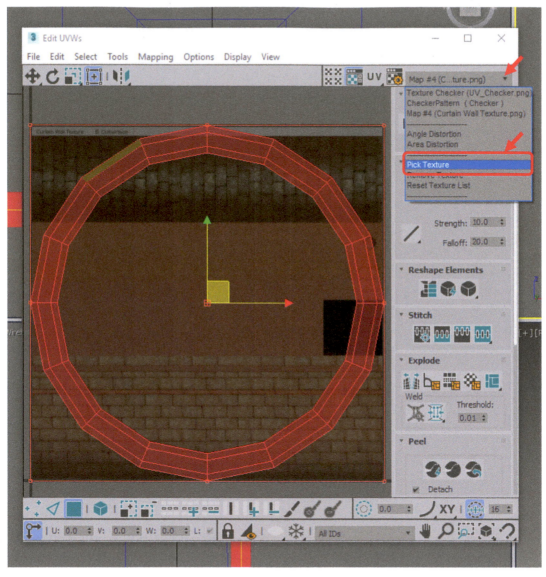

IMAGE 7.32

Using the Scale Selected Sub-object tool and the Move Selected Sub-object tool, scale the rings to a smaller size and fit them into the black box area of the texture map in the window as shown.

Note: Sometimes, for some reason, when you select one of the transform tools (move, rotate or scale), it will not work in the Edit UVW's window. Here's a fix… select one of the Polygon, Edge or Vertex icon buttons at the bottom of the UV Editor window, and then reselect the desired sub-object level (one of the same icon buttons). The Transform tool will now work.

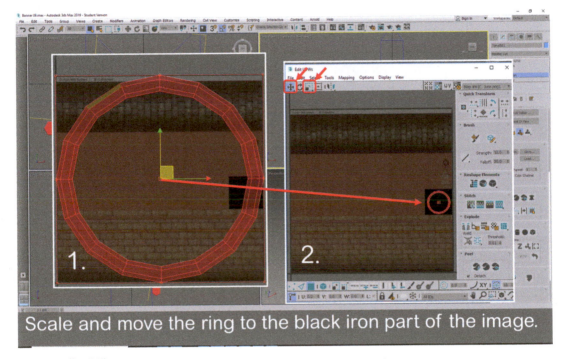

Scale and move the ring to the black iron part of the image.

IMAGE 7.33 (Save 7-12)

Open the Material Editor and assign the CurtainWallTexture to the ring.

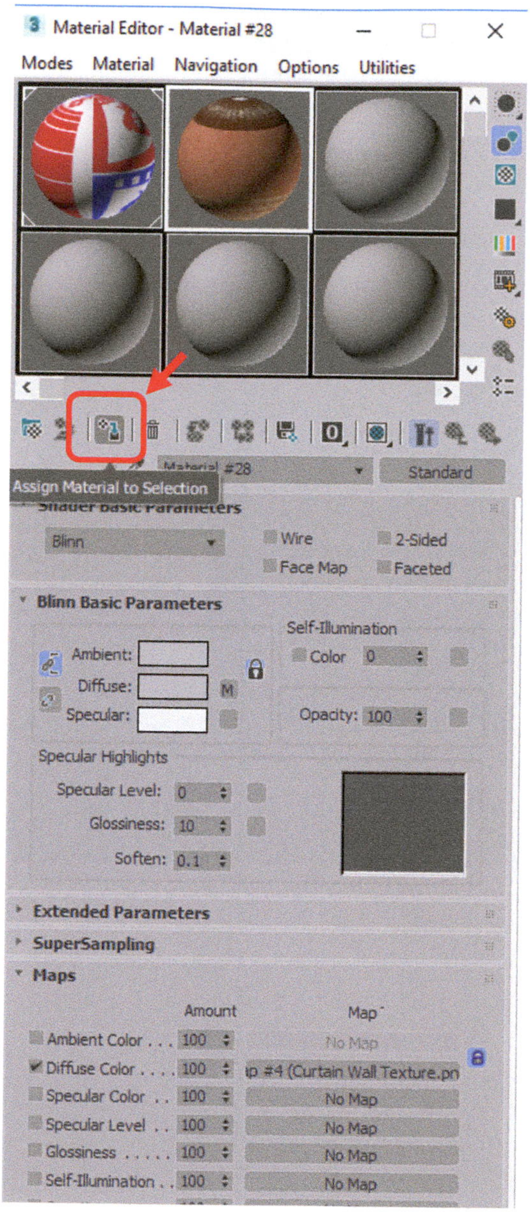

IMAGE 7.34

Next, we'll unwrap the ring holder. Select the three-sided cylinder, and convert it to an Editable Poly. While in the object mode, add an Unwrap UVW modifier to the Editable Poly. Select the Polygon sub-object level of the modifier (not the Editable Poly!)

Turn off the Ignore Backfacing button, and then select the whole mesh.

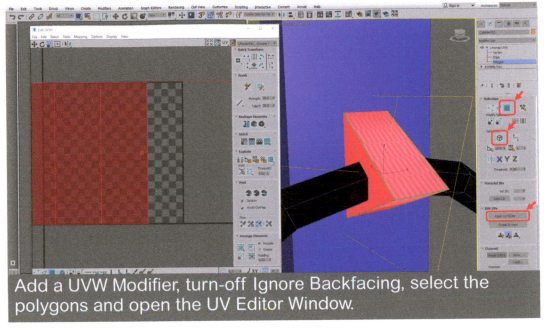

Add a UVW Modifier, turn-off Ignore Backfacing, select the polygons and open the UV Editor Window.

IMAGE 7.35

This time, we will use another mapping type, Normal Mapping. On the top tool bar of the UV Editor window, select the "Mapping" tab and then choose the "Normal" option from the drop-down. In the pop-up window, hold down the drop-down menu in the top left corner and choose "Box Mapping," and then click the OK button.

Normal Mapping

Normal Mapping is one of the most basic methods of procedural mapping. It relies on vector-based projections of the texture. The textures can be distorted with this method depending on the possible angling of polygons from the perpendicular angle to the projection.

In the Normal Mapping drop-down list, the first three items in the list allow you to specify six different side orientations, front/back, left/right and top/bottom. The next two will create box projections in five and six sides, all at once in one step. The last option is Diamond Mapping, which will rotate polygons to fit the space utilizing the least amount of unused space. Although it creates quick solutions, the Normal Mapping projections are not always the best method for unwrapping. Use caution, evaluate the model to determine if most of the important surfaces are going to provide perpendicular surfaces to the projections (square sides). If there are important angles polygons or cylindrical or spherical shapes, it might be best to consider other methods.

The polygons are separated and flattened in projections 90 degrees from the six sides of an imaginary box around the mesh. The six sides are all in scale with each other, so, usually, for subsequent operations, it's best to scale them all together if necessary to maintain the texture size on the polygons.

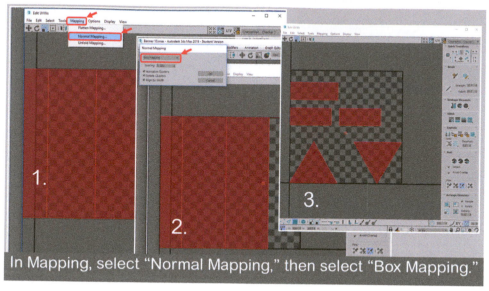

In Mapping, select "Normal Mapping," then select "Box Mapping."

IMAGE 7.36 (Save 7-13)

Using the "Move Selected Sub-objects" tool, stack the six polygons together, roughly as shown.

Next, add the CurtainWallTexture.png image to the background as before, and using the transform move and scale tools, fit the polygons into the black area of the texture image as shown.

Assign the material texture to the mesh from the Material Editor.

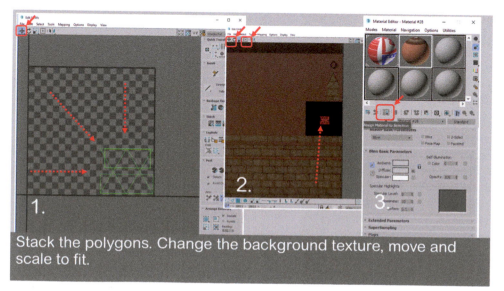

Stack the polygons. Change the background texture, move and scale to fit.

IMAGE 7.37 (Save 7-14)

Now, we will unwrap the post. The two previous meshes were relatively small and utilized the same texture across their surfaces. The post will have a different texture on the front side than the other three sides. With a larger mesh, we also need to consider how it will appear in the game. When a small item has shadows cast on them from the lighting, the shadow is usually not that noticeable. A larger mesh will cast and accept shadows cast upon them more noticeably. When lights are cast on baked textures that are "stacked" in the UV Editor window, all the sides will receive the same shadow cast upon the mesh. Basically, sides that should not have a shadow will have them. Bottom line is, we shouldn't stack the polygons, when practical, for larger meshes.

At some point, you might be unwrapping meshes with dozens of polygon groups or "islands." To manage the groups, it is highly recommended that you name the groups, creating sets that can be easily selected while working. We will use names for the sides of the Post, so you can see how that part of the process works. It might seem unnecessary with this simple mesh, and it's the understanding of the concept that we are after.

Select the Post, and convert it to an Editable Poly. Add an Unwrap UVW modifier to the Modifier Stack. Select the Polygon sub-object level of the Unwrap UVW modifier (not the Editable Poly!).

Select the polygon that has the ring on it. In the Named Selection sets box on the Main Menu, type in the name "side 1" and then hit the Enter-key on the keyboard. If you don't use the Enter-key, the name you typed will not be saved. After naming the first side, continue to name the other sides: rotate the viewport to select the side adjacent to the side 1, select it and name it "side 2" and hit the Enter-key. Continue rotating and naming the two remaining sides.

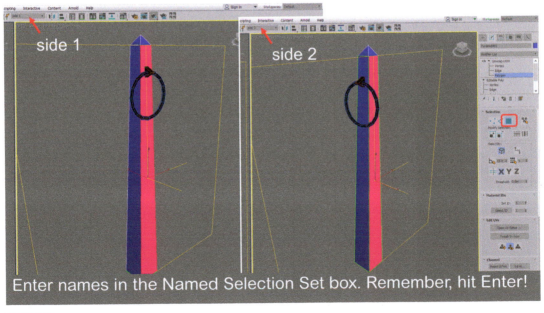

IMAGE 7.38

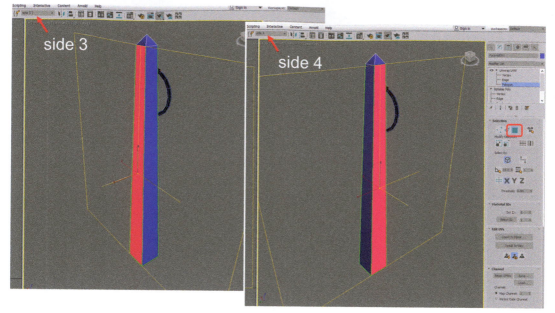

IMAGE 7.39

Next, select the top triangular polygon above "side 1." Name it "top1." Continue around the top, naming the polygons. Be sure to hit the Enter-key to set each name. If you need to re-name or edit an entry, click on the icon button to the left of the Named Selection set box, the Edit Selection Set dialogue box. Also, select the four polygons on the bottom and name them "bottom."

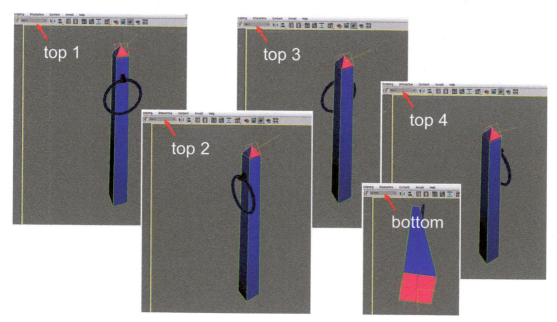

IMAGE 7.40 (Save 7-15)

If you hold the drop-down arrow on the Name Selection Sets box, the names will all be listed.

Open the UV Editor window and from the dropdown list, select "side 1." You could have just selected the polygon, but, remember, you are using the names to get the concept for later complex projects.

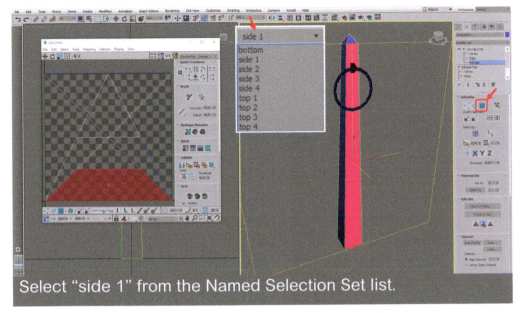

Select "side 1" from the Named Selection Set list.

IMAGE 7.41

Click on the Quick Planar Map button to map the polygon. The polygon in the Edit UVW's window of the UV Editor will change to the proportions of the polygon on the mesh.

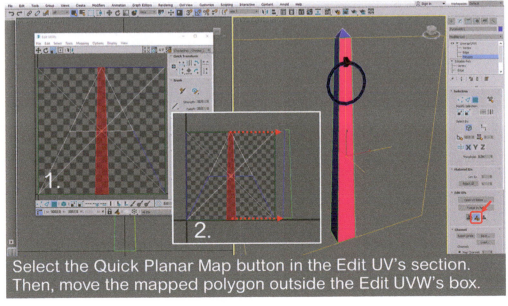

Select the Quick Planar Map button in the Edit UV's section.
Then, move the mapped polygon outside the Edit UVW's box.

IMAGE 7.42

Using the Move Selected Sub-object tool, drag the "side 1" polygon outside the texture map box as shown. Repeat the process of selecting the polygon sets from Named Selection sets box, applying the Quick Planar Map and moving the polygon sets outside the Texture Window Box as shown below.

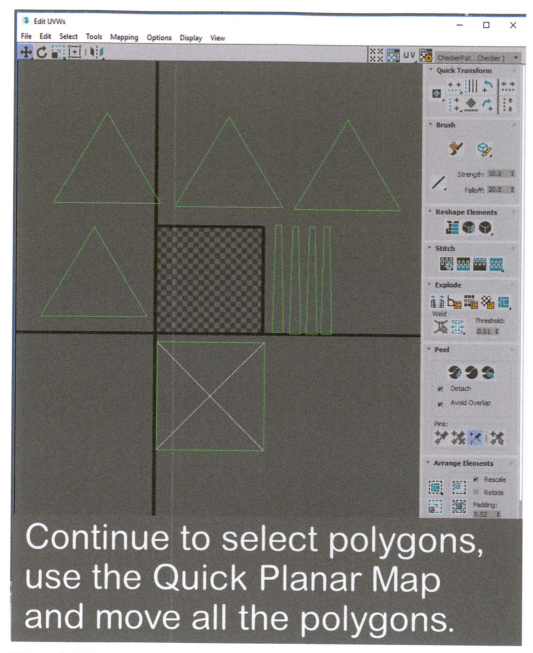

IMAGE 7.43 (Save 7-16)

Using the move, scale and rotate transform tools position the individual pieces as shown. "Side 1" should be the top long section with the top end of it covering the small lion head image. When rotating a piece, you might want to turn on the Angle Snaps on the Main Tool bar to control the rotation.

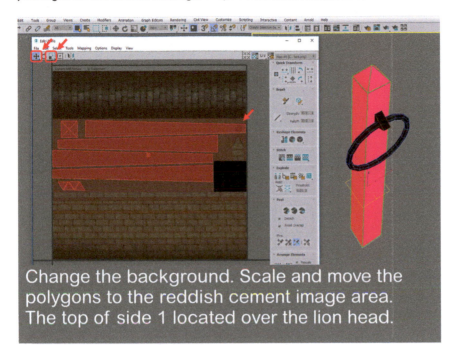

IMAGE 7.44

Once they are in position, zoom in to the area with the lion head image using the mouse wheel. With a closer view, position the "side 1" piece as shown so the lion image will be located correctly.

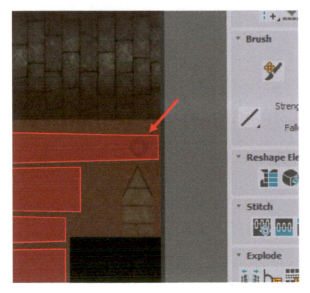

IMAGE 7.45 (Save 7-17)

When everything is in position, open the Material Editor and assign the CurtainWallTexture.png to the mesh.

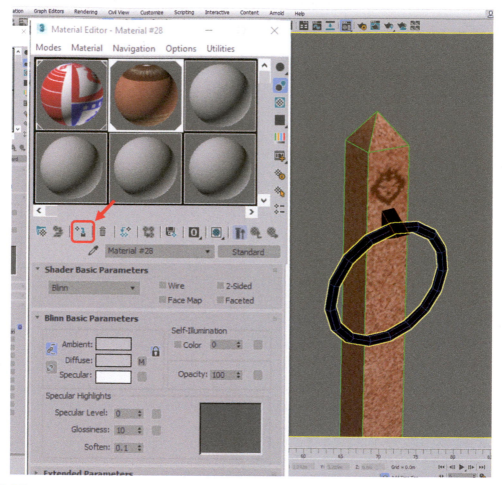

The image in the perspective viewport doesn't look that great. Render the viewport to see how it will look. On the main Tool bar click on the Render Setup icon button (F10). The render set-up will be the same as you set it before when you rendered the banners. Next, you can select the Render button at the top of the window and the image will be rendered, though the image will not be saved. To save the image, if you choose to, or the previous file will be over written, scroll down the window to the Render Output box. To the right, click on the "File" button and navigate to where you want to save the image and name it. You will also need to specify what kind of file type you want. If it is a still image, you will likely choose a .jpg, .png or a .tga.

The default color for the background of a rendering is black. Sometimes it makes it hard to clearly see the edges of a model. Let's make it lighter. To change the background color of the rendered image, open the

Rendering tab on the Main Menu and select Environment from the menu list. Click on the color picker box located below "Color" in the Background section of the Common Parameters. Change the color as desired and close the window. Re-render to see the results.

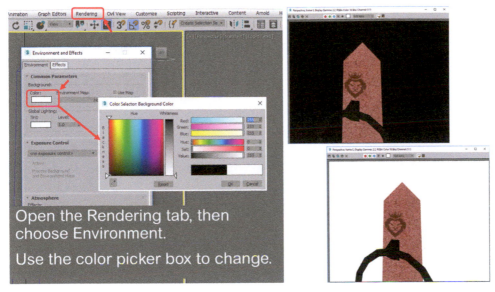

IMAGE 7.47

Unwrapping the Curtain Wall

Next, we will unwrap and texture the Curtain Wall module. Open the final modeling iteration of your Curtain Wall. Select the mesh and add an Unwrap UVW modifier. Make sure that you are not in a sub-object level mode before adding the modifier. As before, select the Polygon sub-object level of the modifier.

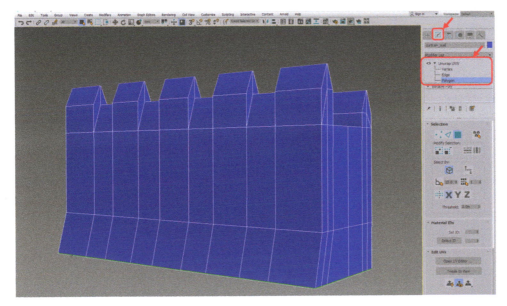

IMAGE 7.48

First, let's go through the mesh and create polygon sets with names in the Name Selection Set box on the Main Menu. Select the front wall polygons as shown. In the box, name the set "front wall face." Remember to hit the Enter-key to set the entry. Continue to select polygon groups and name them. The next few images show how I broke the mesh into groups and the names I used.

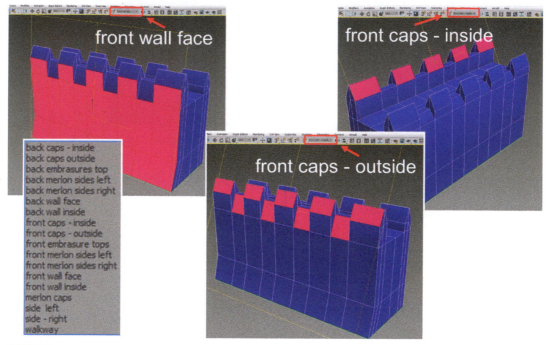

IMAGE 7.49

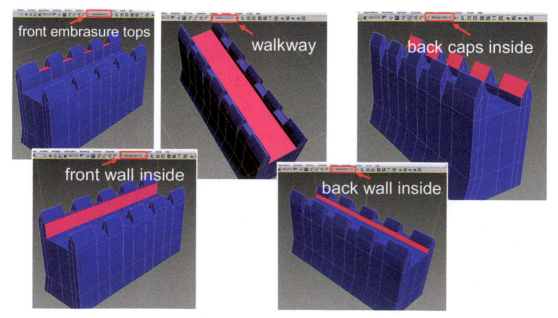

IMAGE 7.50

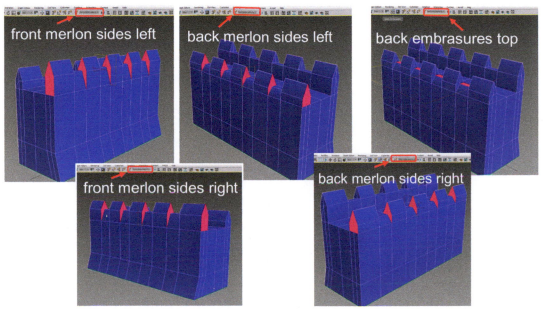

IMAGE 7.51

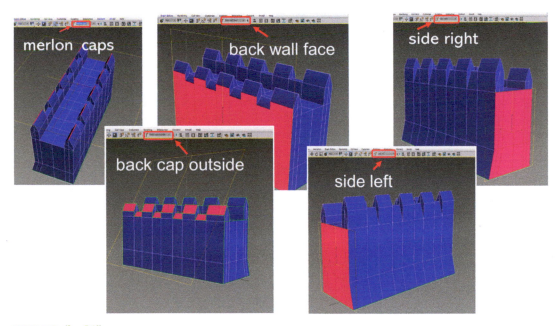

IMAGE 7.52 (Save 7-18)

Between the Banners and the Hitching Post, we used several different methods of planar unwrapping and mapping. For the Curtain Wall let's use the method using the Mapping tab, Normal Mapping. From the Name Selection Set list, select the "front wall face" set in the list (the list will only be available when you are in the Unwrap UVW Polygon Sub-object level). Open the UV Editor window.

On the top tool bar of the UVW Editor Window, select the "Mapping" tab and then "Normal Mapping…" from the drop-down list.

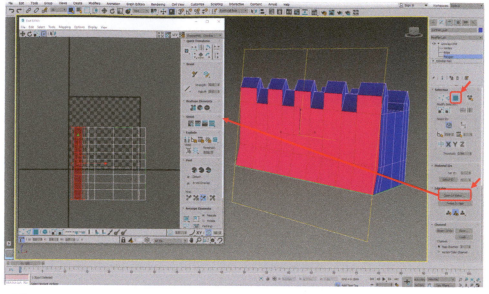

The Normal Mapping pop-up window will open. Click on the drop-down arrow to open the list of planar projection directions.

With the "front wall face" still selected, click on the Left/Right option from the drop-down list, and then click the OK button. The polygons will take on the shape of the wall face. If you select the Front/Back or the Top/Bottom options, the polygons would take on shapes that don't look like the wall face, indicating they would be the incorrect choice. Use the Move tool to move the polygon cluster outside the Edit UVW's window, as shown.

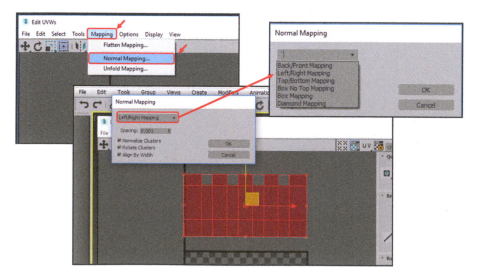

IMAGE 7.54

Repeat the procedure with all the named sets in the Names Selection Set drop-down list: Select the named set, open the Mapping tab to select the Normal Mapping option, then select the proper choice of one of the first three mapping orientations from the Normal Mapping pop-up window drop-down list. This will take a few minutes, work carefully and methodically. When you are finished the UVW Editor should look something like the image below: all the polygon sets are outside the Texture Map box with no overlapping of the sets.

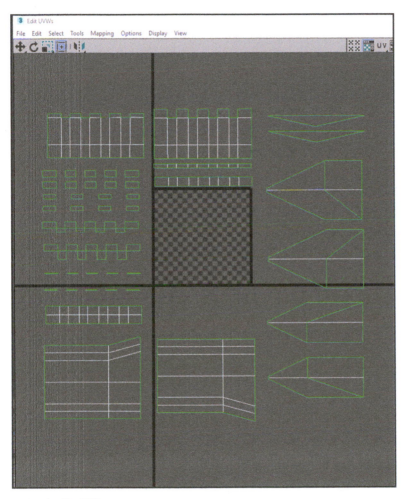

IMAGE 7.55 (Save 7-19)

Did you notice the two triangular polygon groups in the upper right corner? After completing the unwrapping procedure for all the named sets, there were some small green dots remaining, representing polygons. Using the Front/Back option, these became visible. They are the small triangular polygons that were created when we did the chamfer on the top peak edge of the merlons when we were modeling.

Next, change the background image in the Edit UVW's window using the Pick Texture option in the upper right corner drop-down box of the UV Editor. Select the CurtainWallTexture.png that you downloaded earlier.

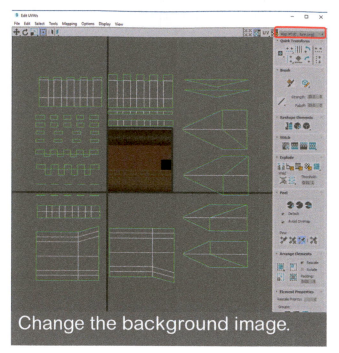

Change the background image.

IMAGE 7.56

Select the "front wall face" name set and using the Scale Selection Suubset tool (Scale tool), and the Move Selection Subset tool (Move tool), relocate the polygons to the Edit UVW's window as shown.

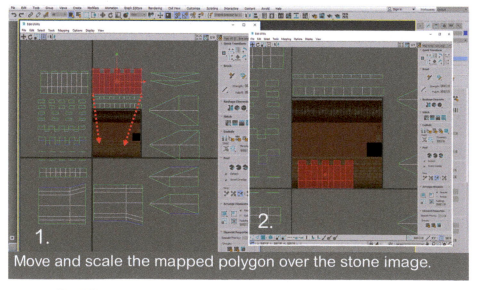

Move and scale the mapped polygon over the stone image.

IMAGE 7.57 (Save 7-20)

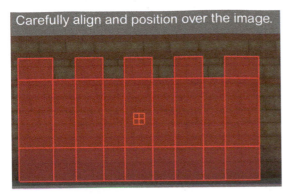

Carefully align and position over the image.

IMAGE 7.58

Apply the CurtainWallTexture.png to the mesh from the Material Editor so we can see the results of the mapping. You will probably need to create the texture map in the Material Editor as we did not do that when we were modeling this module. If so, follow the same steps as before when you created the Banner material.

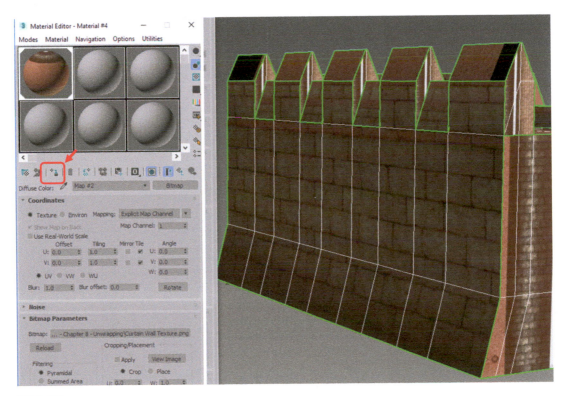

IMAGE 7.59

Taking a closer look at the positioning of the front wall face in the Edit UVW's window, notice how the top edges of the merlons are positioned. The edge is positioned into the reddish area of the image slightly. This will create the illusion that the merlon caps have a bottom edge, creating a small shadow line. We can create the illusion that there are more polygons creating the form than there really are.

Note also the position of the edge of the embrasure (the lower area between the merlons). The edge is aligned with the top of the horizontal reddish row of bricks. The reddish row will also give the perception that there is more detail in the model than there really is. The task is to adjust the scale, so the proper alignments are made.

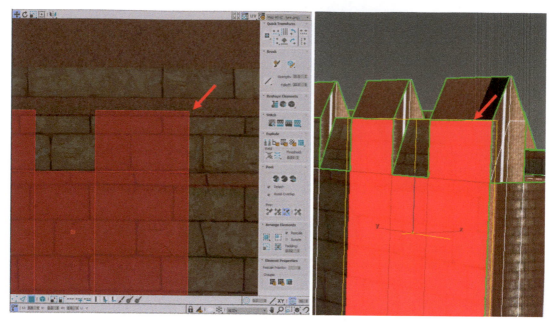

IMAGE 7.60 (Save 7-21)

To help you, when I did my unwrapping of this piece, I found the following orientations of Normal Mapping for the named sides:

Front/Back	Left/Right	Top/Bottom
back merlon sides left	front wall face	back embrasure tops
back merlon sides right	back wall face	front embrasure tops
front merlon sides left	front caps—inside	walkway
front merlon sides right	front caps—outside	merlon caps
side left	back caps—inside	
side right	back caps—outside	
merlon side top triangles	front wall inside	
	back wall inside	

back caps – inside
back caps outside
back embrasures top
back merlon sides left
back merlon sides right
back wall face
back wall inside
front caps – inside
front caps – outside
front embrasure tops
front merlon sides left
front merlon sides right
front wall face
front wall inside
merlon caps
side left
side – right
walkway

Next, select the "back wall face" from the Name Selection list. Scale and move it as you did with the front wall face, locating it on top of the front wall face.

Carefully scale and position it as shown, aligning the edges of the embrasure tops with those of the front wall face. The bottom edge needs to align with the bottom of the front wall face. When these two elements are aligned with the front wall face, the rest should align, except for the top of the merlons, which are shorter on the back side.

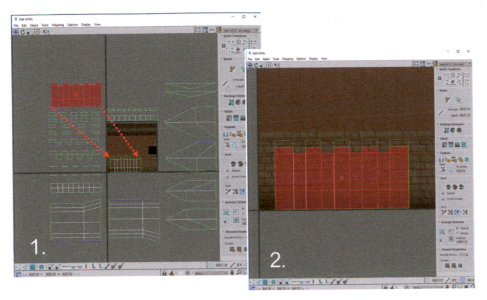

IMAGE 7.61

We can select the merlon caps together and scale them as a group. Select the "back caps—inside," " back cap—outside," front caps—inside," "front caps—outside," back embrasure tops" and the "front embrasure tops." Scale and move this selected group of named sets to the location shown in the image. Scale the polygons so that the width of the merlon cap polygons is about the same that of the merlon extensions on the front wall face. This will keep the image projection on these parts the same scale as the rest of the mesh.

Once the width is correct, select each row individually and move them closer together to "pack" them in the reddish concrete looking image area as shown.

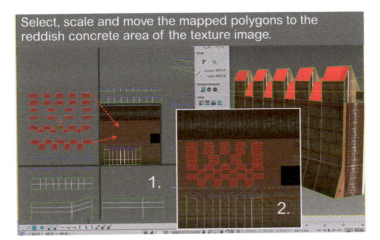

IMAGE 7.62

Next, select the "front wall inner." Move and scale it to the position shown, making it the same width as the front wall face to replicate the scale. Align the top edge with the top of the reddish row of stones as you did with the front wall face.

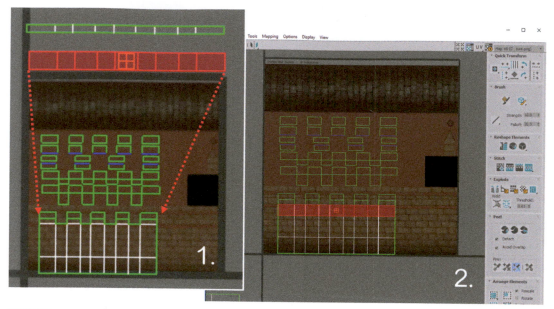

IMAGE 7.63

Repeat the same steps with the back inner wall piece, aligning the top edge with the top of the reddish stones.

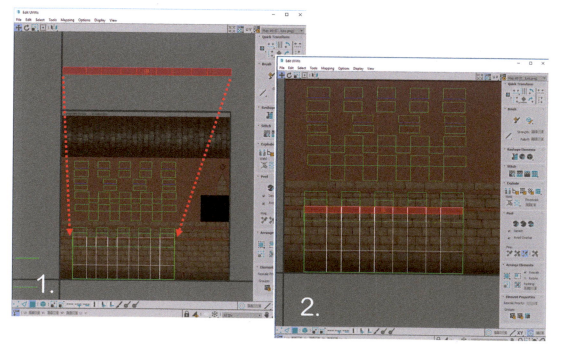

IMAGE 7.64

Next, we'll do the walkway on top of the wall. Select the walkway, and move it to the top image area with the dark gray stones. The center of the walkway has lighter stones to give it a walked-on, used look, bare to the stone. You might need to scale it slightly smaller to make sure it fits within the Edit UVW's window border.

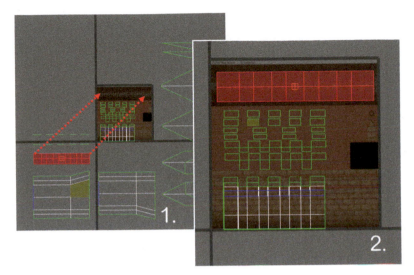

IMAGE 7.65

The two end walls of this module will typically not be seen in the game, but we'll map them just in case they are used. The two end walls are mirror images of each other. We can stack these to take up less space on our texture map. Rotate the two end walls ("side left" and "side right") so that they are oriented correctly, like the other walls, as shown. You might want to turn on the Angle Snaps to control the rotation to 90-degree increments. After rotating both, move one on top of the other, aligning the top and bottom edges.

Scale and move the end walls to the space next to the front and back wall faces in the Texture Map area, aligning the top edge with the top of the reddish row of stones and the bottom aligns with the bottom of the other wall. Check the model in the viewport to see if any adjustments are needed to align the horizontal stone lines as they wrap around the mesh corner to the front wall face.

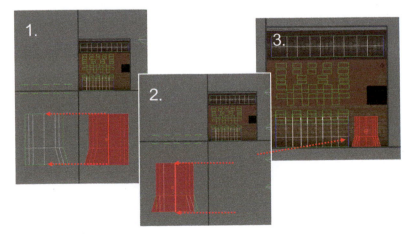

IMAGE 7.66

Select the merlon caps, and move them into the reddish concrete image area.

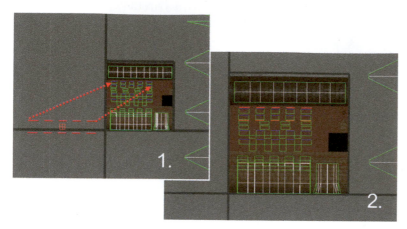

IMAGE 7.67 (Save 7-22)

The merlon sides will take some careful scaling and positioning. First, stack the four name selection sets for the merlon sides into one, being careful to align the pointed ends as best as you can. Notice that the ones for the back wall merlon sides are a bit longer and will overhang the wider front merlons.

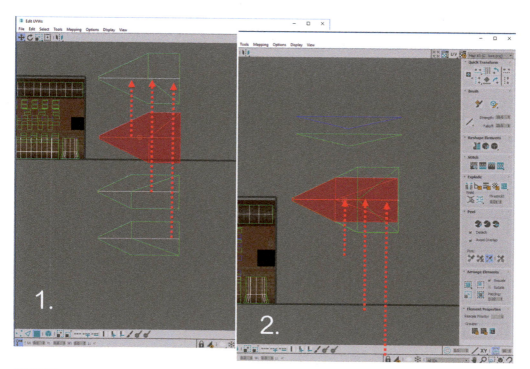

IMAGE 7.68

Rotate the stacked merlon polygons sets 90 degrees so that the pointed end is up as shown.

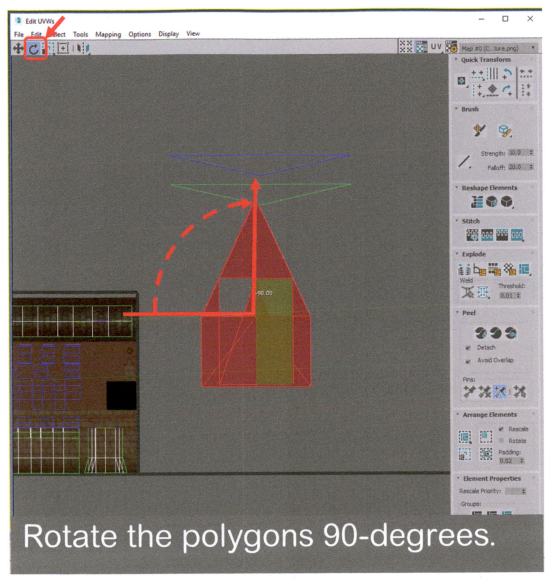

Rotate the polygons 90-degrees.

IMAGE 7.69

Now comes the delicate part… scale and position the stack of merlon sides over the image in the Edit UVW's window as shown. The image has an upside-down, brown "V" shape. Like the shadow line on the front wall face that gives the impression of an overhanging cap, the brown "V" shaped line will create the illusion of an edge on the sides of the merlons created by the cap. It adds visual depth to the model if positioned correctly. Check on the model in the viewport to see if the bottom of the upside-down "V" aligns with the front wall face shadow line for the merlon cap. Adjust if necessary.

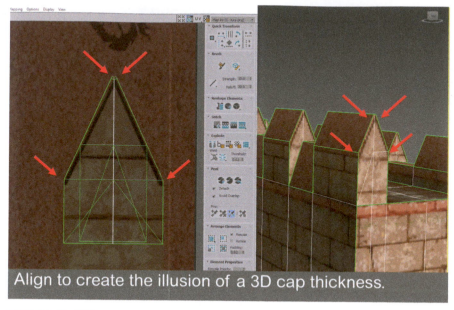

Align to create the illusion of a 3D cap thickness.

IMAGE 7.70 (Save 7-23)

Lastly, scale and position the two triangles, locating them in the reddish concrete area. Remember, they are very small in on the model.

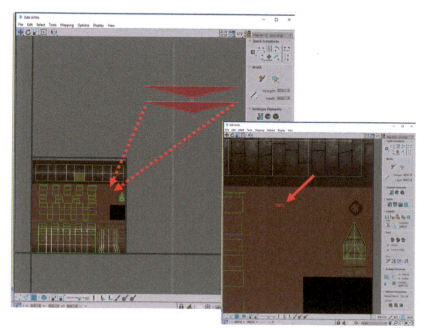

IMAGE 7.71

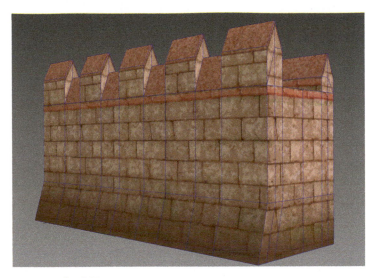

IMAGE 7.72 (Save 7-24)

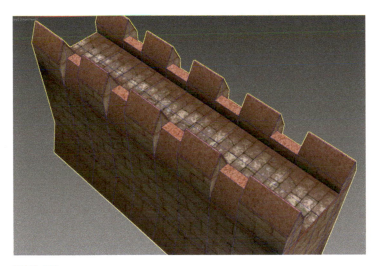

IMAGE 7.73

That completes the unwrapping and mapping of the Curtain Wall module. It looks very different from the un-textured mesh we started with. It was a lot of work, but the results are worth the effort. As you do more unwrapping projects, you will become better at foreseeing where seams should be, designing your models with the unwrapping in mind and you will get quicker as you get accustomed to the steps and the tools. Remember, there are several ways to do normal mapping. We have just completed a basic unwrapping and applying a basic bitmap as a diffuse texture. It is about as simple as unwrapping can get. In time you will learn about shaders, bump maps, specular maps and more. These examples of more advanced texturing can greatly enhance the model's look and how it reacts visually to the different types of lighting available in the games.

Another aspect to consider with this process, we used a prepared texture bitmap. Preparing for the project, I made the texture map knowing what we would need. To create the texture map I used Photoshop, creating new textures and modifying existing ones. When you start working on your own projects, you will be making your own texture maps.

Unwrapping the Fixed Bridge

Next, we will unwrap the Bridge End module from the Fixed Bridge. We are going to add another tool to your unwrapping skills, the checkerboard texture and to reinforce the skills you've learned. Open the final version of the Fixed Bridge we made in Chapter 4.

When it is open, turn off the Bridge Span layer, leaving the Bridge End layer on and active.

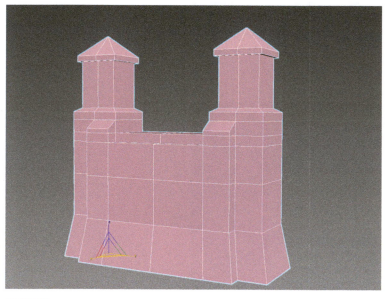

IMAGE 7.74

Open the Material Editor, and select the first material slot sphere. Click on the "Get Material" button to open the Materials/Map Browser. In the Materials/Map Browser, select a "Standard" type map in the Scanline section. Next, click on the Maps drop-down list and select the "None" value box in the Diffuse row.

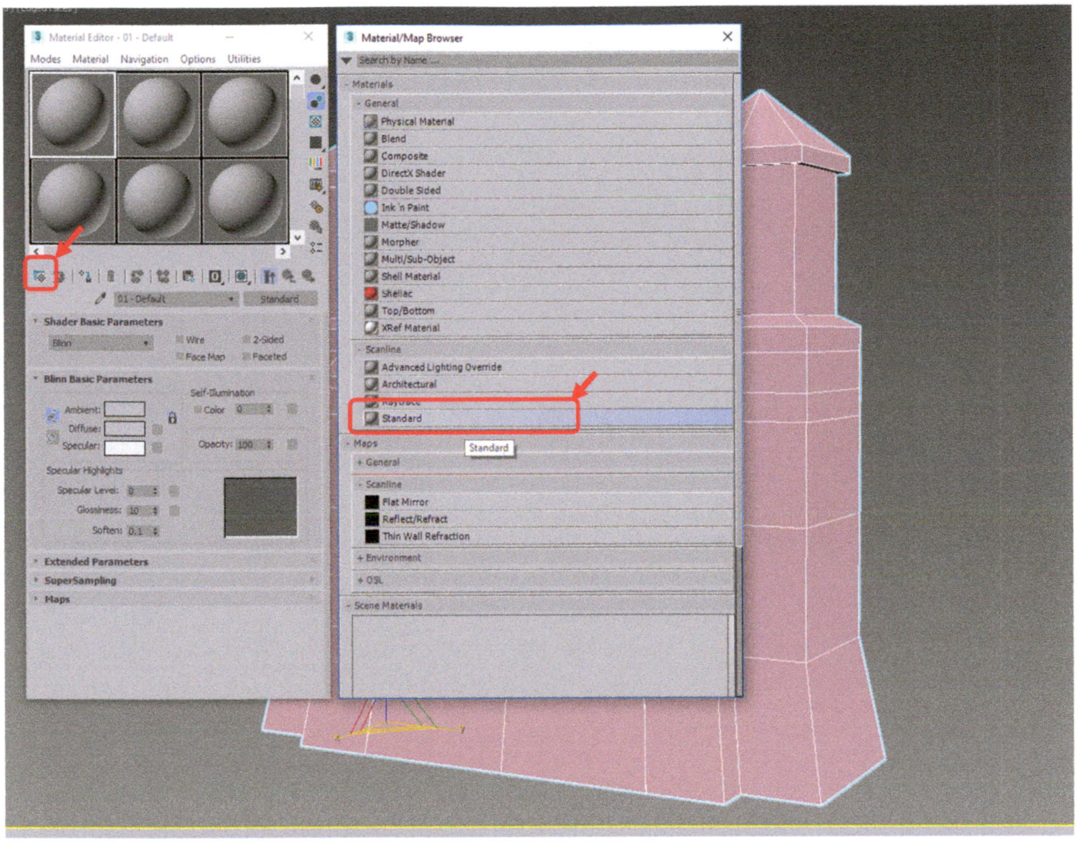

IMAGE 7.75

This time instead of selecting a "Bitmap," select the "Checker" option. The material slot will now have a checkerboard pattern. Find the U and V value boxes in the Coordinates section of the Material Editor. Change the values in each box to 15 as shown. This will make a checkerboard pattern an appropriate size for what we will be doing.

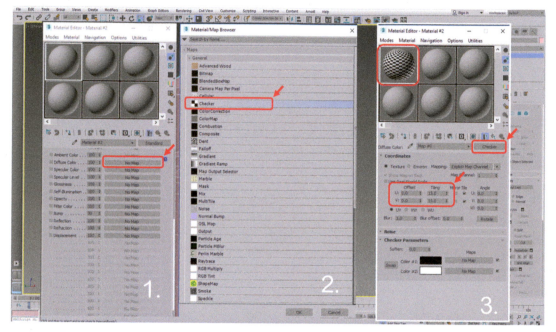

IMAGE 7.76 (Save 7-25)

Assign the material to the mesh in the viewport using the "Assign Material to Selection" button, or click on the material slot window and drag it on to the mesh.

We're ready to add the Unwrap UVW modifier to the Editable Poly in the Modifier Stack. Before you add it, make sure that you are not in a sub-object level mode.

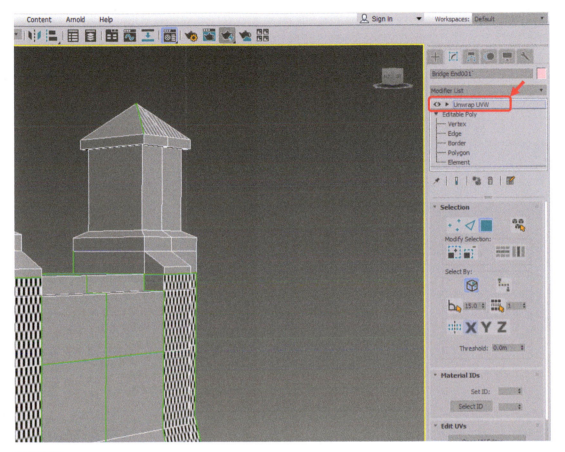

IMAGE 7.77

Like with the Curtain Wall, we want to create, and name polygon group sets to make it easy to select the groups when unwrapping and to keep things organized. Start the selection and naming process. Work methodically and use names that roughly describe the sets. Remember to hit the Enter-key to set the name after you type it in the Name Selection Set box. Below are the names I used and the pictures following shows the selections. I have arranged the images in the same order they appear in the list, not the order I made them in. (col = column; lt = left; rt = right; drbrg = drawbridge)

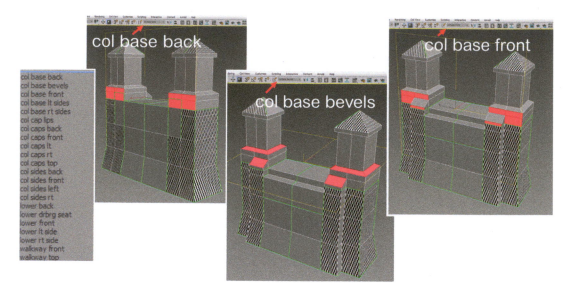

IMAGE 7.78

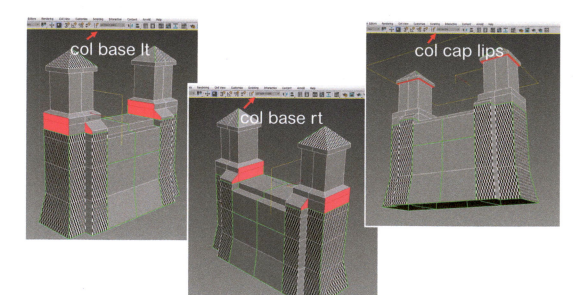

IMAGE 7.79

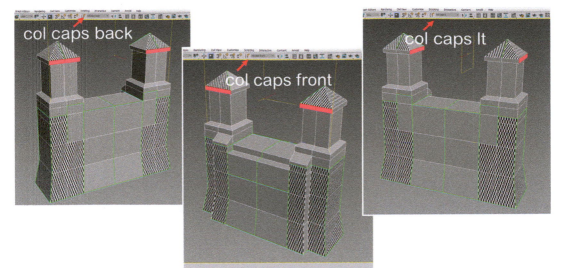

IMAGE 7.80

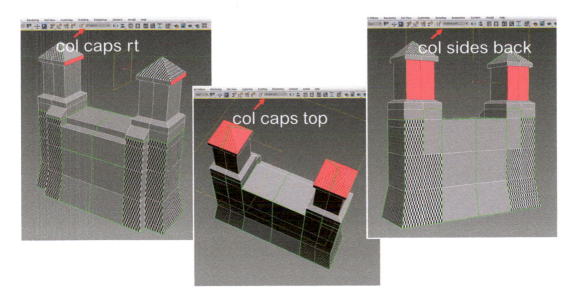

IMAGE 7.81

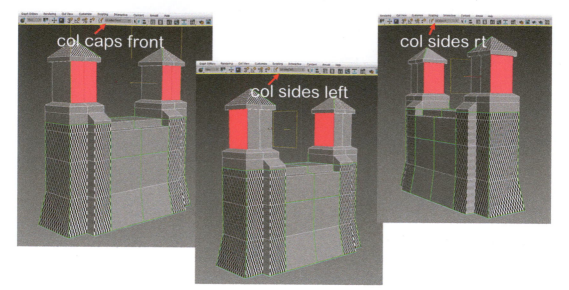

IMAGE 7.82

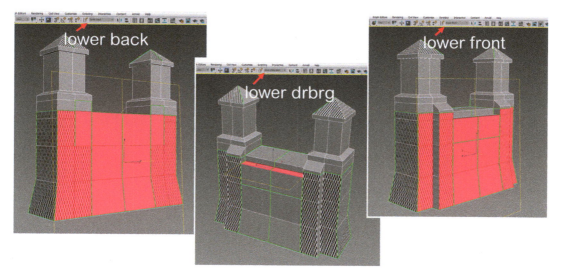

IMAGE 7.83

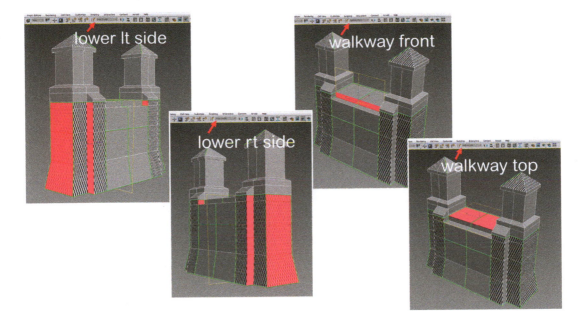

IMAGE 7.84 (Save 7-26)

Next, open the UVW Editor window. Just like we did with the Curtain Wall, start at the top of the Named Selection sets selecting and mapping the mesh groups. As a reminder, select the Named Selection set, click on "Mapping" on the top tool bar of the UV Editor, and then select "Normal Mapping." In the Normal Mapping dialog box, select the appropriate mapping orientation from the drop-down menu.

When I mapped my selection sets, the orientations I used were as follows:

Back/Front	Left/Right	Top/Bottom
col base rt sides	col base back	col cap lips
col base lt sides	col base front	col caps top
col rt side	col caps back	col base bevel
lower sides rt	col caps lt	lower drbrg seat
lower lt side	col caps rt	walkway
lower rt side	col caps front	
	col sides front	
	col sides back	
	lower back	
	lower front	
	walkway front	

As you map the named groups, move them outside the Edit UVW's window. Separate them into groups of the lower wall section, the column bases and caps, the middle columns and the walkway. This will make it easier to stay organized.

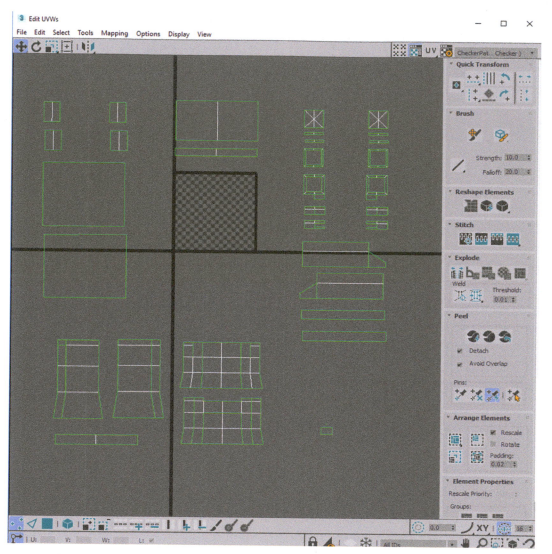

IMAGE 7.85 (Save 7-27)

In the lower right corner, I have a collection of two stray polygons that were left over after all the named sets were mapped. These two are located inside the mesh, hidden from view. The strays can be scaled down and placed anywhere, and they will not be seen in the game. They were probably the result of a modeling operation. If we were to delete them, we would lose all the unwrapping we have done. We would need to go back to when we applied the Unwrap UVW modifier. It is possible to go into the Editable Poly sub-object level to *move* vertices, edges or polygons without losing the unwrapping and mapping. It is not possible to *add or subtract* (weld, delete or insert) vertices, edges or polygons: the unwrap UVD will be broken and lost.

Luckily, Unity, the game engine we will use, can deal with stray vertices like these, hidden from view. Earlier engines had a difficult time working with them in a mesh. These are definitely here in error. Before exporting to a game, I would want to go back and delete the polygons and reapply the unwrap UVW. I'm using them as an example of what might happen as you work. This is not uncommon.

Before we start moving and scaling the named sets into the Edit UVW's window, open the Material Editor, and in a new material slot, create a new texture using the "bridge-gate house texture map.png." We will be using it along with the checker board texture. Also, change the background of the UV Editor to the same image using the Pick Texture option from the drop-down menu in the window.

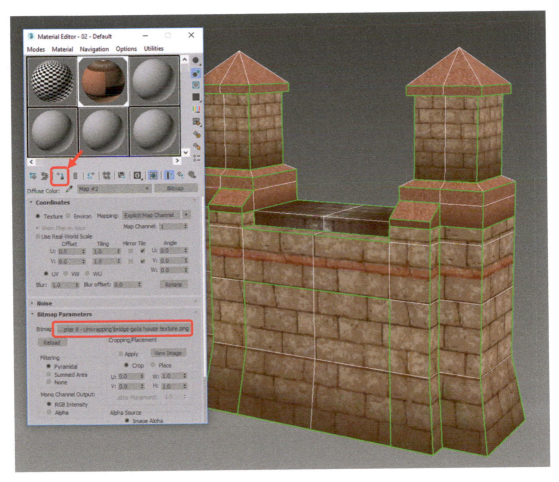

IMAGE 7.86

Checkerboard Utility Material

Arrange the position of the UV Editor in the user interface (UI) so that it is on the left half of the screen (scale the UV Editor by dragging the corners diagonally). Position the mesh in the Perspective viewport so that it can easily be seen. You might want to use the maximize viewport toggle in the lower right corner to make viewing better. With the texture image in the background, we can move our first name set into the Edit UVW's window scale it to fit the texture map. Select the "lower front" selection set to move and scale into position as shown. Note that the top of the polygons extends from the bottom of the reddish row of bricks to the line of the last row of stones and the bottom of the image.

Notice the size of the checkerboard squares. We can use the size of these as a tool for scaling the other three sides of the lower part of the model by scaling the squares of the other three sides to match this one. Sometimes this will be the best method to use for matching the scale of multiple polygon sets. In this case, with our current meshes, we have the advantage of working with geometric, rectangular parts. With organic polygon sets, often found with a character, using the checkerboard is the best tool. Using a checkerboard texture, sometimes called a "utility material," is also useful for finding anomalies in the mapping of faces. The objective in evaluating the applied texture is to get the checkerboard to have uniform squares, not rectangles. The line patterns of the checkerboard should be straight, not waving or curvy. If they are not straight, the image will be wavy or curvy in those areas. By adjusting the vertices, edges and polygons of the mapped image (not the actual mesh), the textures can be manipulated to project without or with minimized distortion on the actual mesh.

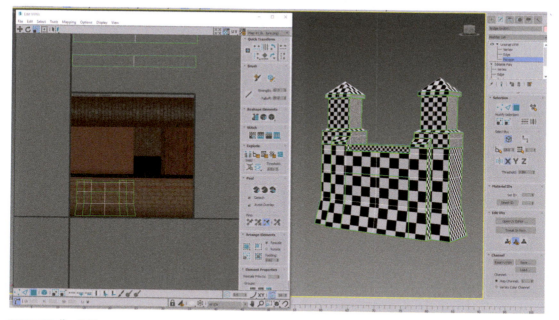

IMAGE **7.87** (Save 7-28)

Next, select the two "lower side" sets and rotate them 90 degrees to orient the top of the selections correctly (top is up). Move one of the sets to overlap the other to stack them as shown. Using the Scale Selected Sub-object tool, adjust the scale of the two lower side sets so that in the viewport, the checkerboard squares match the size of the lower front checkerboard. When they are the same size, the texture maps, when applied will be the same scale. Now, if you haven't already, you can move them into the Edit UVW's window next to the lower front polygon set. Notice that the height of the new scaled set matches the lower front set. Position it to align with the lower front set so that the stone wall horizontal lines will align at the corner where they intersect vertically.

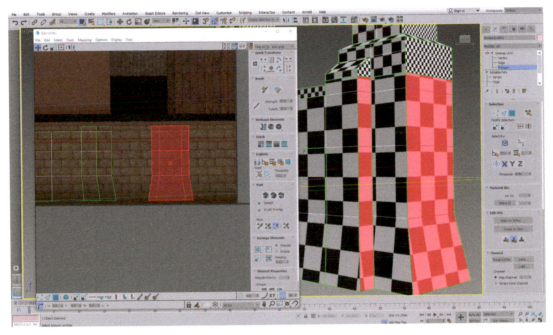

IMAGE 7.88

Rotate the Perspective viewport to view the back side of the mesh. Repeat the scaling of the checkerboard texture on the "lower back" set. When the squares match in size, move the lower back set to the Edit UVW's window and locate it over top of the lower *front* named set. The main walls of the lower part of the module are now mapped. In the Material Editor, assign the "bridge-gate house texture.png" map to the mesh to view your progress. The mapping of the lower section should show the horizontal alignment the stone wall on the four wall sides. Switch back to the checkerboard pattern texture by reassigning it to the mesh.

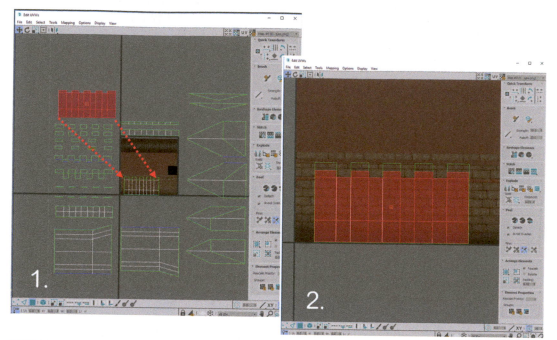

IMAGE 7.89

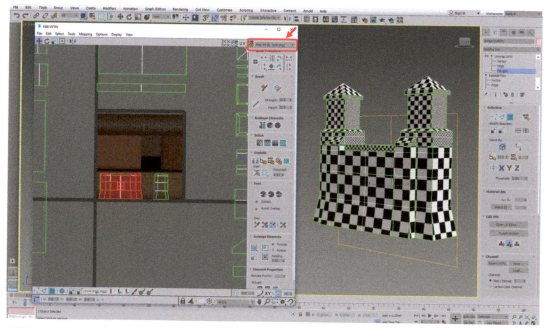

IMAGE 7.90

The lower part of the mesh uses the stone wall section of the texture image. The base and cap parts of the two columns will use the reddish concrete area of the texture map image. For these parts on this mesh, if we use the same scale that we did for the lower sections, the concrete texture will be too large. They will be a larger scale than the reddish concrete scale texture we used on the merlon caps of the Curtain Wall. So, we can use the checkerboard square size as a guide. Working with the column base sets, select the "col base lt front" and the "col base rt front" named sets and stack them. Next, scale them so that the checkerboard size on these parts appears to be a little more than one-half the size of the checkerboard squares on the lower sections. This will make the texture smaller, although the polygon sets will actually be larger in the Texture Map window. They are covering more area on the texture image, creating a denser texture. Locate the scaled polygons in the Edit UVW's window to complete the mapping.

Continue with the other Named Selection sets for the column bases, the sides and the beveled name set, scaling the checkerboard squares to match. When locating the base sets in the Edit UVW's window, align the bottom edges with the bottom of the reddish concrete image area of the texture map. This will give the polygons a "dirty" look, appropriate for the lower parts of the columns where they would typically get covered with dirt. After positioning these polygons, switch the assigned image in the Material Editor from the checkerboard map to the real image. Then, rotate the perspective viewport to make sure that the polygons around the column bases are oriented correctly with the dirtiest area at the bottom of the polygons. If they are oriented incorrectly, rotate them to the proper position in the UV Editor window. When complete, reassign the checkerboard texture to the mesh to continue assigning and scaling.

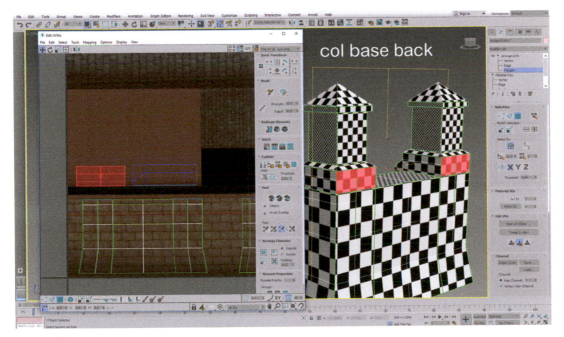

IMAGE 7.91

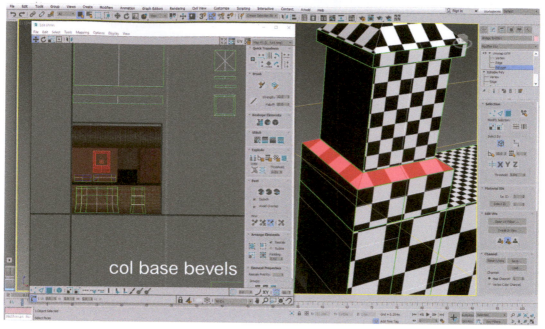

IMAGE 7.92

Next, map the "top cap" named sets for the columns. The checkerboard squares should be sized to match the column base square sizes to ensure that the image scales are the same.

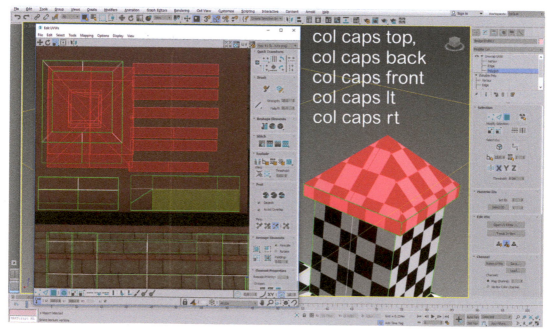

IMAGE 7.93

The next section to map will be the center sections of the columns. We will utilize the same image area as the lower wall section of the mesh. To add visual interest, we will scale the stones to be smaller than the lower section stones. Select the eight "column" name selection sets, and stack them. Select the stack, and scale the checkerboard squares so that they appear slightly less than one-half the size of the lower wall section checkerboard squares. The polygon selections will actually get larger to scale the image smaller. When ready, move them into the Edit UVW's window, aligning the bottom edge of the selection sets with the bottom of the lower wall polygons. This will create the "dirty" look to the bottoms of the polygons like you did with the column bases.

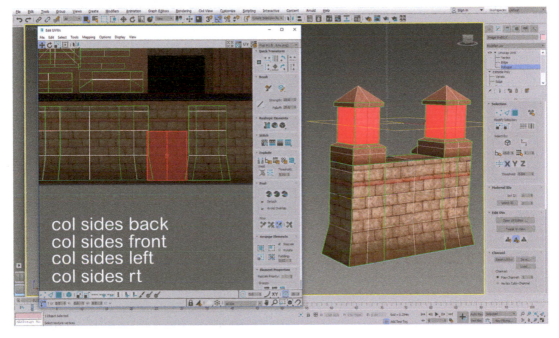

IMAGE 7.94

IMAGE 7.95 (Save 7-29)

Select the "lower drbg seat" name set. This is where the drawbridge rests when it is open. Position and scale the polygons to fit within the gap area in the top side of the "lower front" name set. When you get close to the position, carefully match the checkerboard square scales in the viewport. When you change the Material Editor assigned material to the "bridge-gate house texture.png," check to see if the horizontal joint lines between the stones align with the vertical joint lines on the lower front mapping.

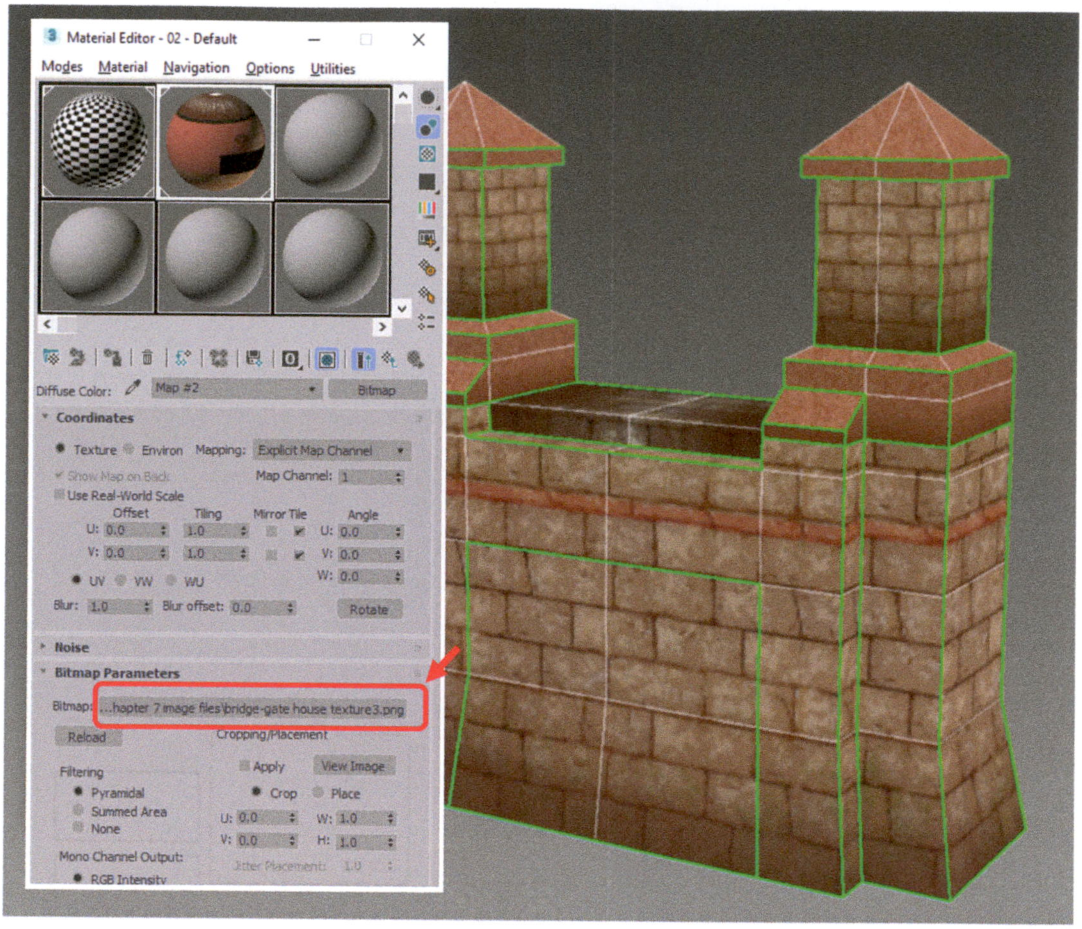

IMAGE 7.96

Align the stone lines to wraps the image around the mesh.

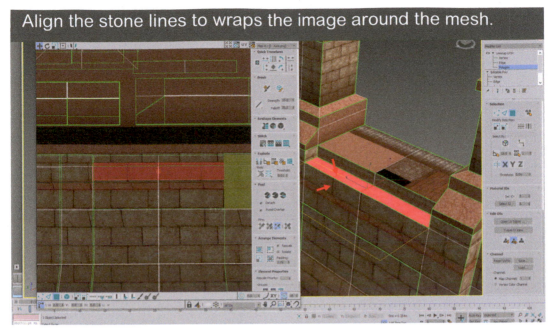

IMAGE 7.97

Select the walkway and walkway front .

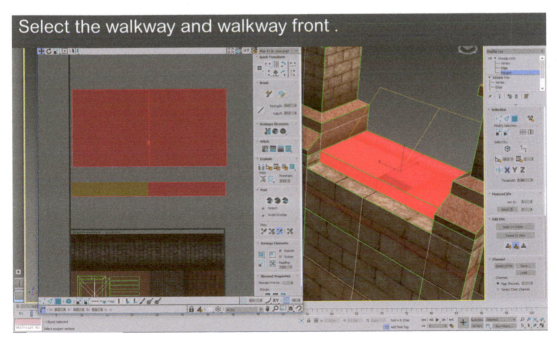

IMAGE 7.98

Lastly, we need to map the "walkway" and the "walkway front." Select both these name sets, and arrange them as shown in the image, aligned and spaced a short distance apart. On the mesh, these two sets have a common edge between them. In this particular instance, we can "stitch" the two sets together as one. It will make the mapping easier as the texture will wrap around the edge continuously.

Switch to Edge sub-object level in the Unwrap UVW modifier (not the Editable Poly level). Select the bottom two edges of the "walkway." They will turn red. Notice that two edges on the "walkway front" turned blue. The red and blue edges indicate that these edges are common with each other on the mesh. They are the same edge. With both selected, click on the "Tools" tab on the top menu bar of the UV Editor. Select "Stitch Selected" from the drop-down menu. A small dialog box will pop up, just click on the OK button to complete the stitching. The two parts are now one.

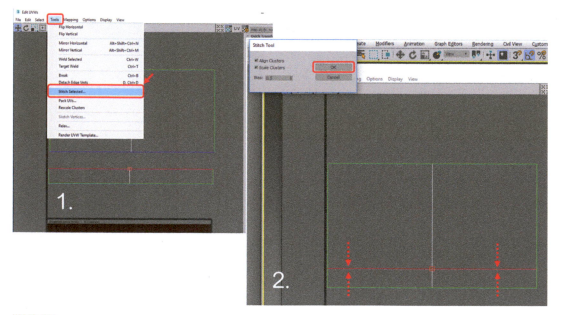

IMAGE 7.99

Rotate the polygons 90 degrees to orient them correctly with the walkway texture, and then move and scale them to the walkway texture area at the top of the Edit UVW's window. Note that the walkway texture in this map is one-half the scale of the walkway part of the Curtain Wall Texture we used before.

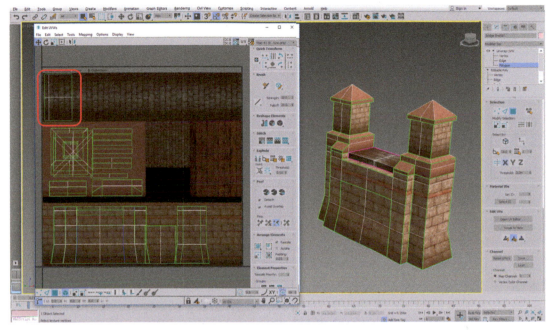

IMAGE 7.100

IMAGE 7.101 (Save 7-30)

That completes the unwrapping and mapping of the Bridge End. There is one more basic unwrapping thing you should know how to do: creating a texture map. For all the previous unwrapping projects we have done, I have supplied the texture maps that you used. For the next exercise, you will be creating your own texture.

The Banner-Flag

In our game, we need a banner-flag for the teams to capture (it's a capture the flag game). Find the "Flag-Banner.max" file in the companion file folder for Chapter 7 (or open Save 7-31), and open it in 3ds Max. For this final unwrapping exercise, I am providing a model, so we can get right to the unwrapping.

IMAGE 7.102 (Save 7-31)

With the file open, select the banner mesh. Add an Unwrap UVW modifier to the Modifier Stack. Get into the Polygon sub-object layer of the modifier. Click the Ignore Backfacing button off.

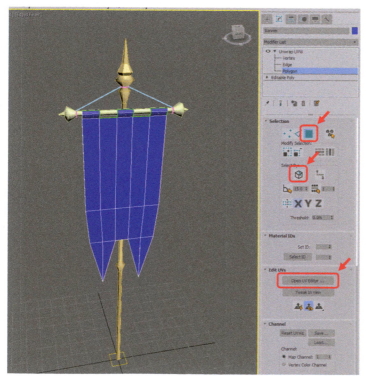

IMAGE 7.103

Select the whole mesh, and then open the UV Editor. Apply Normal Mapping to the polygons as you've done previously, using the Normal Mapping option under the Mapping tab of the UV Editor tool bar. Select the Front/Back orientation in the Normal Mapping dialog box that appears and then hit OK.

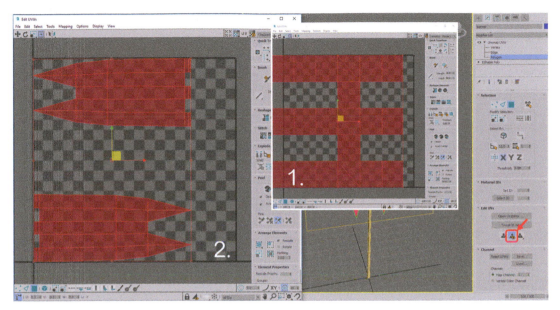

IMAGE 7.104

Scale, rotate and move the two polygon sets to the location as shown.

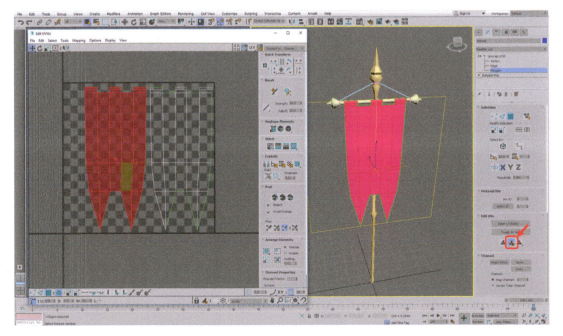

IMAGE 7.105 (Save 7-32)

Next, we will create an image template of the Edit UVW's window that we can use in Adobe Photoshop or another graphics editor program. Click on the "Tools" tab on the Top tool bar of the UV Editor to open the drop-down menu. Select the last one in the list, "Render UVW Template…."

The Render UVW's dialogue window will open with a list of options for the template it will render. In the width and height parameter boxes, we want to enter only numbers that are a power of 2's (256, 512, 1024, 2046). These determine the size of the image in pixels. As stated earlier, game engines work best with images for textures with dimensions that are powers of two. Typically, most images are square. However, rectangular images will work, as long as the width and height are power of two numbers. In our case, for the Flag-Banner, we will use a 1,024 × 1,024 image.

In the "Fill" section, change the "Mode:" value box to "Solid." This is my personal preference; you might find one of the others works best for you. This time though, use "Solid" so you can follow along. When the image renders, the polygons will appear solid gray (the color in the color picker box) against a black background. You can uncheck the "Show Overlap…" and also uncheck the three check boxes in the "Edges" section. Unchecking these will visually simplify the template image when it is rendered. We won't need any of these features with this image.

At the bottom of the window, click on the "Render UV Template" button to create a 2D image of the normal mapped polygons.

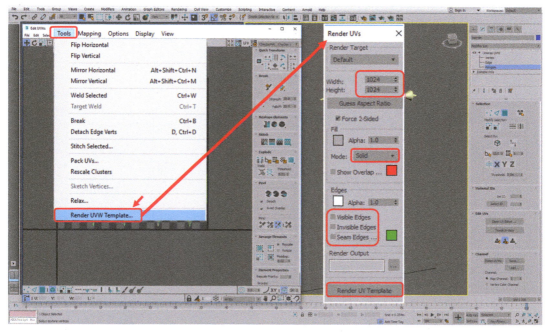

IMAGE 7.106

The image below shows the rendered template. If you'd like to explore, try turning some of the unchecked boxes in the Render UVW's window back on and re-render to see what the results are. In the upper left

310

corner, click on the save icon button and save the image file with a name of your choice as a .png, .jpg or .tga file. You might want to get in the habit of using only .png or. tga files as they have Alpha channels, useful for creating transparent backgrounds.

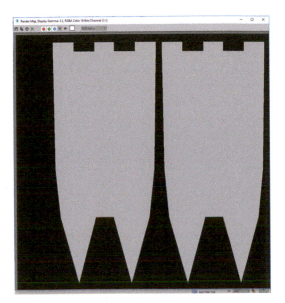

IMAGE 7.107

Open the template file in Photoshop if you have it or in another program like the free and open-source image manipulation software, Gimp. For the next step, everyone has their own preferences; I prefer to open a new layer on top of the template layer, creating my image over it. Some may prefer to add the layer under the template. Regardless, add a layer to start working on so you do not alter the template layer. If you need to come back and make changes, the original layer with the template will be preserved.

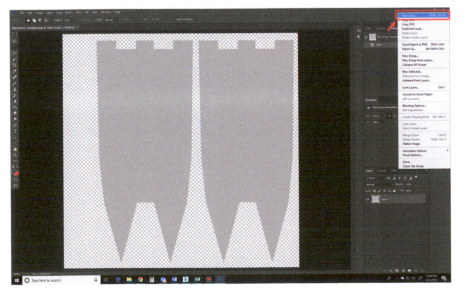

IMAGE 7.108

Looking at the template image, the banner areas, which are gray in color, are easy to determine. From this one template, in 3ds Max we only unwrapped the banners part of the model, and we can create the textures for the other parts of the model too on this map. We will need a texture for the other parts of out model, the ropes and rope loops, a texture for the pole and crossbar, and if we separate the ornamental pieces on the ends of the crossbar and pole, an area for them. The rope texture area needs to be long and narrow, the shape of the ropes. The same goes for the pole texture area: long and narrow. The ornament texture area can be smaller and rectangular. We can fit those three shapes on the left side of the template in the open area next to the banner texture area. The size of the pole and ornament areas isn't critical, and the colors will be solid: no pattern or details. The rope will have a texture, so the bigger it can be the better. However, we need to recognize that the ropes holding the banner crossbar are very thin and small relative to the rest of the model. The texture for the ropes is not the primary area for detail, the banners, the main focal point are. They are the biggest, filling the most area of the texture map.

For source images, open both the "banner_02.png" and the "bridge-gatehouse template.png" images in the program. We can use these to create a new image by using copy and paste, with some modifications. There will be three images open in Photoshop.

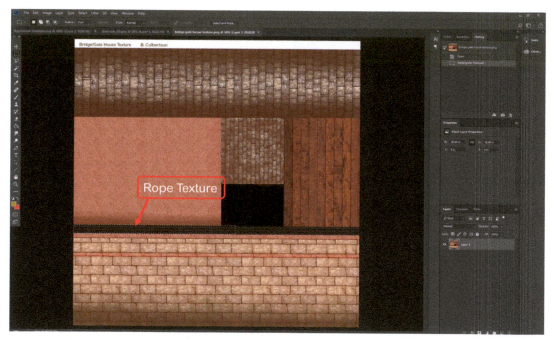

IMAGE 7.109

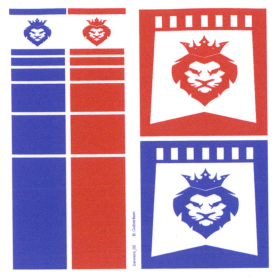

IMAGE 7.110

Use the Photoshop eyedropper tool to change the foreground color to the blue color used on the "banners_02.png" image by sampling it. Switch back to the new template, and on the new layer you added, use the Rectangular Marquee tool (box) to create a rectangle over the two banners. Fill the rectangle with the blue color using the Fill tool. We can no longer see the banner shapes, so reduce the opacity of the new layer with the blue fill to 50 percent to see the banner shapes in the layer under it. Next, going back to the "banners.02.png" image, copy just the blue lion head. Return to the template image, and paste the lion head icon into the image on a new layer (just paste). Scale and position the head as shown.

IMAGE 7.111

If you want to do so too, I added a layer below the lion head icon and added a few white colored rectangles to add some more visual finish to the banner. When ready, return the blue layer from 50 percent to full opacity.

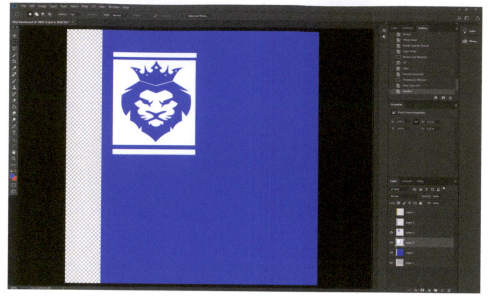

IMAGE 7.112

Switch to the bridge-gate house texture.png image, and create a marquee rectangle over one-half the horizontal length of the ropes in the middle of the image. Copy them and paste them into the new texture image. Next, rotate them vertically using the Edit > Transform tool. Scale and position as shown. Once in position, go to the top tool bar and select Image > Adjustments > Hue/Saturation to slide the "Hue" slider to alter the rope color to make them blueish.

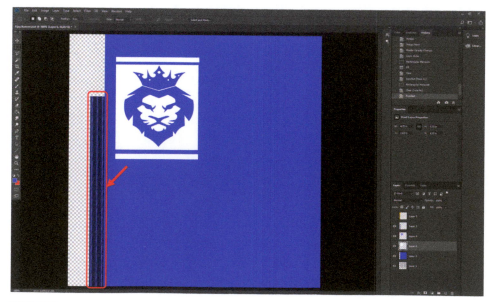

IMAGE 7.113

Add another new layer and create the two yellow-gold areas, a long rectangular darker yellow gold for the poles and a smaller rectangle for the lighter yellow gold. Save the image as a Photoshop file and as a .png file named "flag-banner_blue."

IMAGE 7.114 (Save 7-33)

Back in 3ds Max, create a new material in the Material Editor using the new texture we just made and apply it to the banner.

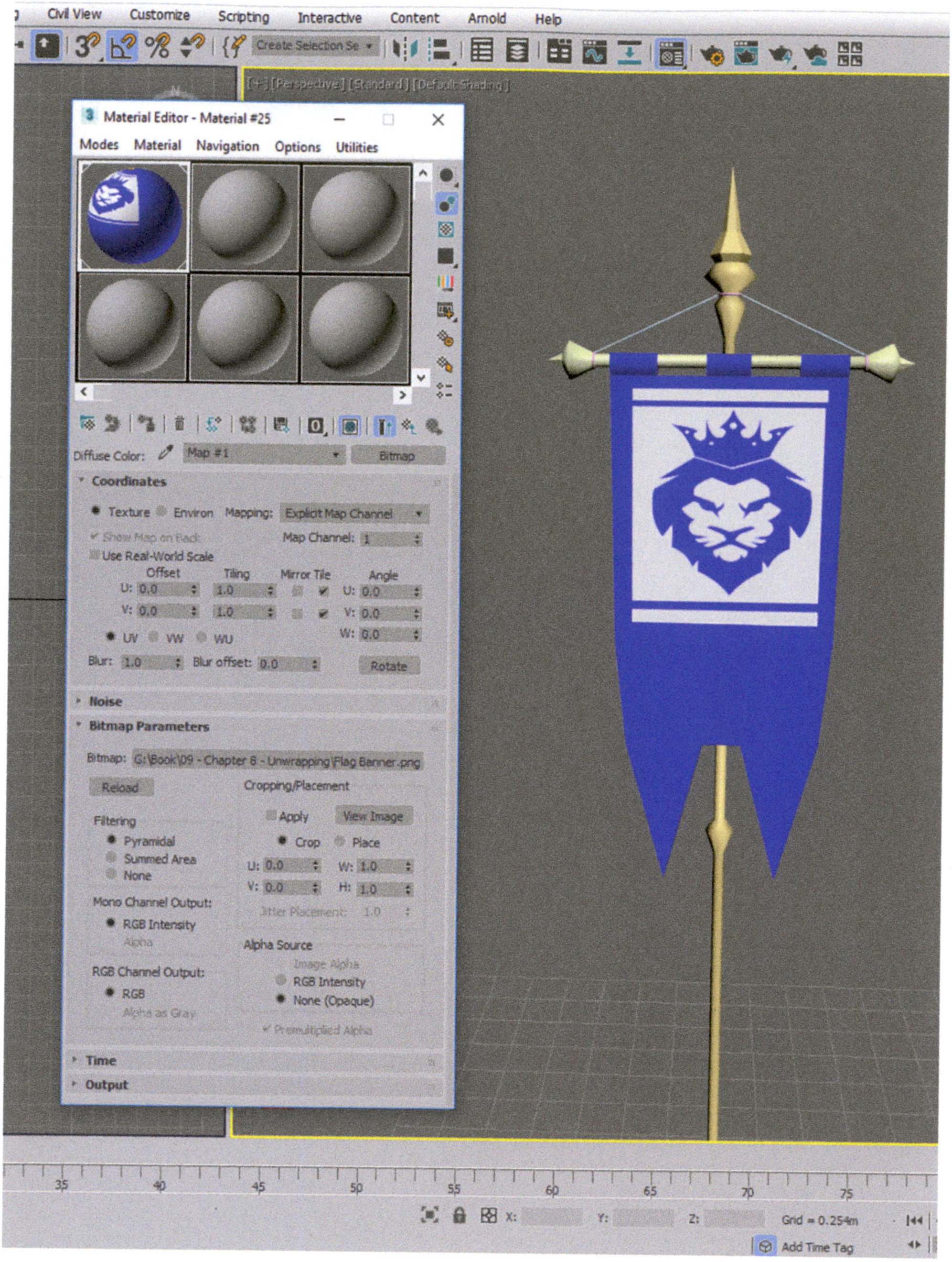

IMAGE 7.115

Select the pole mesh. Add an Unwrap UVW modifier. In Polygon sub-object level of the modifier, turn off the Ignore Backfacing and select the whole mesh. Open the UV Editor, and go to Mapping > Normal Mapping. In the Normal Mapping dialogue window, select the Front/Back mapping orientation.

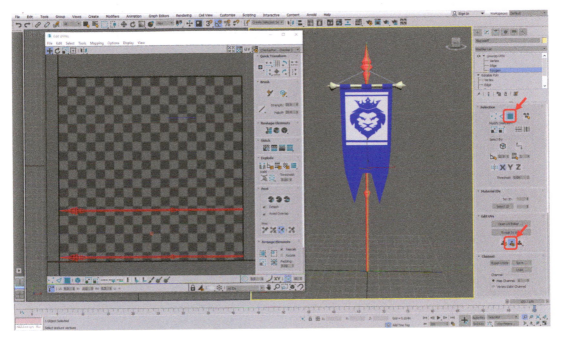

IMAGE 7.116

Rotate the mapped pole polygons to vertical, and select just the top ornament parts as shown.

We want to move just these polygons over to the light gold image area. We cannot move them alone because they are attached to the polygons of the pole below them. In the Editor, on the right-hand tool bar, find the "Break" icon button in the "Explode" section. Click on this button to detach the selected polygons from the ones below it. Move the detached polygons over to the light gold image area as shown.

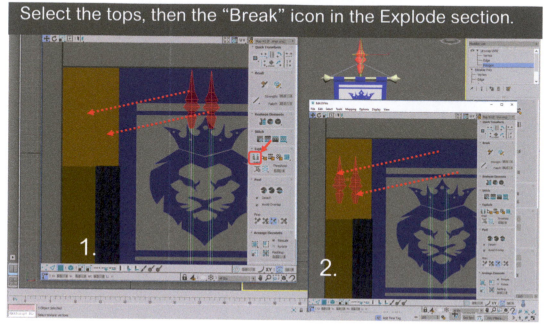

IMAGE 7.117

Detach the middle ornament polygon areas using the "Break" icon button, and move them over to the light gold image area. Then, move the four remaining pole polygon parts over to the darker gold image area.

IMAGE 7.118

Next, select the crossbar mesh. Repeat the same process you just did on the pole:

- Add an Unwrap UVW modifier.
- Turn off the Ignore Backfaces.
- Select the whole mesh.
- Unwrap using the Front/Back normal map orientation.

- Rotate the polygons to a vertical orientation.
- "Break" the ornament polygons, and move them to the light gold image area.
- Move the crossbar parts to the darker gold image areas.

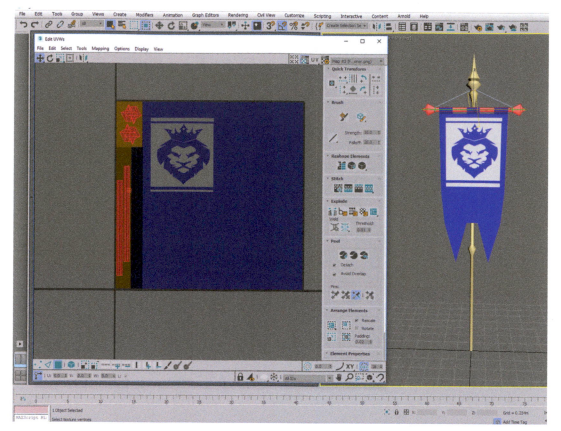

IMAGE 7.119

Repeat the same process (minus the "break" step) on the two rope meshes and the three rope loops. To save some work, you could unwrap and map one of the ropes and one of the rope loops and then clone and scale, if necessary, to replace the others. Note that when you apply the normal map the rope loops, choose an orientation that places them on their side as shown to use the rope texture.

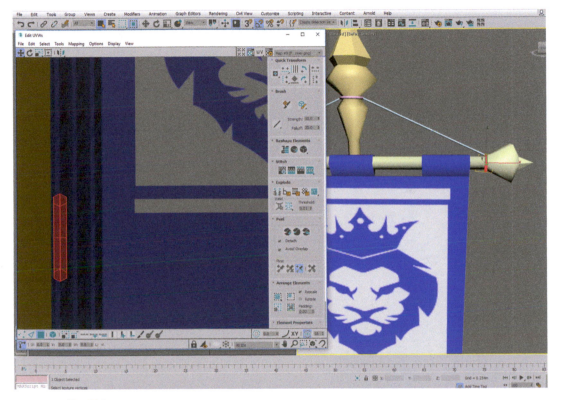

IMAGE 7.120 (Save 7-34)

This will complete the blue Flag-Banner. In the photo-editing program (Photoshop), create another texture, "flag-banner_red.png" by changing the blue areas to red, using the banners_2.png image to eyedropper for the red color and adjusting the rope color to reddish with the saturation tool.

In this chapter, we used several different basic unwrapping and mapping methods, and created a new texture using a template from the UV Editor. Unwrapping, creating textures and mapping are all much more complex subjects than what we covered. We couldn't possibly cover the topics in the depth they deserve here. Hopefully, you have a good grasp of the concepts we used so you can get your mapped meshes successfully in the game engine.

Chapter 7 Exercise: Texture the Modules

Now, here's the big challenge… go back and unwrap and map the remaining modules we made up to now: The Fixed Bridge, the Gate House, the two Turrets, The Table and Chair, the Wall Torch, and the Cannon. Set up a schedule to do them, say over a week's time, and come back to pick up with Chapter 8, the Castle Keep. You will need them to complete the Castle project. As an aid, I have unwrapped them and saved file iterations as I did them. They can be found in the online companion file folder for the book.

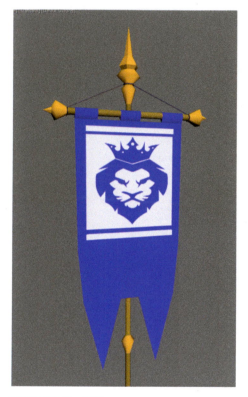

IMAGE 7.121 (Save 7-35)

Modeling the Castle Keep

Concepts/Skills/Tools Introduced in This Chapter

- Reinforcing of Acquired Skills and Tool Use
- Straight Staircase

The final major piece to the castle project will be the Castle Keep. This is the inner fortress for the King, within the castle walls. Creating the Castle Keep will utilize your previously learned modeling skills. Instead of going through its construction step-by-step, the instructions will be limited. You will be required to analyze the images and do the operations necessary to achieve similar results. You are not expected to duplicate the castle exactly, but to improvise when necessary to get the model done while meeting the specifications. Remember, you can always access the saved files for the project to monitor the iterations.

For this last major model, I have done the preliminary research and developed a sketch to work from. Referring to our GDD, the keep requirements are as follows:

Gate House module:

- Height from ground- to upper-level deck: 10–15 meters
- Overall height: 25 meters
- Module width: up to 40 meters

- Module length: up to 40 meters
- No "batter" at the bottom of the structure
- Player access to inside by one entrance
- Stair access to upper level by player
- Castle Flag (goal) located on upper level, accessible to player
- Hand-painted textures
- Polygon count: under 4,000

Note: The characters in the game will be scaled to 1.15 meter; short, stocky, fantasy dwarf styling. The structures in the environment should be scaled accordingly.

As before, below are five of the images that I used for reference when designing the Castle Keep.

IMAGE 8.1

IMAGE 8.2

IMAGE 8.3

IMAGE 8.4

IMAGE 8.5

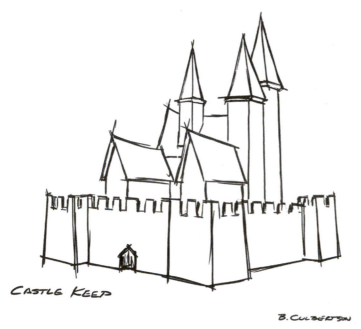

CASTLE KEEP

B. CULBERTSON

IMAGE 8.6

Prepare a new scene in 3ds Max. We will need a "Placeholder" layer, a "Castle Keep Level 1" layer and a "Castle Keep Level 2" layer in the Scene Explorer. Name and save the file as "lastname_castlekeep_01."

The Castle Keep Placeholder

To begin the Placeholder, I made a box with parameters as shown in the image below.

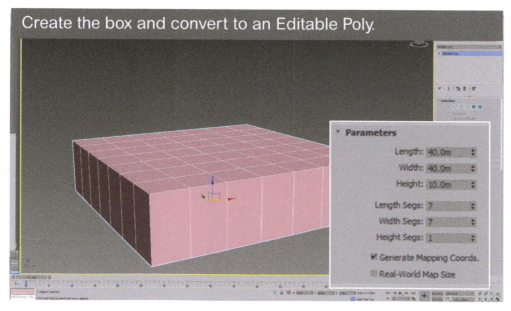

IMAGE 8.7 (Save 8-1)

Center the box at (0, 0, 0,), and convert it to an Editable Poly. Using the Extrude tool in the Polygon sub-object level, create the structure block-out as shown. The following images show the extrusions I made to create the body of the mesh.

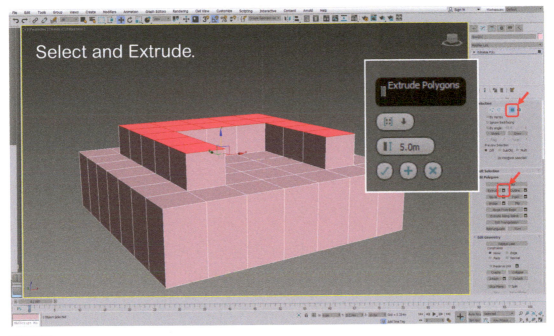

IMAGE 8.8

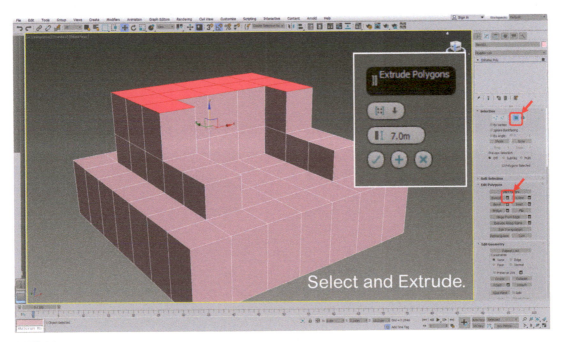

IMAGE 8.9

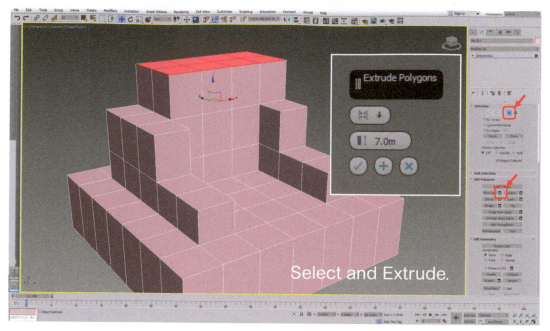

IMAGE 8.10

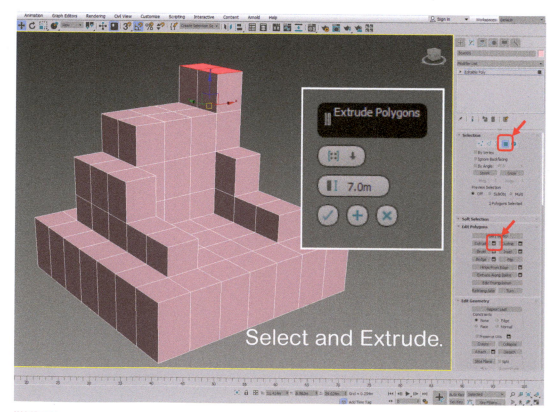

IMAGE 8.11

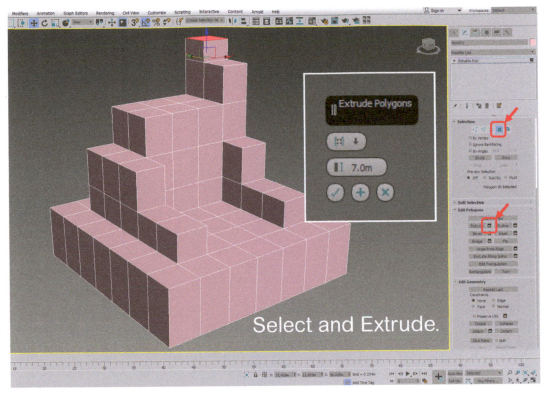

Select and Extrude.

IMAGE 8.12

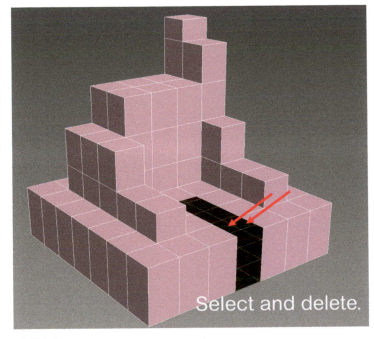

Select and delete.

IMAGE 8.13

Delete the polygons as shown to create a space for the ramp to the upper level. Extrude the edges on the side using the select, shift and drag method in Edge sub-object level mode to create the side walls and the ramp.

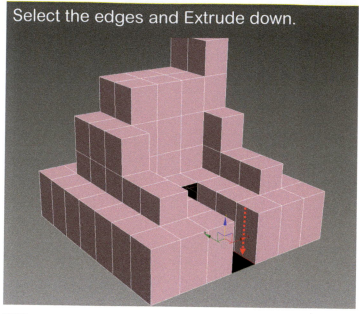

IMAGE 8.14

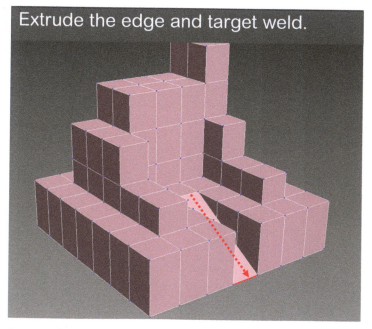

IMAGE 8.15 (Save 8-2)

The Castle Keep Model

That's all for the placeholder. Change the active layer in the Scene Explorer from Placeholder to the Castle Keep Level 1, turning off the Placeholder layer. Like the Gate House module, we will build one-quarter of the lower section of the Castle Keep and use the Symmetry Modifier to fill out the remaining three sides. Start with a box with the following parameters.

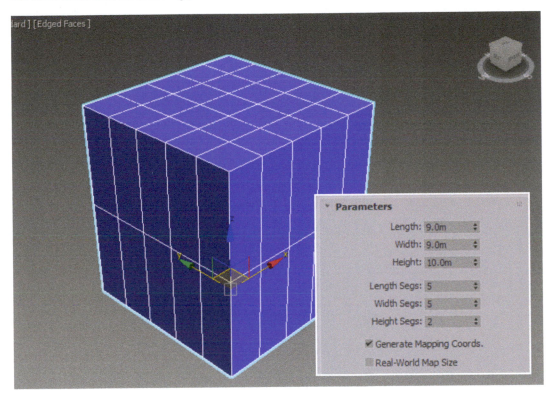

IMAGE 8.16 (Save 8-3)

Center it at (0, 0, 0), and convert it to an Editable Poly. Move the middle row of vertices to a new Z-Coordinate Display value of 2.5 meters. Lowering these vertices will allow us to create the entrance doors.

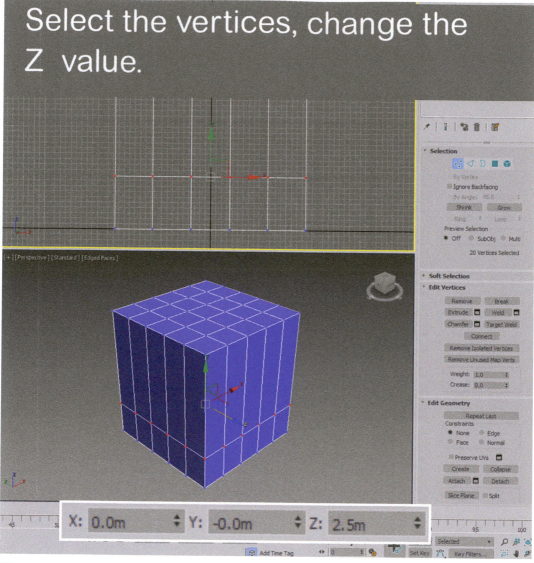

IMAGE 8.17

Rotate the perspective viewport to view the bottom of the mesh. Select and delete all the bottom polygons on the mesh. This will lower the polygon count.

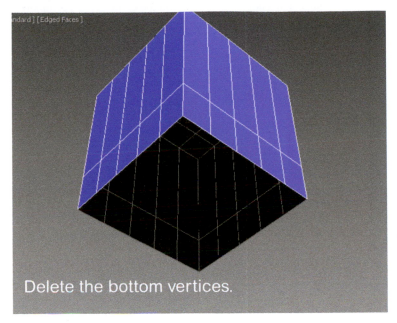

Delete the bottom vertices.

IMAGE 8.18

Next, on a corner, Target Weld the second vertical row of vertices from the corner to the corresponding corner vertices. Do the same to the row on the adjacent side around the corner as shown. This is to reduce vertices on the upper walkway that will extrude from here.

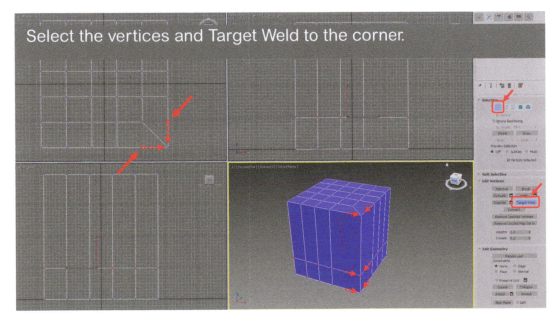

Select the vertices and Target Weld to the corner.

IMAGE 8.19

Select the vertices as shown, and extrude them 2 meters. Using the green plus (+) button on the Extrude Caddy, extrude them six more times for a total of seven times (14 meters). Delete the end polygons. Repeat the same extrusions, and delete on the polygons on the adjacent side around the corner. When complete, delete the polygons of the two extrusions on the bottom of the mesh.

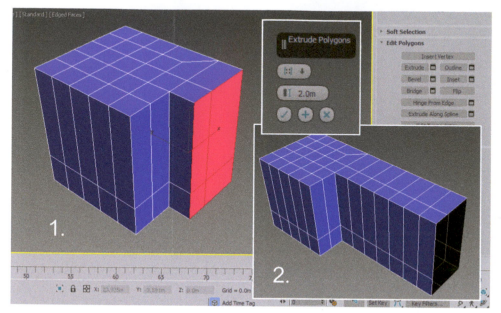

IMAGE 8.20

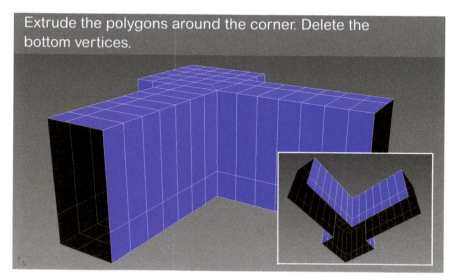

IMAGE 8.21 (Save 8-4)

Next, we will create the top of the wall with the embrasures and the merlons. Select the polygons on the top of the mesh as shown. Extrude them, and then use the Cut tool in Vertex sub-object level to create a row of edges along the wall top where shown. Don't cut the corner polygons; they will be extruded to make columns. Remember to turn on the 3D Snaps when using the Cut tool, and the Snap Settings should be on Midpoint and Endpoint.

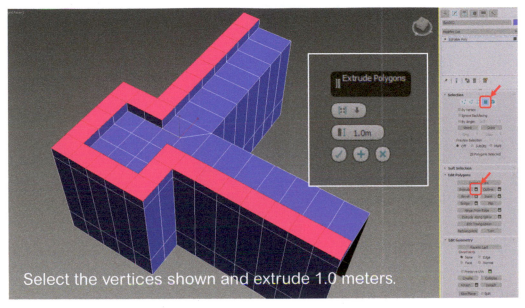

IMAGE 8.22

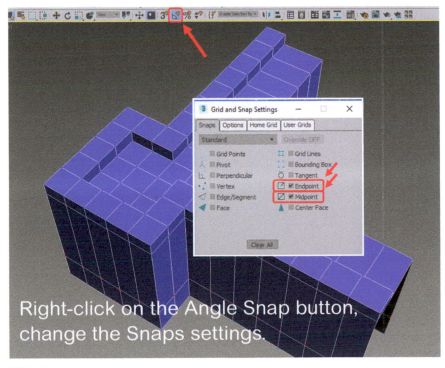

IMAGE 8.23

335

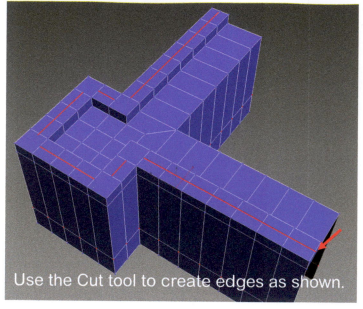

Use the Cut tool to create edges as shown.

IMAGE 8.24

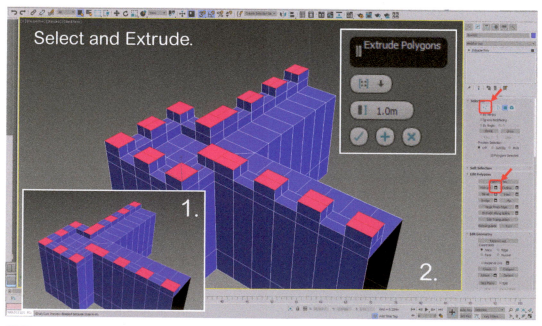

Select and Extrude.

IMAGE 8.25

Next, Target Weld the vertices along the embrasures to the vertices below them to create the beveled embrasure as we did on previous modules.

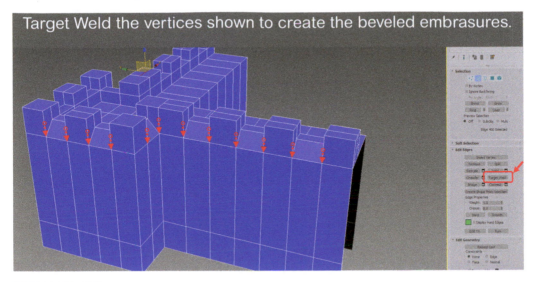

IMAGE 8.26 (Save 8-5)

Select the top polygons on the corner tower's corners, and extrude them up 1 meter. If we do this before raising the merlon center edges, the side faces of the corner columns will stay flat.

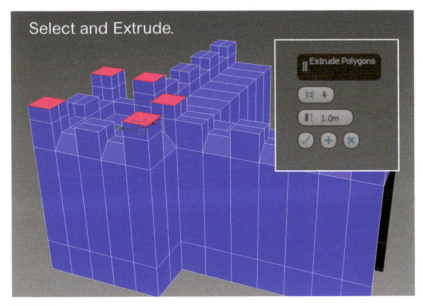

IMAGE 8.27

Select the center edges on the tops of the merlons as shown. Drag them up in the Z-axis until they meet the tops of the corner columns.

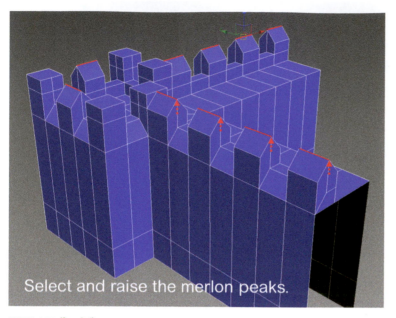

Select and raise the merlon peaks.

IMAGE 8.28 (Save 8-6)

To make pointed caps on the corner columns, we need to create a vertex in the center of the top polygons. Use the Cut tool again to create crisscross edges on the column tops as shown. Then, select the center vertex of each column top (where the cuts intersect, creating an "x"), and together, drag them up the Z-axis to a height you desire to create pointed caps.

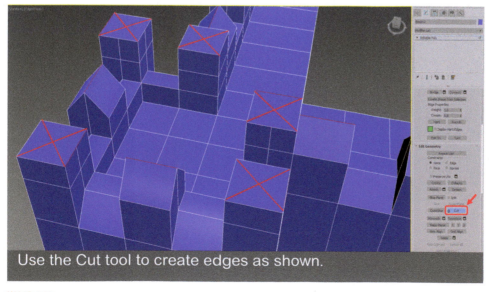

Use the Cut tool to create edges as shown.

IMAGE 8.29

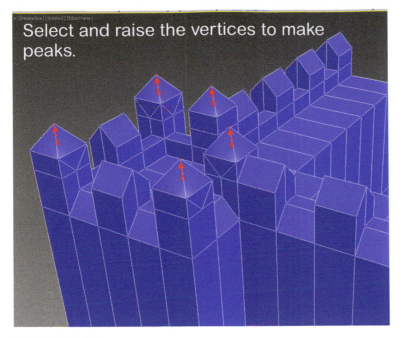

IMAGE 8.30 (Save 8-7)

Remember the last thing we did to the merlon peaks in previous modules. We used the chamfer tool to soften the top edge where the player will have access to them. Go ahead, and use the chamfer tool on all the merlon peak edges.

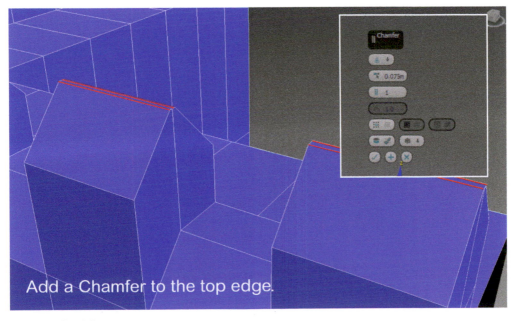

IMAGE 8.31 (Save 8-8)

Next, we will create the entrance doorway to the structure. There will be two entrances, on the front and the back sides. Select the vertex at the top of where the center of the door will be and change its Z-Coordinate Display box value to 3.5 meters to give the door some height. Remember, we will be using the Symmetry Modifier to fill out the building sides.

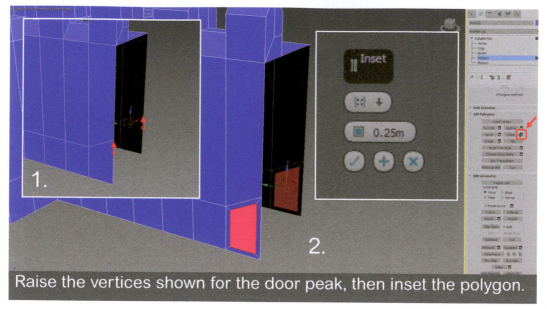

Raise the vertices shown for the door peak, then inset the polygon.

IMAGE 8.32

Select the doorway polygons on both the outside and inside walls. Create an inset with the Inset tool as shown. Then, as with the other door and window openings we have created previously, drag the faces toward the center to create a bevel doorframe. Next, delete the inset polygons and the bevel sides along the vertical centerline of the mesh (the symmetry line).

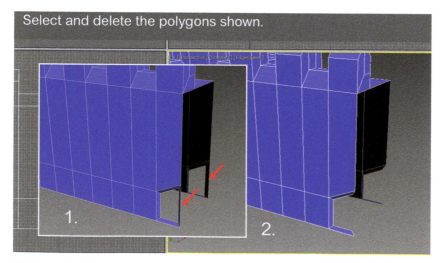

Select and delete the polygons shown.

IMAGE 8.33 (Save 8-9)

The bevel at the top of the doorframe has a vertice that is not in line with the other end vertices. To fix it, select all the end vertices in the left viewport. Then, right-mouse click in the Front viewport to change to a perpendicular angle to the row of vertices and to keep them selected. In the Modify panel, select the Align View button to bring all the selected vertices into alignment. This will be important to make sure the Symmetry Modifier will work correctly later.

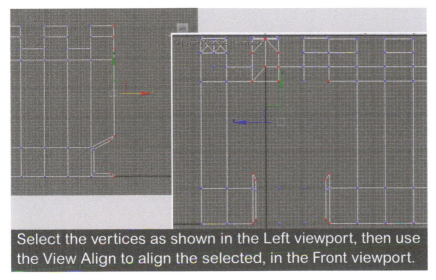

Select the vertices as shown in the Left viewport, then use the View Align to align the selected, in the Front viewport.

IMAGE 8.34

The next step will be to bridge the front and back doorway openings. Select the three edges on both the front and back opening, and then click on the Bridge button.

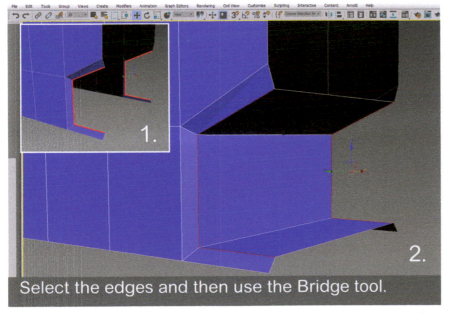

Select the edges and then use the Bridge tool.

IMAGE 8.35

The lower vertices of the top of the doorframe are slightly out of alignment due to the View Align tool use. The beveled polygon has a slight twist to it which creates a visible diagonal line through the polygon. By raising the two vertices in the Z-axis slightly, you can eliminate twisting in the polygon.

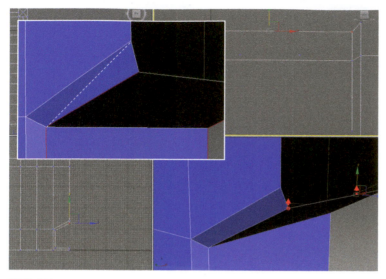

IMAGE 8.36

To add some visual interest to the walls, let's add a slight bevel to the outside walls. Carefully select the two bottom rows of outside vertices of the corner tower (not including the vertices of the two side walls). From the front view, scale the vertices in the X-axis and then in the left viewport, in the Y-axis. If the corners where the side wall meets the corner wall did not react as expected, it is likely that some unwanted vertices are selected. Use the undo, and then reselect the vertices to make the correct scaling. When complete, move the bottom two outside rows of vertices (one wall at a time) to create an angle parallel to the cornet tower bevel.

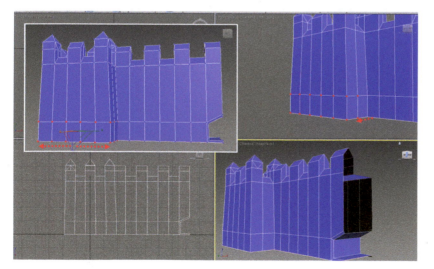

IMAGE 8.37 (Save 8-10)

When we add the Symmetry Modifier to the mesh, the entrance doorway is going to be 3.5+ meters wide (double the current width). That's a wide doorway. Select the end row of vertices that include the centerline of the doorway. In the Y-axis Coordinates Display box subtract 0.5 meter to move the vertices toward the corner tower for a narrower doorway.

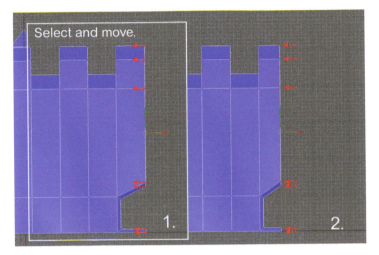

IMAGE 8.38 (Save 8-11)

We're ready to add the Symmetry Modifier to the mesh to create the other three quadrants. We will not be collapsing the stack after we add the modifier until the model is unwrapped and mapped. Later, we'll be able to unwrap and map just one-quarter of the section instead of the whole model.

Select an edge of the open end above the doorway. Add a Symmetry Modifier, and find the correct Mirror Axis in the parameters section of the Modifier panel. This will complete the front half of the Castle Keep wall. Drop down in the Modifier stack, clicking on the Edge sub-object level of the Editable Poly. Next, click on an edge on the open end of the other side wall. Add another Symmetry Modifier to the Modifier stack. Find the correct mirror axis to form a complete four-walled, closed structure as shown. As you can see, it is possible to stack modifiers on the Editable Poly. The program first calculates the Editable Poly, then recalculates the mesh with the modifier above the Editable Poly, and then adds the next modifier in succession up the stack.

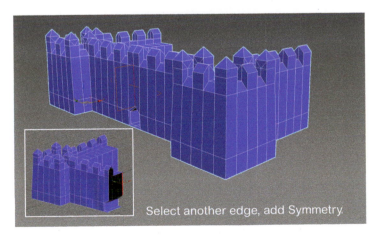

IMAGE 8.39

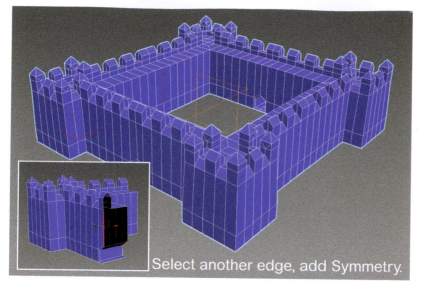

IMAGE 8.40 (Save 8-12)

We could go into the mesh and reduce the polygons on the inside of the wall, deleting them to reduce the polycount. If we leave them, the mesh can be used as a stand-alone piece, increasing its versatility. We will not be modeling an elaborate interior for this module.

In the game, we need to provide an opportunity for the player in the game to get inside the Castle Keep and up to an upper level. Next, we will fill the interior with boxes to create a platform for the upper level.

In the top viewport, create a box with the parameters as shown in the image below.

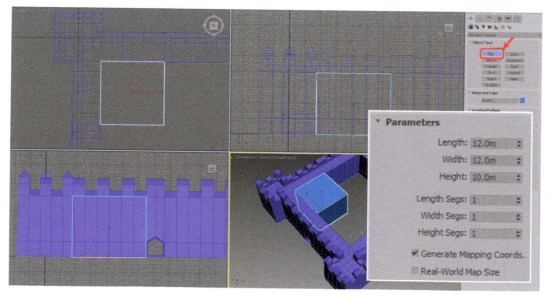

IMAGE 8.41 (Save 8-13)

Locate the box in an inside corner of the lower wall. Clone the box three times, and position in them in the other three corners, to make a total of four boxes, using the "hold the Shift-key, select and drag" method.

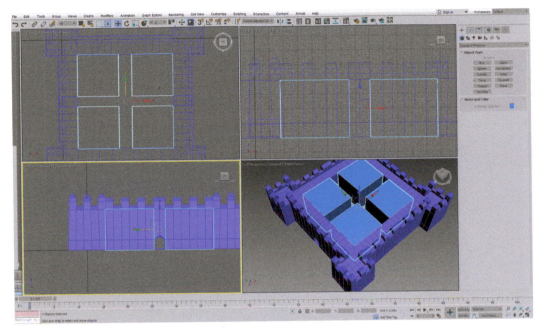

IMAGE 8.42 (Save 8-14)

Next, make a box in the center of the four boxes to be a mid-floor landing for staircases (shown as a cream-colored box in the image below).

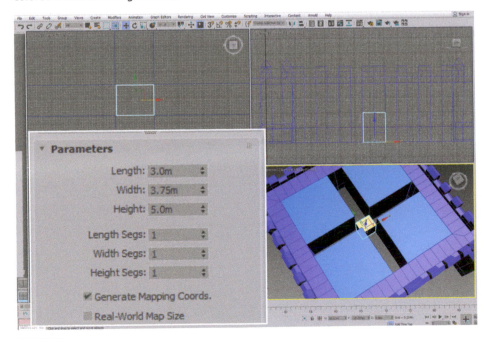

IMAGE 8.43

We will utilize the spaces between the boxes for staircases. Next, add a straight staircase on the lower level up to the middle landing as shown (change from Standard Primitives to Stairs in the Geometry tab drop-down menu in the Command Panel). When the staircase is positioned properly, use the mirror tool to make an instance clone and position it on the opposite side of the middle landing box.

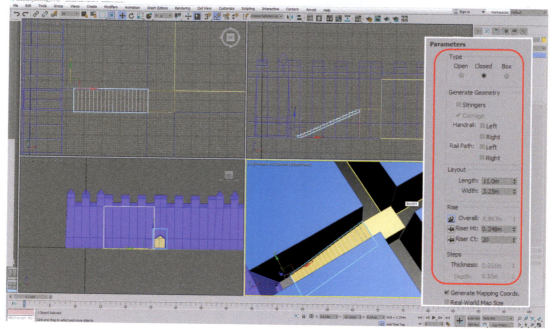

IMAGE 8.44

Then, make a copy clone of the staircase and rotate it 90 degrees, and move it up so that the bottom step is on the middle landing box, and up to the top of the lower level as shown. Widen the staircase to fit the wider opening, and lengthen it to reach the inner wall. Mirror the staircase as you did with the lower staircase to fit the remaining slot on the opposite side.

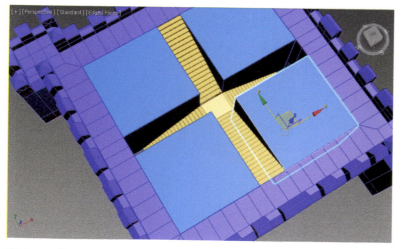

IMAGE 8.45 (Save 8-15)

Together, these four staircases are 640 polygons. If we needed to reduce the overall polycount in the future for this module, we could replace these with single polygon ramps, reducing the count to 636 polygons. For now, we will continue to use them.

We will create the upper structure, the second floor, using the four boxes. The player will not enter any of the upper structure buildings, so we do not need to create interiors or make access to them. We do need to create a place of prominence for the kingdom flag-banner to sit as part of the upper level of the Keep, awaiting to be defended or captured. Before starting the upper level, switch to the "Castle Keep Level 2" layer in the Scene Explorer.

We'll start with one of the two front boxes. While they are still Standard Primitives we can alter the creation parameters, add 2 length segments and 3 width segments as shown to each. To the two back boxes, add 3 length segments and 2 width segments, the opposite of the front boxes. Then, convert all four of them to Editable Polys.

Select the three polygons on top of the front left box, and extrude them 6 meters as shown. Then, delete the three selected polygons on top.

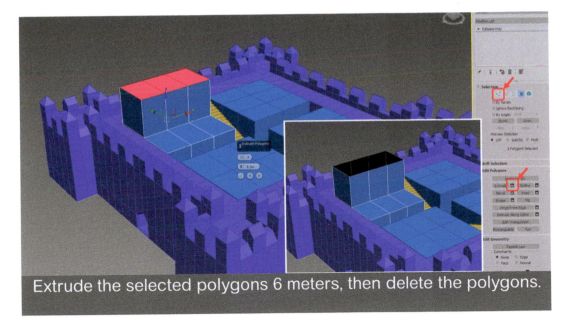

Extrude the selected polygons 6 meters, then delete the polygons.

IMAGE 8.46

Next, we will create a roof on top of this raised box shape through a sequence of steps. In Edge sub-object level, select the three top edges along the long side and extrude them a short distance as shown using the "Hold down the Shift-key and drag the Select and Move gizmo"method along the X-axis (horizontally). Repeat on the opposite side, extruding them the same distance.

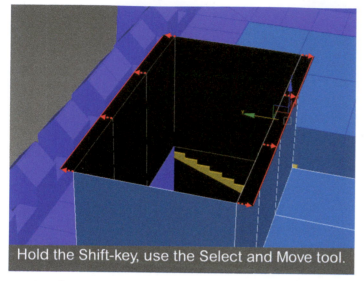

Hold the Shift-key, use the Select and Move tool.

IMAGE 8.47 (Save 8-16)

Then, select the outside perimeter with the Border tool, and use the "Hold Shift-key" and drag the gizmo up on the Z-axis to create another box shape on top of the lower one. Raise it approximately to twice the height of the lower box, about 12 meters.

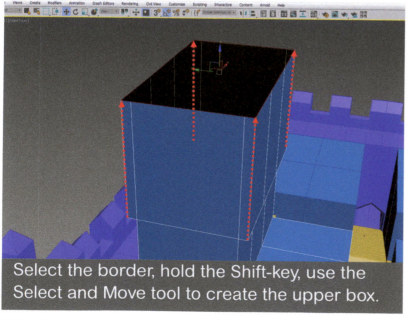

Select the border, hold the Shift-key, use the Select and Move tool to create the upper box.

IMAGE 8.48

Select the top inside vertices on the two end walls (in from the corners), and then move them down in the Z-axis as shown in the image (1). We are creating the roof thickness. Select the top edge vertices, and use the Select and Uniform Scale tool to move the vertices together in the middle of the box using the X-axis of the gismo. Weld these vertices together (2). Using the gizmo will ensure the peak of the roof will be centered.

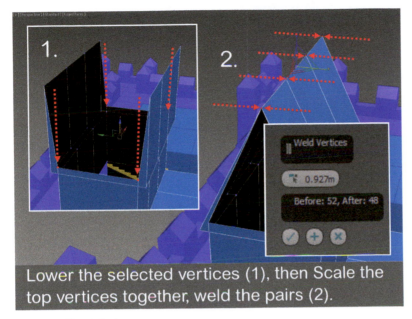

Lower the selected vertices (1), then Scale the top vertices together, weld the pairs (2).

IMAGE 8.49 (Save 8-17)

Next, select the four vertices that we lowered a few steps ago (Image 8.73). Use the Select and Uniform Scale tool again to bring these together in the middle, and weld them. Select the one vertex just created, and bring it up toward the peak as shown to create an even wall thickness on both slopes of the roof.

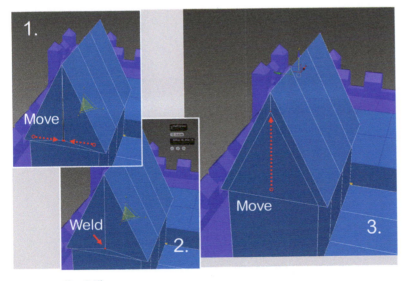

IMAGE 8.50 (Save 8-18)

Now, we can select the new roof end polygons and extrude them a short distance to create the roof gable overhang. Repeat the extrusion on the opposite gable end.

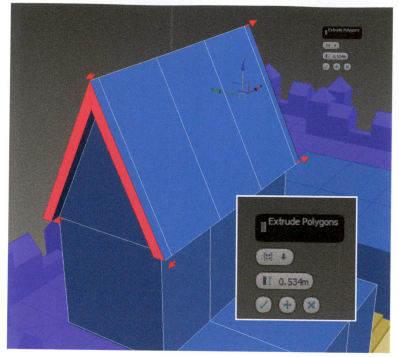

IMAGE 8.51

Let's give the top roofline a little character. Select all the vertices along the top peak, and use the Select and Uniform Scale tool to widen them slightly in the Y-axis. Then, use the Select and Move tool to lower the middle vertices to create sway back shape. Adjust the end vertices to accentuate the curve. Be careful not to move the top vertex of the end wall.

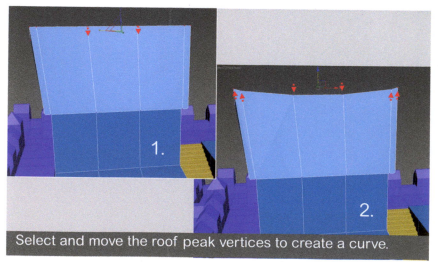

Select and move the roof peak vertices to create a curve.

IMAGE 8.52 (Save 8-19)

To create the other front structure on the right, we can save some time by cloning this box mesh with the building modeled to replace the box opposite it on the other side of the staircase. Delete the right front box, and use the mirror tool to create the new one and position it in the empty space.

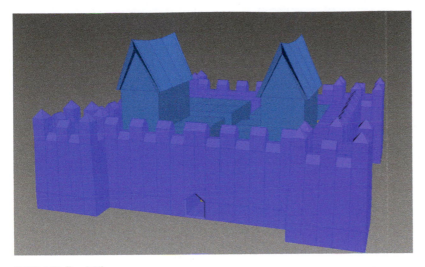

IMAGE 8.53 (Save 8-20)

Rotate your view to the back side to work on the back blocks. Select one of them, and convert it to an Editable Poly. Scroll down the Modify Panel, and click on the "Attach" button to activate it. Select the other box in the front half as shown. It will become part of the first box, an Editable Poly.

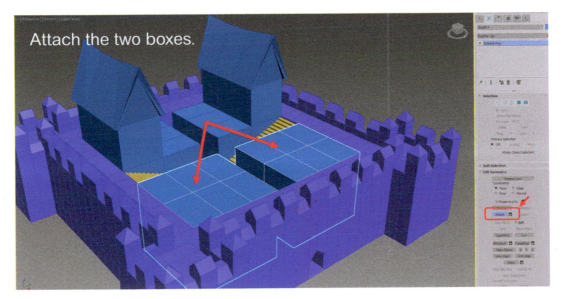

IMAGE 8.54

We are going to extrude the top polygons up 12 meters, and then delete the upper-level side polygons between the two box shapes.

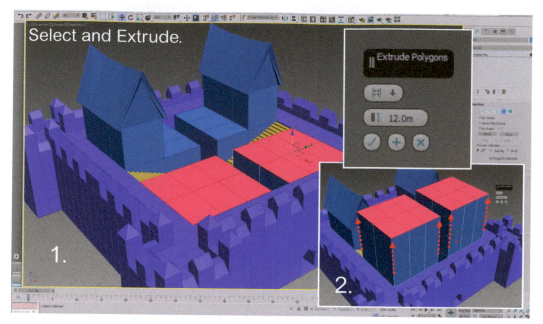

IMAGE 8.55 (Save 8-21)

Select the border edges of the two holes you just created, and use the Bridge tool to connect them. This will cover the staircase without blocking it and give us working space for the building on top.

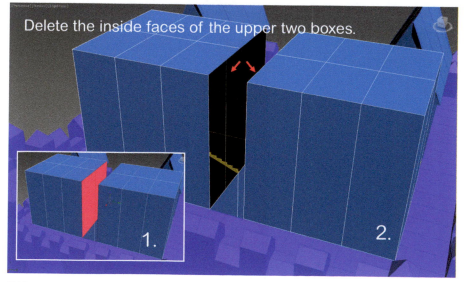

IMAGE 8.56

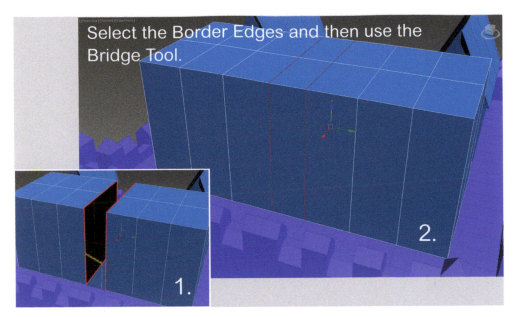

IMAGE 8.57 (Save 8-22)

The next steps will shape the roof of the long part of the building. Select the ten polygons as shown and delete them.

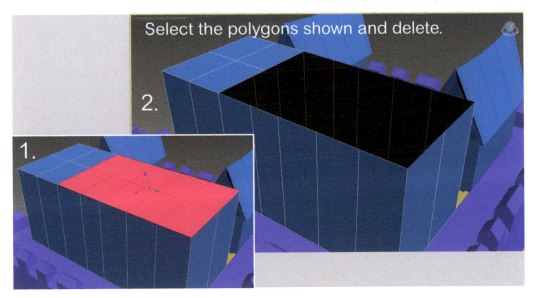

IMAGE 8.58

Create a roof the same way we did, using the same steps, with the first block. In Edge sub-object level, select the five top edges along the long side of the opening and extrude them a short distance as shown using the "Hold down the Shift-key and drag the Select and Move gizmo" along the X-axis. Repeat on the opposite side. Next, select the outside perimeter with the Border tool, and use the "Hold Shift-key" and drag the gizmo up on the Z-axis to create another box shape on top of the lower one.

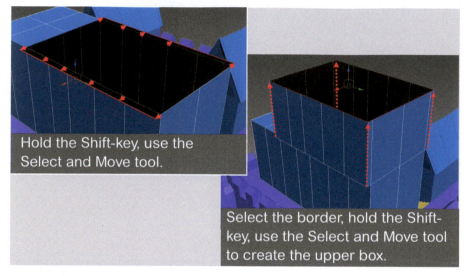

Hold the Shift-key, use the Select and Move tool.

Select the border, hold the Shift-key, use the Select and Move tool to create the upper box.

IMAGE **8.59** (Save 8-23)

Select the top edge vertices and use the Select and Uniform Scale tool to move the vertices together in the middle of the box using the X-axis of the gismo. Weld these vertices together. Using the gizmo will ensure the peak of the roof will be centered.

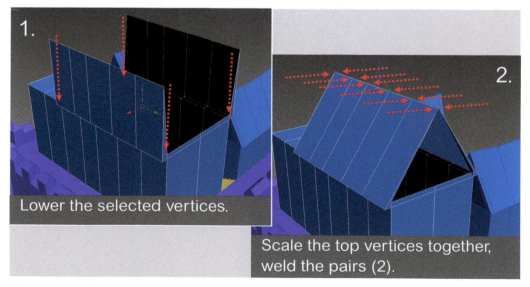

1.

Lower the selected vertices.

2.

Scale the top vertices together, weld the pairs (2).

IMAGE **8.60** (Save 8-24)

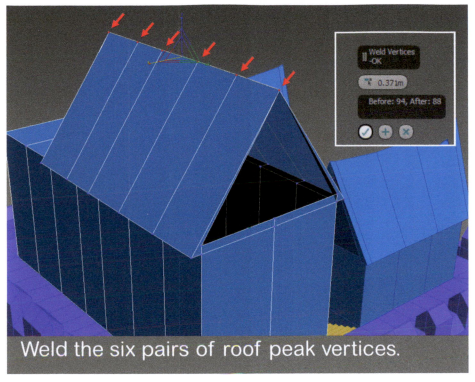

Weld the six pairs of roof peak vertices.

IMAGE 8.61

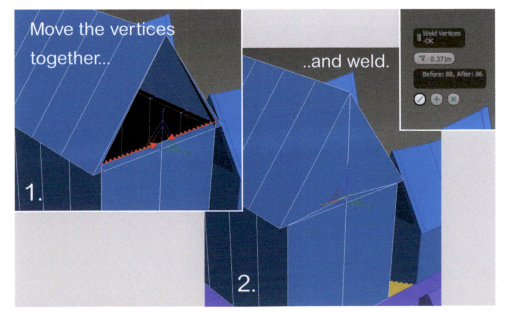

IMAGE 8.62

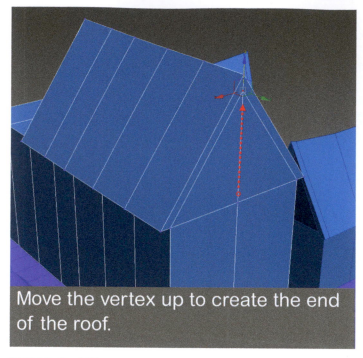

Move the vertex up to create the end of the roof.

IMAGE 8.63 (Save 8-25)

Now, we can select the new polygons and extrude them a short distance to create the roof gable overhang. Repeat the extrusion on the opposite gable end.

IMAGE 8.64

Then, give the roof peak a sway back curve like the previous roof peak by adjusting the roof peak vertices.

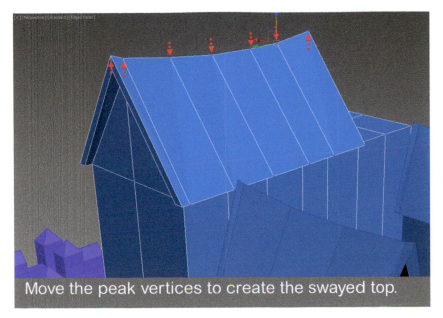

Move the peak vertices to create the swayed top.

IMAGE 8.65 (Save 8-26)

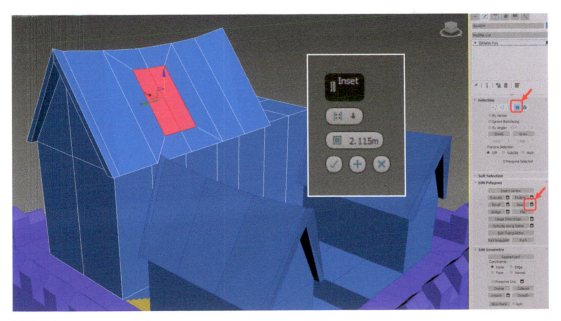

IMAGE 8.66

Next, we'll make a tower coming out of one of the roof sections. Select the two polygons as shown and extrude them. Switch to the Front viewport, and move the lower vertices of the top angled polygons up so that they are level with the top two. Select all four top vertices in the Front viewport and right click in the Top viewport. Click the View Align button in the Modify panel to get the vertices all on one plane.

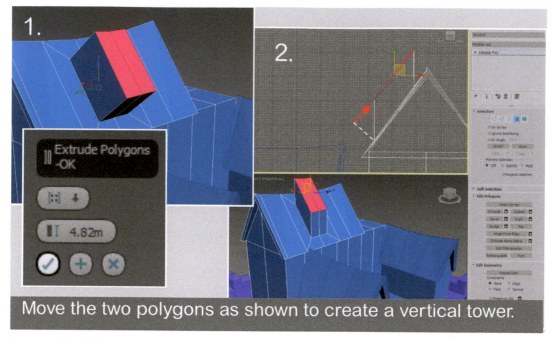

IMAGE 8.67 (Save 8-27)

The top vertices of the tower are likely not on the same plane. Select the four top vertices of the tower in the Front viewport, switch to the top viewport and apply a View Align.

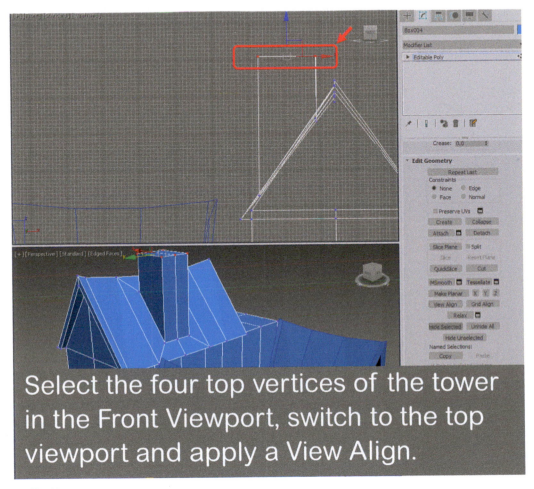

Select the four top vertices of the tower in the Front Viewport, switch to the top viewport and apply a View Align.

IMAGE 8.68

Select the two polygons on top of the new tower and delete them. Next, use the Border tool to select the edges around the opening, and then hold down the Shift-key and use the Select and Scale tool to extrude a lip around the outside of the hole. Use the Select and Move tool to raise the new border slightly, and then hold the Shift-key and drag the border up to create a box shape on top of the beveled edges. This will be the roof. Switch to Vertex sub-object level mode to select the four vertices, and use the Select and Scale tool to bring the four sides together in the middle, creating a pointed peak in the roof.

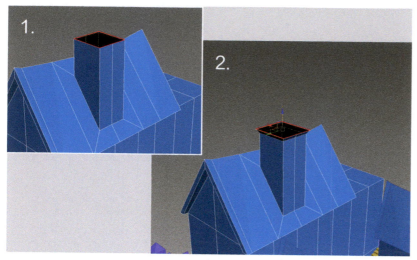

IMAGE 8.69

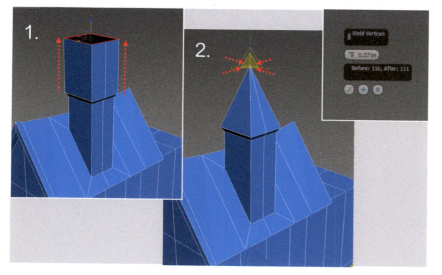

IMAGE 8.70 (Save 8-28)

If you haven't done so already, create the gable end on the end of the roof as shown.

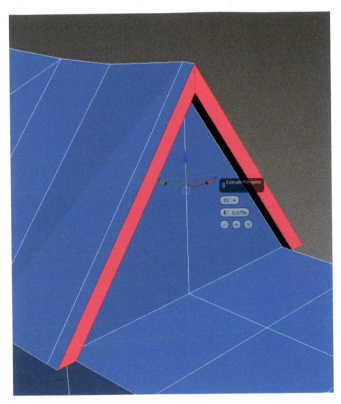

IMAGE 8.71

Create a 0.7-meter inset on the polygons as shown to start the first of two towers. Then, extrude the polygon 10 meters and delete the two polygons.

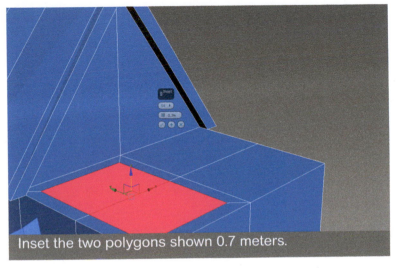

Inset the two polygons shown 0.7 meters.

IMAGE 8.72

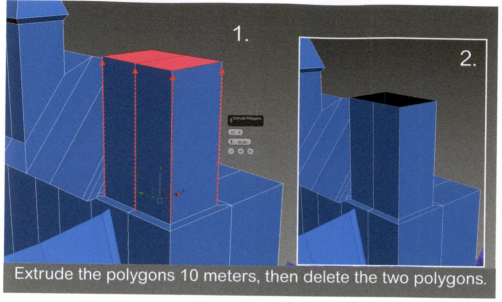

Extrude the polygons 10 meters, then delete the two polygons.

IMAGE 8.73

Create the peaked roof the same way, with the same steps, as the last roof. With the border edges selected, using the Select and Scale tool, hold the Shift-key and then drag the edges to extrude them horizontally a small distance. Then, using the Select and Move tool, lift the selected border slightly to create a bevel edge. Extrude up a box shape, and then weld the vertices to a point.

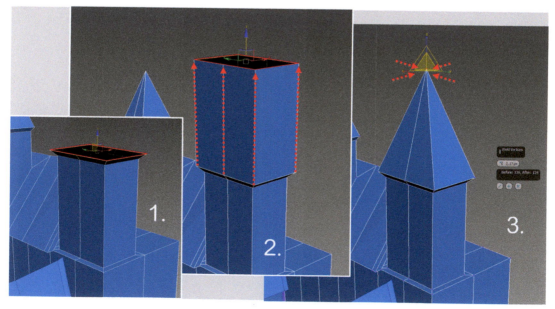

IMAGE 8.74 (Save 8-29)

Finish the remaining tower next to the one we just finished using the same steps, extruding the height of the inset polygons 14 meters. Complete the tower roof using the steps in the previous image.

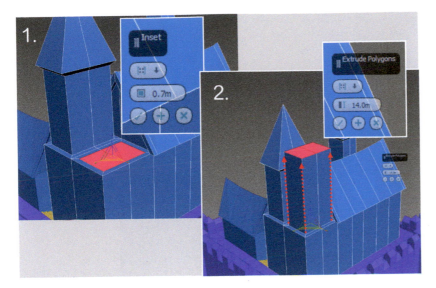

IMAGE 8.75 (Save 8-30)

To finish the Castle Keep modeling, we will make a prominent place for the Flag-Banner in the area between the two front buildings and covering the staircase below.

Create a straight staircase with the approximate dimensions and position as shown. Remember the "Stairs" tool set is in the drop-down list in the Create > Geometry tab. Note the "Stringers" box is checked, the parameters being at the last section in the modifier list.

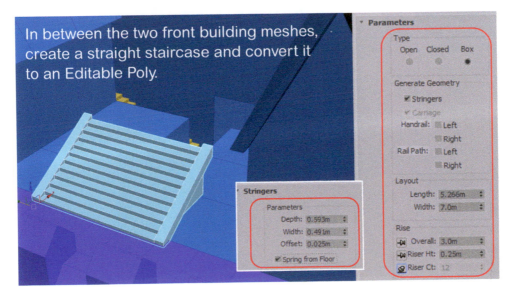

IMAGE 8.76 (Save 8-31)

Convert the Straight Staircase to an Editable Poly. This will allow us to extrude the back side along with the end caps of the two stringers all the way to the back to meet the back building wall.

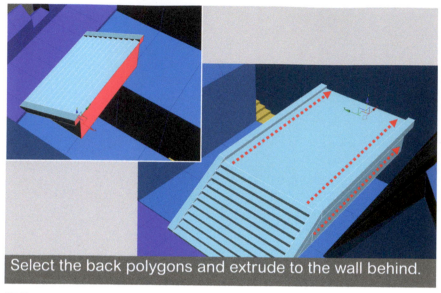

Select the back polygons and extrude to the wall behind.

IMAGE 8.77

To create a platform for the Flag-Banner, use the Inset tool on the long-extruded polygon. Then, move the two vertices as shown toward the far end to create a small polygon that can be extruded up to create a platform for the flag pole.

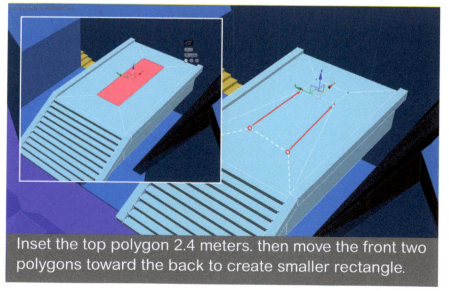

Inset the top polygon 2.4 meters. then move the front two polygons toward the back to create smaller rectangle.

IMAGE 8.78

Extrude the new polygon up a short distance to create a small platform for the Banner Flag to stand.

IMAGE 8.79 (Save 8-32)

That completes the modeling of the Castle Keep. Next, you can unwrap and texture the module parts, and map them to complete the texturing. You can fund the textures needed in the companion file for the book online.

After you complete the unwrapping of the Castle Keep, use the Group tool to group all the elements, naming it "Castle Keep Group." We will be using the group in the next chapter.

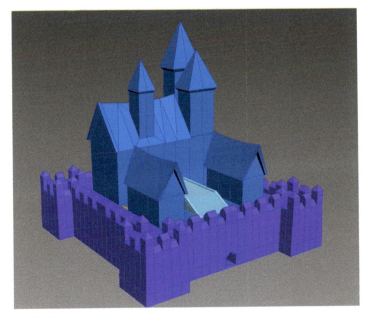

IMAGE 8.80

Chapter 8 Exercise: Water Well

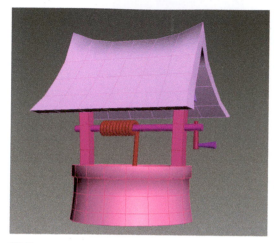

IMAGE 8.81

Every castle needs a water well, so design and model one! The design can be of your choice or you can follow the example I made. Be sure to do some research to define your design. For mine, I created a cylinder, and used the Select and Scale tool to shape the well wall. For the rope (I made it thick to be more toon-like), I made a torus primitive and split one side. Then, twisted it like a lock washer so that the open ends were next to each other. Then cloned it, fitting the nine new pieces to look like a continuous rope. There is an easier way of creating it, by using the loft tool and the helix, but we have not covered that process yet, so I am not using it. When you complete Chapter 7, Unwrapping the Model, you can return to the finished wall torch model and complete the unwrapping and texturing of your model.

In the companion folder online, you will find the 3ds Max file iterations saves from when I modeled a water well and the texture file, "accessory_textures.png" for your use.

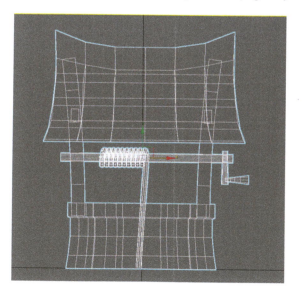

IMAGE 8.82

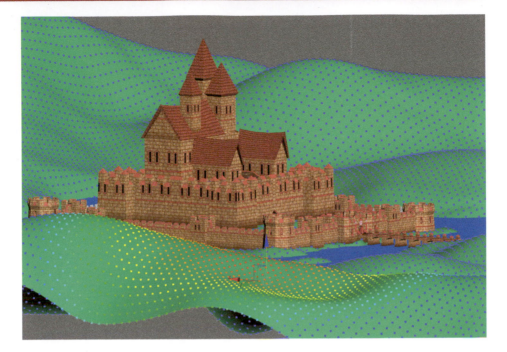

Lights, Cameras, Scene

Topics in This Chapter

- Cameras
  - Target Camera
- Render
  - Render Setup
  - Stills
  - Animations
  - Camera
  - Direct Target
  - Lens
- Foliage

With all the castle assets complete, we can assemble the castle environment. All the work you've done will soon come together. As part of this scene, we will add some lights and a camera, so that you will know how to create and utilize them. With the collection of modules that we made, there are endless ways to combine them to create a layout. Of course, you are free to arrange them how you like. I will continue with a basic layout that you can follow if you choose.

To start, create a new file scene, naming it in the "lastname_castlescene_01.max" format. Create a green-colored Plane object in the top viewport to be our ground surface with the following parameters.

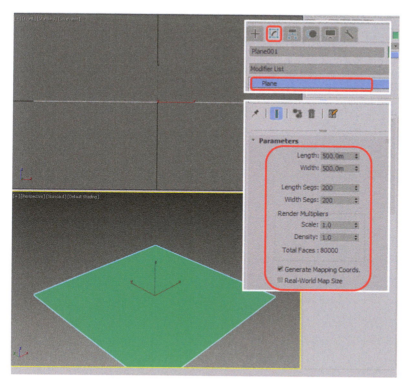

IMAGE 9.1 (Save 9-1)

Notice that the Height and Width segments are 200 each. We will need these to create the landscape. Convert the plane to an Editable Poly.

Merging Scenes

In 3ds Max, there are several different kinds of Import types. When importing, we are bringing something from one scene into another scene. If we are bringing an object from a 3ds Max scene into another 3ds Max scene, we use the Merge option: 3ds max file into a 3ds Max file use Merge.

If we are bringing a file from another program into our 3ds Max scene, we use the Import option. Depending on the program type, we generally import objects using the .3DS, .OBJ or .FBX file types. FBX was developed by Kaydara for their Filmbox (later renamed Motion Builder) software. The format saved an object's motion properties. Kaydara was acquired by Alias in 2002 and by Autodesk in 2006. With its features expanded, FBX allows you to move files between Autodesk products while maintaining the file contents properties. Using the .3DS format is limited to retaining only geometry, texture and lighting data. The .OBJ has similar limitations. Optimally, use the .MAX or .FBX file format when possible.

Since we modeled in 3ds Max and are continuing with it, we can use the Merge option for lossless transfer.

Go up to the top tool bar, and navigate to the Merge option: File > Import > Merge…

Click on "Merge" to open the file navigation box. Find the last version of the Castle Keep (the grouped one, "Castle Keep Group"), and select it. If you don't have the elements grouped, please do so now, and then proceed.

The Merge dialogue box will appear on the screen. In the left-hand column of the dialogue box, select the Castle Keep Group and then select OK.

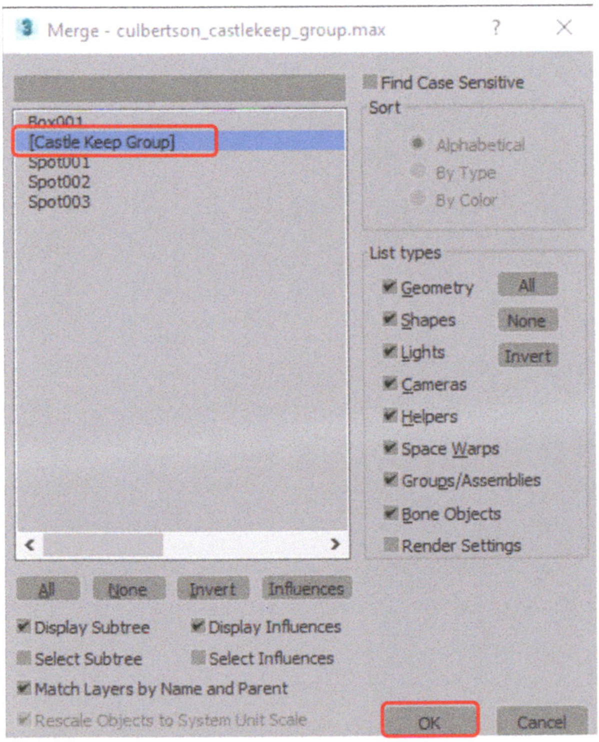

IMAGE 9.2

If the castle merges into the scene with no textures, open the Material Editor and create new textures using the ones from the scene. Apply the textures to the models where necessary. Once the models are mapped, the textures should apply readily. Some of the modules are grouped. If you are applying the textures to a grouped module, you might need to go up to the "Group" tab on the top menu and select "Open" from the drop-down menu. This will allow you to work with the individual objects within the group, in the case of the Castle Keep, applying the two textures that are used for the Castle Keep. When textured, go back to the Group tab and select "Close" to return the module to the closed state.

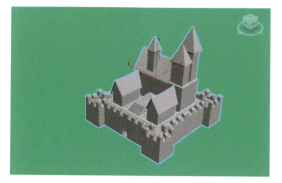

IMAGE 9.3

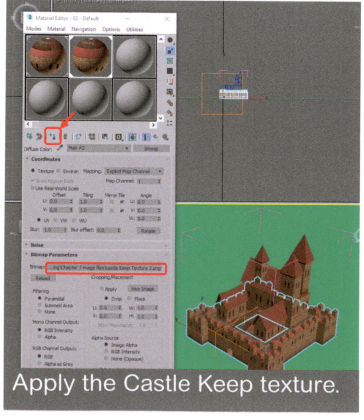

Apply the Castle Keep texture.

IMAGE 9.4

The Castle Keep's base should be resting on the terrain plane. Next, let's merge the Gate House module into the scene. Follow the same steps to merge the module as you did for the Castle Keep, navigating to the Gate House final module: File > Merge > Gate House file. When you get to the Merge dialogue box, select the Gate House module from the list, and then select OK. Position the Gate House module in front of the castle as shown. This will be the start of the outer-wall defense.

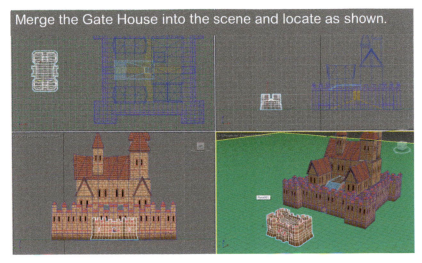

IMAGE 9.5

The next module to merge in will be the Curtain Wall. Repeat the merge process. Locate it into position next to the Gate house so the walkways on to align for the player to move from module to module easily.

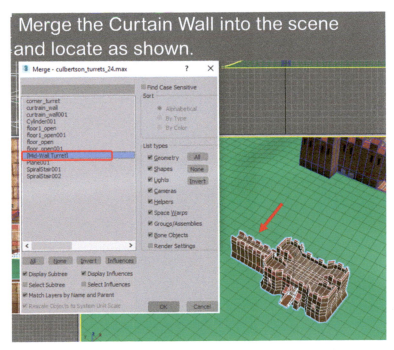

IMAGE 9.6

The next module to merge is the Mid-Wall Turret. Align it with the open end of the Curtain Wall. We will need another Curtain Wall module for the other side of the Mid-Wall Turret. We don't need to merge the next one into the scene. We can clone the existing one by selecting it, using the Select and Move tool while holding down the Shift-key to drag it along the X-axis. Position the new cloned piece in line with the others as shown.

Merge the Mid-Tower module into the scene.

IMAGE 9.7

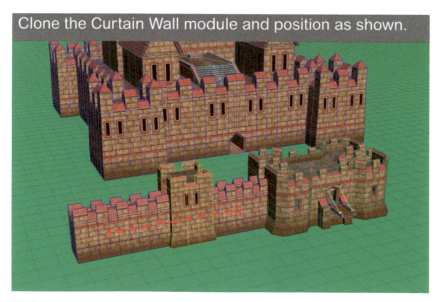

Clone the Curtain Wall module and position as shown.

IMAGE 9.8

Time to create the anchor to our outer wall, merge in the Corner Turret Group. Position it so that the upper-level door to the left of the lower door is aligned with the Curtain Wall. With the access from the ground level and the spiral staircase, the players can now move to the top of the outer wall.

Merge the Corner Tower module and place.

IMAGE 9.9

Now that all the major modules for the perimeter wall have been merged into the scene, completing the wall around the castle is just a matter of cloning, moving and aligning modules as needed. Take your time, and carefully finish the outer-wall enclosure around the Castle Keep.

IMAGE 9.10 (Save 9-2)

With the outer wall set, we can merge the Fixed Bridge modules into the scene. Merge the Bridge Span and the Bridge End, and align them with the drawbridge. The Bridge end should fit nicely with the drawbridge. When the Bridge Span is in position, you are all set to clone six or seven more spans to create a long-raised approach to the drawbridge.

IMAGE 9.11

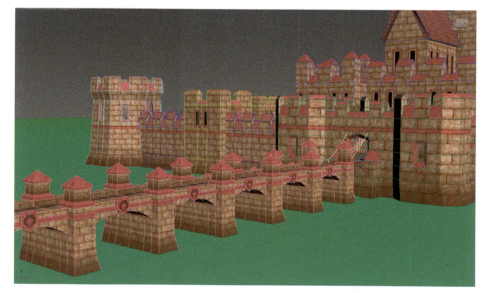

IMAGE 9.12

Soft Selection

Let's raise our Castle to an elevated plateau so that it will have an area of prominence. To do this, we will use a new tool in the Vertex sub-object level, "Soft Selection." To start, select the Castle Keep group and raise it a short distance up in the Z-axis, up from the plane.

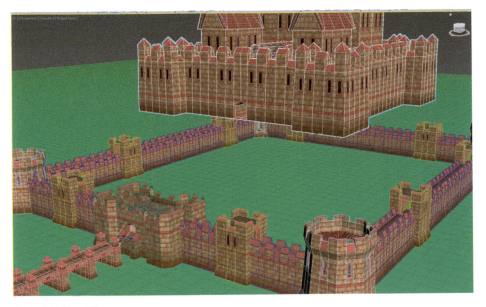

IMAGE 9.13 (Save 9-3)

With our plane converted to an Editable Poly, in Vertex sub-object level use the "Select Object" tool on the main toolbar (to the left of the Select and Move tool) to select a boxed area on the plane around the Castle Keep group in the top viewport at shown (close to the perimeter of the Castle Keep).

Next, scroll down the modify panel to the "Soft Selection" section, and click on the "Use Soft Selection" option and raise the Falloff value box to 9.0 meters or until the bright green outline of bright green vertices comes close to the inner side of the outer wall, roughly as shown in the image. rainbow-colored gradient has appeared around the vertices selected, which are red in color. The gradation of color indicates the

375

amount of influence the selected red vertices will have in pulling the neighboring vertices around them. The closer to the red vertices, the more influence the selected vertices will have.

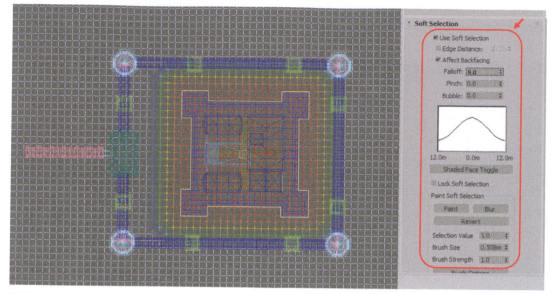

In the Z-coordinate Display value box, change the value to 4.0 meters and select "Enter" on the keyboard. The selected red vertices will rise, pulling the rainbow-gradient ones along with it, creating a gentle transition between the ground level and the new plane of the red selected vertices. Changing the parameters of the Falloff and the height change will alter the transition. Move the Castle Keep back down to rest on the new plateau.

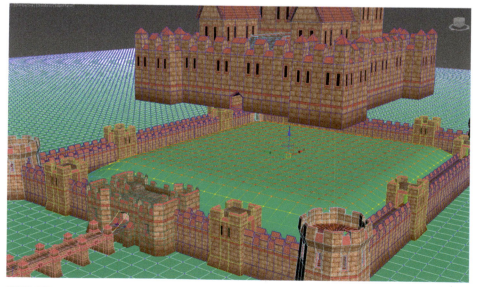

IMAGE 9.15

Looking inside the outer wall at the Gate House, there is a falloff from the doorway to the ground. Players coming out of the Gate House inside the wall will need a bridge span to walk out onto. Clone two sections of the Bridge Span, and locate them at the drop-off so that the players can leave and enter the structure. Use the Soft Selection with a much smaller Falloff setting to adjust the terrain vertices at the end of the Bridge Span to fill any gap in the transition from walkway to ground.

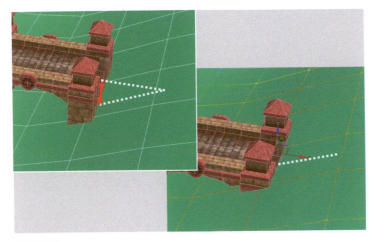

IMAGE 9.16

At the four corners of the outer wall, bring the terrain vertices up in the Z-axis to meet the doorways of each Corner Turret. Take your time making the adjustments. Control your adjustments to keep the transitions inside the wall, not affecting the outside wall ground level.

IMAGE 9.17

Next, we will raise the terrain around the castle wall perimeter. Select the terrain vertices as shown. This will take a few minutes, don't rush it. You need to use the Select Object tool again. Zoom-in using the Top viewport enough to see between the vertices. When selecting, click between the vertices, not directly on the vertices. Use the Soft Select tool with a Falloff setting of 6. Again, make the selection roughly like as shown.

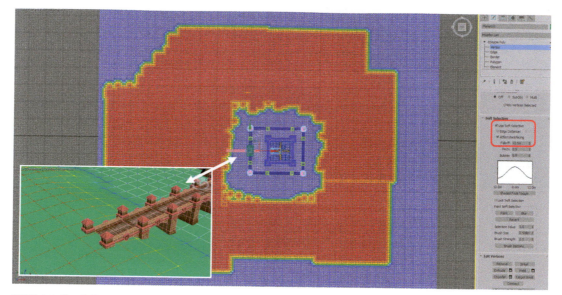

IMAGE 9.18 (Save 9-4)

Once selected, use the Select and Move tool to raise the selection in the Z-axis until the new plateau is flush with the walkway of the last Bridge Span module. The depressed area we just created will be the water moat area around the outer wall.

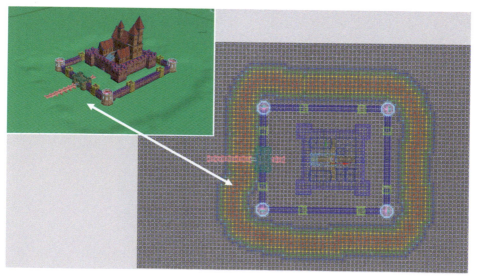

IMAGE 9.19

The main objective of the last procedure was to raise the terrain to the bridge walkway level. It created a moat area, but we need to go back in the moat and sink the vertices a bit more. Set the Soft Selection Falloff value to 12.0 meters, and while holding down the Ctrl-key on the keyboard, carefully click on the vertices near the center of the moat, creating a ring around the outer wall. Once selected, use the Select and Move tool to lower the vertices in the Z-axis to deepen the moat. Be careful not to lower the vertices right next to the outer-wall modules. We don't want gaps under the modules between the ground and the meshes.

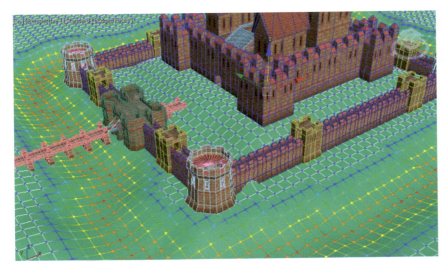

IMAGE 9.20 (Save 9-5)

Time to create some water for the moat. Create a new plane in the Top viewport with the following parameters.

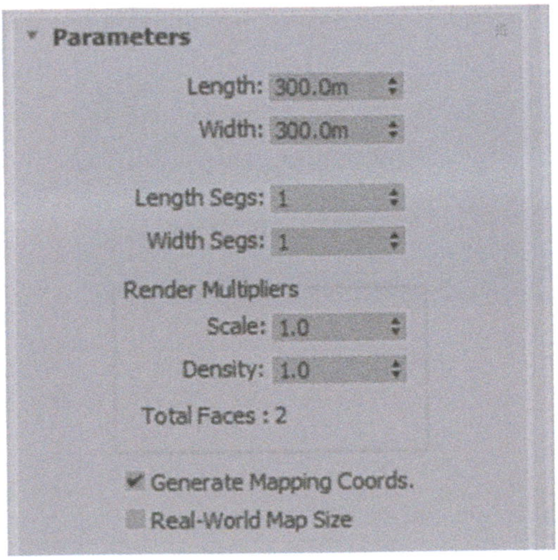

▼ **Parameters**

Length: 300.0m

Width: 300.0m

Length Segs: 1

Width Segs: 1

Render Multipliers

Scale: 1.0

Density: 1.0

Total Faces : 2

☑ Generate Mapping Coords.

☐ Real-World Map Size

IMAGE 9.21

Make the plane a blue color to represent water. Adjust the height of the plane in the Z-axis to "fill" the moat area and be below the surface of the rest of the terrain plane. Once in place, carefully work your way around the perimeter of the outer wall, adjusting the vertices of the ground/terrain plane to add a short shoreline around the base. Adjust the moat area as you like, creating a lake, pond or river.

3ds Max has some amazing capabilities for producing realistic water effects and terrain. We really haven't scratched the surface of the tools available. Knowing how to use the Soft Selection tool will make an great addition to your digital tool box, which is the main reason we went through this exercise. Because we will be taking our scene to the Unity 3D game engine, we won't be using the terrain or water we just created. We will utilize the powerful terrain and water tools in Unity 3D to create the desired effects from within the game engine. They are handled much better there for the game. If we were to complete our terrain and water here in 3ds max for other purposes, like for film, we would use tools and modifiers, like noise, to take them to the next level along with complex textures with reflection and refraction, parametric movement, and more. Beyond the scope of a basic book, but well within your reach with some research. If you explore in the Geometry tab in 3ds Max, open the "Extended Primitives" section in the menu to find the "Foliage" button. You'll find pre-made trees that you can add to the scene. Be judicious in adding them, they take up a lot of resources to render in the viewports and add a ton of polygons to the polygon count.

IMAGE 9.22

Add in the last few accessory items you modeled and mapped: The Banners, Hitching Post and Flag-Banner, and you are ready to export to Unity.

Add the accessory models.

IMAGE 9.23 (Save 9-6)

Lighting

Before we export our project to Unity, let's add a few lights and a camera in 3ds Max so that you know how to work with them. We will not be exporting the lights or camera to Unity. The viewports have default lighting with settings determined by the viewport settings. We have been using the Default Shading setting since Chapter 2. If we add a light to the scene, in addition to the illumination create by the new light, the program will turn on the ambient lighting system. Ambient light is the light that is reflected around the scene, adding light from all directions to every point in the scene. Ambient light intensity and color is controlled using the Global Light settings in the Environment and Effects window, accessed from the Environment selection of the Rendering tab of the main menu

There are several possible lights to choose from in 3ds Max. The two main types of lights are Photometric and Standard. You can create lights in the Create panel using the Lights tab to select the type. Photometric lights create the lighting based on light energy levels as in the real world. They require intensive calculations based on a number of variables. They typically require mental-ray rendering, a slow highly accurate renderer that takes light bouncing off objects in the scene into account. For our purposes, we don't need the highly realistic final rendering that an architect or interior designer might need to sell their concepts. We will use the Standard lights which are more of a simulation of the real world. They are generally much faster to render but are of a much lower quality than the Photometric. In 3ds Max 2018, Autodesk added Arnold to the lighting and rendering package, with powerful tools to enhance the rendering abilities of the program. We will concentrate on the basics here.

In the Create panel of the Command Panel, select the Lights tab and change the default "Photometric" setting to "Standard."

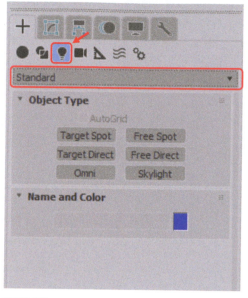

IMAGE 9.24

Let's render an image before we add lighting to see the results with default lighting. So far, we have not rendered images other than when we made a texture. Go to the Render Setup Icon on the Main Toolbar. The Render Setup dialog box will appear on the screen. View the image below for the settings we want to use for this image. The Output size is HDTV, a large image with HD quality. In the Render Output, click the Save File to "on" and click the "Files..." button on the right to open the dialog box to name the file and save it to a location of your choice. Save the files in the .PNG format.

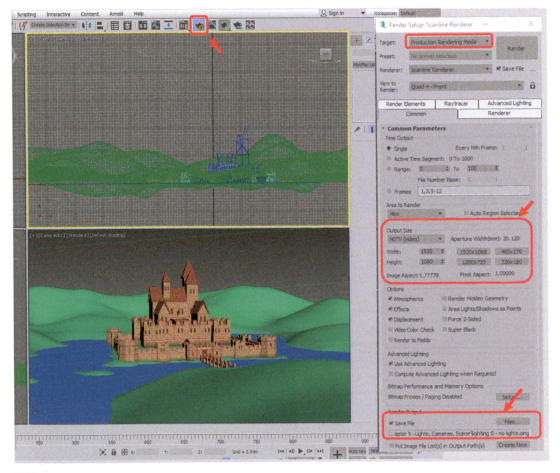

IMAGE 9.25

The renderer renders the active viewport. Right click in the perspective viewport to make it active if it is not already. Render the viewport by selecting the Render button at the top right corner of the Render Setup window, the render Production button on the Main Toolbar or use "Shift+Q." The image is sharper than the viewport images, but the lighting is dull, having a low contrast range.

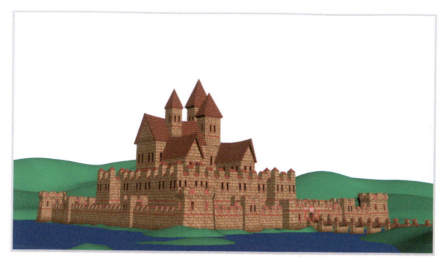

Create a "Lights" layer in the Scene Explorer, and make it active. There are six light options available for placement in the scene. Each has unique properties that determine when they should be used. For brevity here, click on the Target Direct option. This will create a wide beam of parallel light from the source to the target. It simulates the light from the sun, which as you probably know emits essentially parallel light beams to earth due to its distance from us. Click in the top viewport where you want the light source to begin, and then move the cursor to where you want it to end, the target, and click. This will be our main, primary source of light. Lights and cameras are created on the X-axis plane by default. After creating the light and target, use the Select and Move tool to place the light in the location as shown, using both the Front and Left viewports to check the position to locate the light source to the right and in front of the castle. This will be our "Key-light."

Switch to the Select and Move tool to select the light source icon. The parameters rollout will appear in the Modify panel. There are many variables in adjusting a light and fine-tuning how it will light the objects in the scene, light decay, lighting atmospherics (fog, fire and more). The topic of lighting could fill volumes of books. Let's make a few simple adjustments to see the effect on rendering.

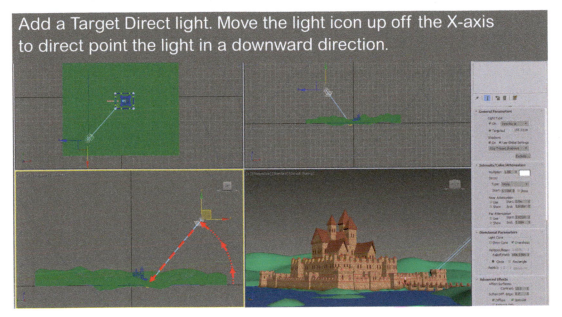

IMAGE 9.27

Three-Point Lighting

When lighting a subject, three-point lighting is the standard setup for lights. In three-point lighting, the first light, typically located in front of and to the side (at about a 45-degree angle) is known as the "Key-Light." It is the brightest of the lights, creating the highlights on the subject surface and the shadows on the opposite side away from the source. The second light is the "Fill-light." The Fill-light adds soft light to the shadow area of the subject creating the light/shadow areas as in chiaroscuro shading. The third light is the "Backlight," located behind the subject. From the front view, the backlight creates a "halo" lighting fringe around the figure that helps to separate the subject from the background. When creating a still shot, setting up a television scene or a film shot, three-point lighting is used. For video games, it's not always easy to set up three-point lighting as the player movement adds variables to the set-up solution. So, lighting is based more on scene location needs.

Next, add another target direct light as the Fill-light, to the left of and in front of the castle. Its intensity level should be 50–75 percent of the Key-light's intensity. Lastly, add a backlight behind the castle with an intensity similar to that of the Fill-light.

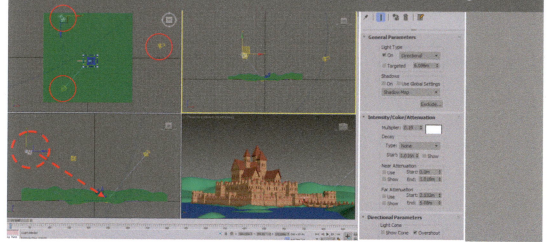

IMAGE 9.28 (Save 9-7)

Open the Render Setup dialog box again. Change the Render Output file name to a new name so that you don't overwrite the first rendered image. Make the Perspective viewport the active viewport, and then render the viewport.

The image has a much wider contrast range. The shadows helping to define the 3D forms. Still not the greatest, but a big improvement over no lighting.

IMAGE 9.29

This is just a quick light placement that will hopefully give you an idea of the potential lighting possibilities for rendering in 3ds Max. The adage that lighting can make or break a scene is all to true. Play with the settings and options, rendering the results. You can uncheck the "Save File" option in the Render Setup dialogue box while experimenting to save time. Try the different types of Standard lights. The interior of the Gate House and the Castle Keep staircases could use some dramatic lighting. Try rendering a night scene, lowering the intensity to near zero. Remember, lighting is only half the visual story. The textures are just as important, the way they reflect, refract and absorb light. Water that does not reflect light on its surface isn't going to look much like water. Metal objects need specular highlights for the light reflect off. It gets complex, but that is what makes the results so believable and challenging to do. From early CGI renderings 25 years ago to the renderings being done today has been an unbelievable leap. Disney's film *Moana* is an example of the cutting edge today… it is simply incredible eye candy. Study the lighting in the movie's beach scenes… the colors in the shadows, the reflections and refractions. So, you have made a start on the journey of lighting. It will be an important tool in your CG tool box.

Cameras

Next, let's add a camera to the scene. Create a "Camera" layer in the Scene Explorer, and make it active. Turn off the Lights layer. The lights will still be active.

Go to the Camera tab next to the Lights tab in the Create panel. Like the lighting tab, the Camera tab offers several options for cameras. We will use the Target Camera. Click on the Target Camera option, and create a camera in the Top viewport, just like you did when creating the Target Direct light. Again, the camera and target are created on the X- and Y-axes, so you will need to move them to usable positions. It is difficult to envision what the camera will be seeing in our current viewport setup. In the Perspective viewport, change the Perspective setting to "Camera." Now, the viewport is what the camera is seeing.

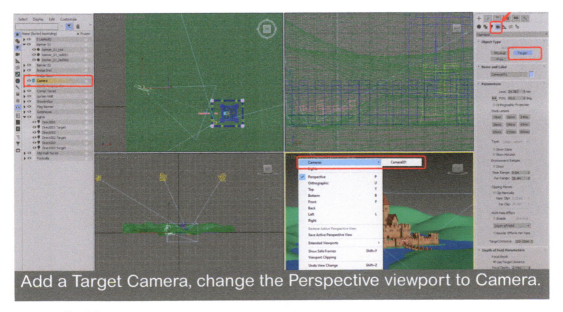

Add a Target Camera, change the Perspective viewport to Camera.

IMAGE 9.30 (Save 9-8)

Move the camera and the camera target to get views that would be very difficult to achieve with the pan and zoom tools of the viewport.

We have already rendered still shots of the viewports using the perspective setting. Now, you can use the render setup to render from the camera. Still shots are done the same way as before. To make an animation rendering, change from the "Single" setting in the Render Setup dialogue box to either Active Time Segment, Range or Frames. In the Render Output, click the Save File button to open the Save dialogue window. Change the Type to an animation type (.AVI, .MOV, etc.), or render a still sequence (.JPEG, .TGA, etc.). For each type, also use the Setup box button to the left side of the window to adjust the options available for the file type.

Additionally, click on the camera icon to view the camera parameters in the modify panel. There are controls to adjust the camera as you would a high-tech SLR or video camera. If you are familiar with cameras, this will be an easy learning curve. If you are not, play with the different settings to see what they do. Remember, almost everything in 3ds Max is animatable. For instance, you could start an animated scene with a long 100 mm lens shot, pan and trolley the camera in close to the subject while transitioning to a close-up 28 mm lens. Very controllable and highly dynamic. Animating the scene through the scene to do a "fly-through" can be done by manually moving the camera and target while keyframing or using a much easier method by making the camera follow a spline using a path constraint. It is possible to set up multiple cameras, each with different animation settings to create multiple clips for a movie. Using the Batch renderer, 3ds Max will automatically render the camera cuts and even email you when it is finished.

As with lighting, rendering both still shots and animations is a large topic for exploration.

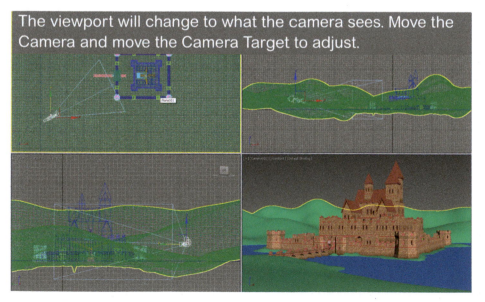

IMAGE 9.31 (Save 9-9)

CHAPTER 10

Export to the Game Engine

Topics in This Chapter

3ds Max:
- FBX Export
- Export Selected
- Hide Selected

Unity:
- Open Unity
- Create a Project
- Import Custom Package
- UI Layout
- Add a Folder
- Inspector Panel
  - Model
  - Rig
  - Animation
  - Materials

- Terrain
  - Edit Texture
  - Add Texture
  - Raise/Lower Brush
  - Paint Texture
  - Paint Height
  - Smooth Height
- Navigation Controls
- Play / CTRL+P
- Maximize on play

In this chapter, we'll prepare the castle project for export to the game engine, Unity, and then import it into the game engine.

Unity is a game engine with cross-platform build capabilities developed by Unity Technologies, first released in 2005. Originally a Danish company, the company moved its home office to San Francisco in 2009. Unity is the premier engine of choice for most indie game developers due to its ability to export games to 27 different platforms: make one game, and release it to multiple platforms. The company has a clear roadmap for the product's evolution with a defined, regular update schedule. The product has a tiered licensing model: Personal, Plus, Pro and Enterprise. For our purposes, we can go with the free Personal version that allows up to $100k in revenue derived from game play before triggering a paid status upgrade.

To acquire Unity, go to www.unity3d.com and navigate to the "Get Unity" button. Downloading and installing are straight forward and simple.

To begin, you will need to create an account on the Unity website. The Unity website has beginner interactive tutorials that are available if you are new to the product. Before continuing here, make sure that you have created a Unity account, and have downloaded and installed the program on your computer.

Preparing for Export

First, we will prepare our files for the export from 3ds Max and the import to Unity.

In the companion files for this chapter, you will find a folder named "Unity Castle Project Files." In your Documents folder or another suitable location, create a copy of this folder. It contains the Unity project template we will use and a folder with copies of the material textures from the projects we worked on in this book.

In Chapter 9, we assembled all our modules into one scene. We have a choice of how we want to export our castle. We can export it as one assembled prefab or as separate modules. With the separate modules, we will need to create the scene in Unity by arranging all the individual modules in the scene like what we did in the last chapter in 3ds Max. Exporting all out castle modules as one prefab will allow us to be able to drag the entire castle into the Unity scent in one step. Once in the scene, we can move or modify individual modules that are part of the prefab.

Open your final 3ds Max file of the assembled scene from the last chapter (or open Save 10-1). Holding down the Ctrl-key on the keyboard, select the ground/terrain plane and the water plane in the scene to select those objects. They will not be part of our export to Unity. Open the Display tab at the top of the Command Panel, and scroll down to find the "Hide Selected" button and click it. The two objects will be hidden in the scene, not deleted.

Using the Select and Move tool, select everything in one of the viewports.

Scroll down to "Export" in the File tab of the top menu. In the Export flyout, click on "Export Selected."

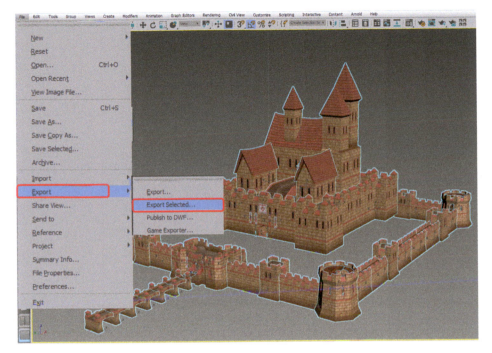

IMAGE 10.1 (Save 10-1)

The Save As window will open, enter a file name, such as "Castle Group." Save it to the Unity Castle Project Files folder for easy locating. Next, the FBX Export dialogue will open. The default settings should be ok, so you can click on the OK button. 3ds Max will create a FBX file in the designated folder.

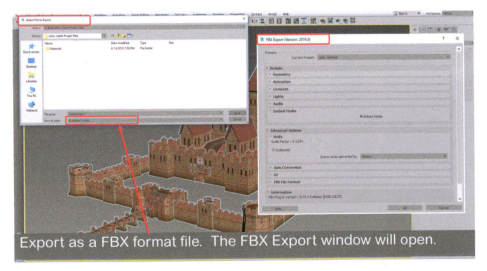

Export as a FBX format file. The FBX Export window will open.

IMAGE 10.2

Open Unity, signing in with your login information if necessary. When the start-up screen opens, select the "+New" button on the top right corner. A window will open asking for a project name and a folder location to create the game files. I created a folder named "Unity Castle Project" and a project name "Castle Project." When ready, click on the Create button and "Hold On" while Unity creates the project. When it is finished, the Unity user interface (UI) will open on the screen.

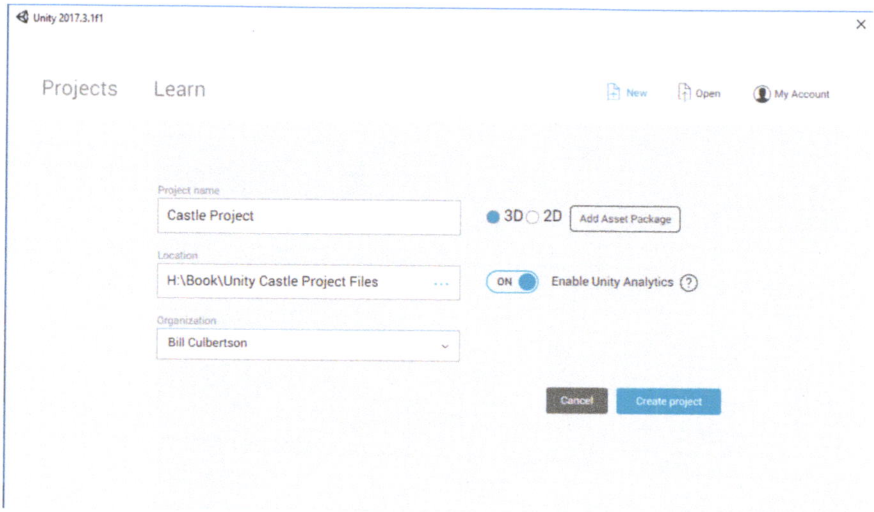

IMAGE 10.3

To unify our screens so that we are looking at the same UI setup, in the upper right corner, select the 2 by 3 option in the Layout drop-down list. Also, click on the "Inspector" tab to the left below the Layout tab.

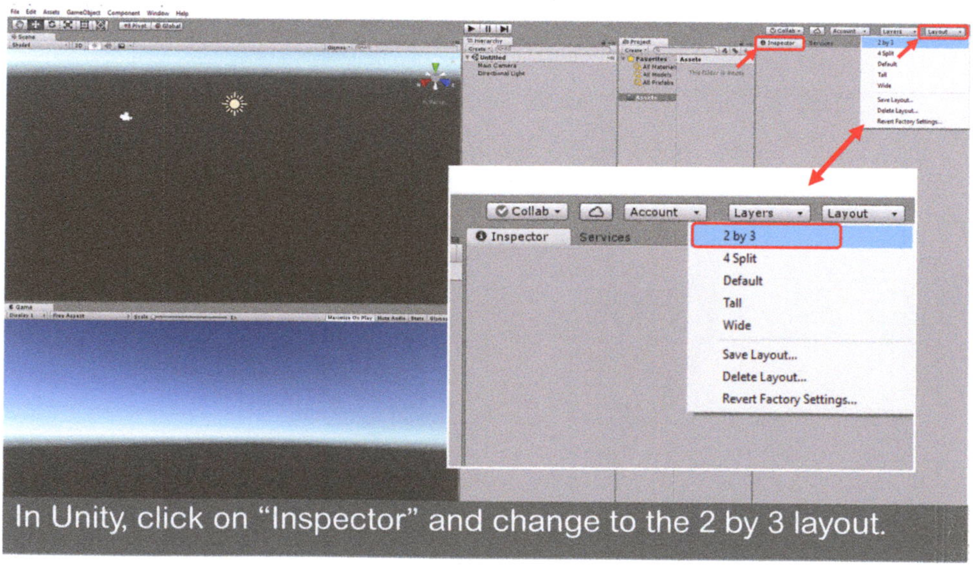

In Unity, click on "Inspector" and change to the 2 by 3 layout.

IMAGE 10.4

On the top menu bar, click on the "Assets" tab, then drop down to the "Import Package" listing, and from it, select the "Custom Package" option. Next, navigate to the project folder, in my case the "Unity Castle Project." In the folder is a Unity project package file named "CastleProjectTemplate." This file was prepared for us to use by my game developer friend and colleague Jordan Dubreuil. Select the file, and click "Open."

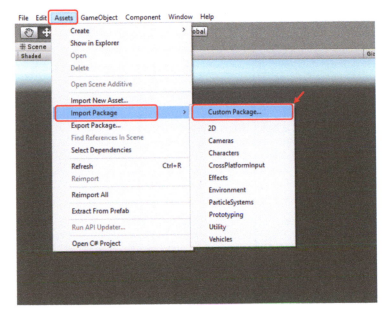

IMAGE 10.5

IMAGE 10.6

When the Import (Unity) Package dialogue box opens, select "All" and then click the "Import" button. The program will complete the import and display the Unity UI with a project open in it.

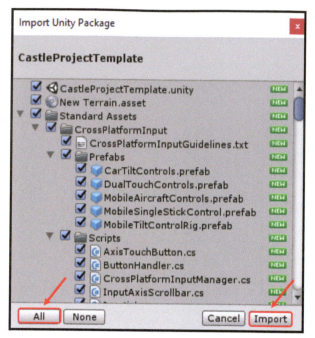

IMAGE 10.7

Double click on the CastleProjectTemplate icon, which is a Scene file in the Assets tab column. The scene will open.

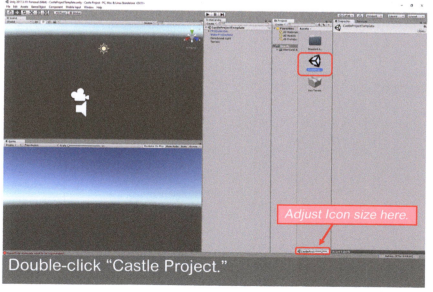

Double-click "Castle Project."

IMAGE 10.8

In the Hierarchy panel, select the "Terrain" listing, and then move the mouse cursor into the Scene window (the upper window on the left side of the UI). Next, click the "F-key" to center the view on the terrain.

In the Inspector on the right-hand side, the parameters and options for the Terrain will be open. Select the "Paint Texture" icon (the paint brush icon in the middle of the "Terrain" row of icons). This gives you options to texture the terrain element. Select the "Edit Texture" button, and choose the "Add Texture" option. A new dialogue box will open.

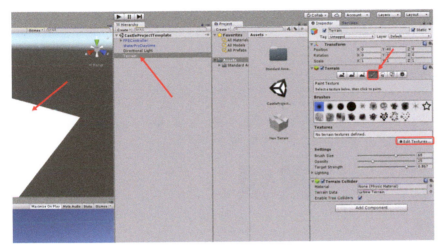

IMAGE 10.9

In the Add Texture pop-up dialogue box, click the "Select" button under the left-hand image. A selection will open with available texture images. Select the GrassHillAlbedo texture, and then click "Add" in the Add Texture window. The grass texture will be applied to and cover the terrain. While we are here, add another texture using the same steps, "GrassRockyAlbedo." We can use this texture later to create a road to the castle. Your Inspector should look similar to the Inspector window on the right of the image below.

IMAGE 10.10

395

Next, we'll bring the Castle into the scene. In the Project tab, click on the Create tab to open a drop-down menu. Select Folder. Name the folder "Models." Then, in the same panel, click on the folder you just created so that it is the only one open in the column to the right (Assets > Models).

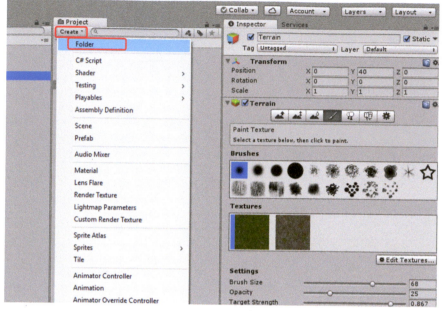

IMAGE 10.11

Open the Castle Project folder, and find the "Castle Group" FBX file that you saved there when you created the FBX file for the castle in 3ds Max. Drag the FBX file into the empty Models folder. Unity will import the FBX file into the scene.

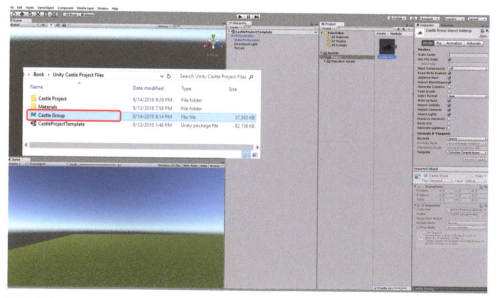

IMAGE 10.12

When the importing is completed, click on the Castle Group thumbnail image. The Inspector panel to the right will show the properties of the model. There are four tabs at the top of the panel: Model, Rig, Animations and Materials. We will make some adjustments in these tabs before bringing the model into the scene window.

In the "Model" tab, find the Generate Colliders item in the list and click on the check box to create colliders. If there are no colliders, the player will pass through the model, not walk on top of it. Then, click on the "Apply" box in the lower right corner of the panel. This is a must do before continuing. In the "Rig" tab, change the Animation Type from "Generic" to "Legacy," and then click the "Apply" button.

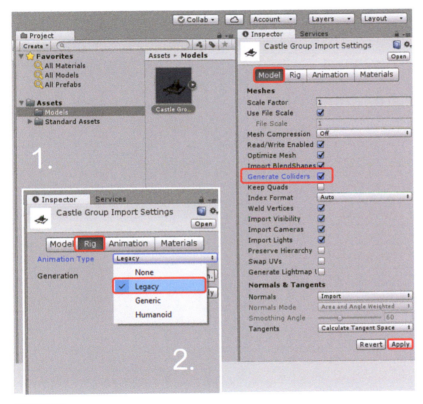

IMAGE 10.13

Next, in the "Animation" tab, scroll down to find the Wrap Mode. Change the Default setting to "Loop," and then click the "Apply" button. This will set the drawbridge animation to run and loop in a cycle endlessly when the game is running.

In the "Materials" tab, we can use the settings to apply all the textures to the meshes of the Castle Group. The Imported Materials check box should be checked. In the Location value box, change the setting to "Use External Materials (Legacy), and then click the "Apply" button.

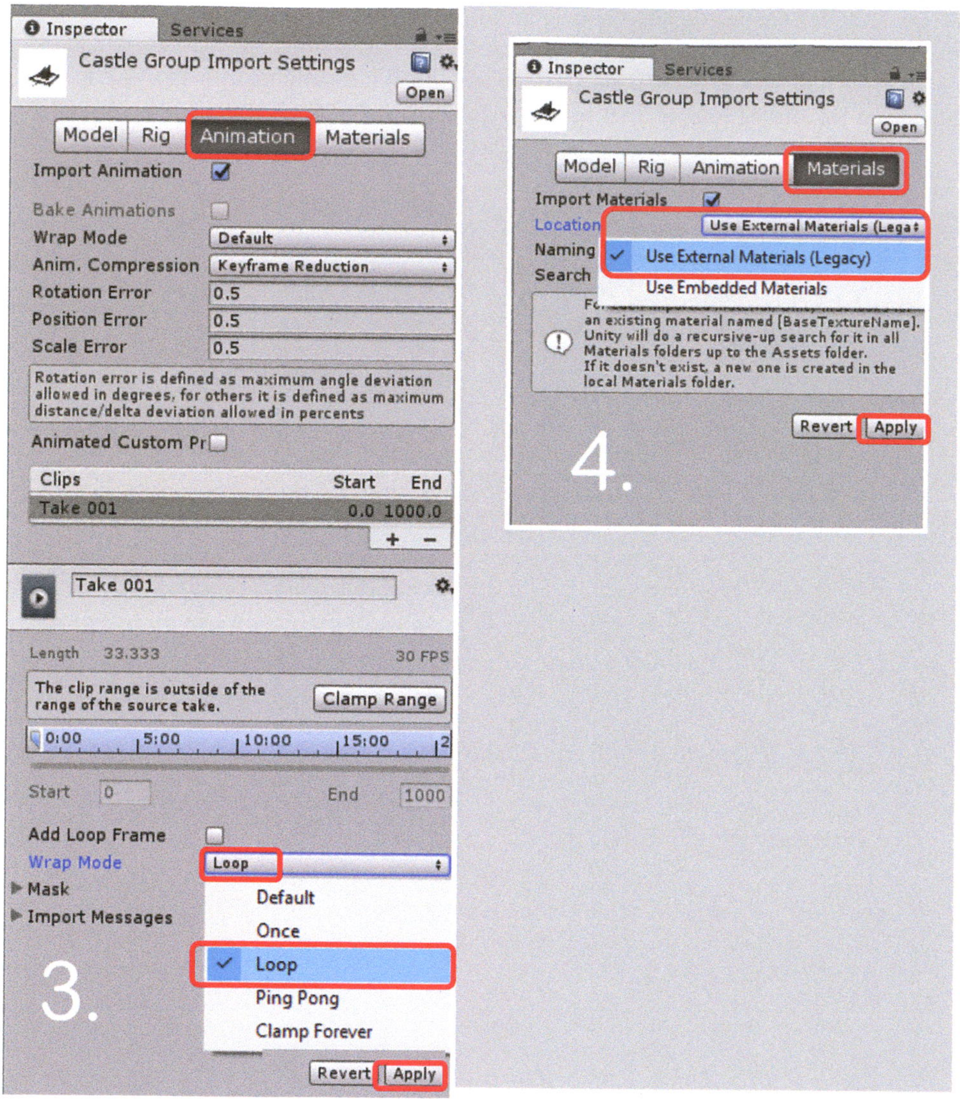

IMAGE 10.14

Time to bring in the model we exported from 3ds Max. Select the Castle Group Icon in the Project panel, and drag it into the Scene window onto the terrain. Notice that the Castle Keep is floating, not in contact with the terrain. Remember, we raised it in 3ds Max to give it some prominence and brought the ground plane up to meet it using the Soft Select tool. Just like in 3ds Max, in Unity, we need to raise the terrain under the Castle Keep.

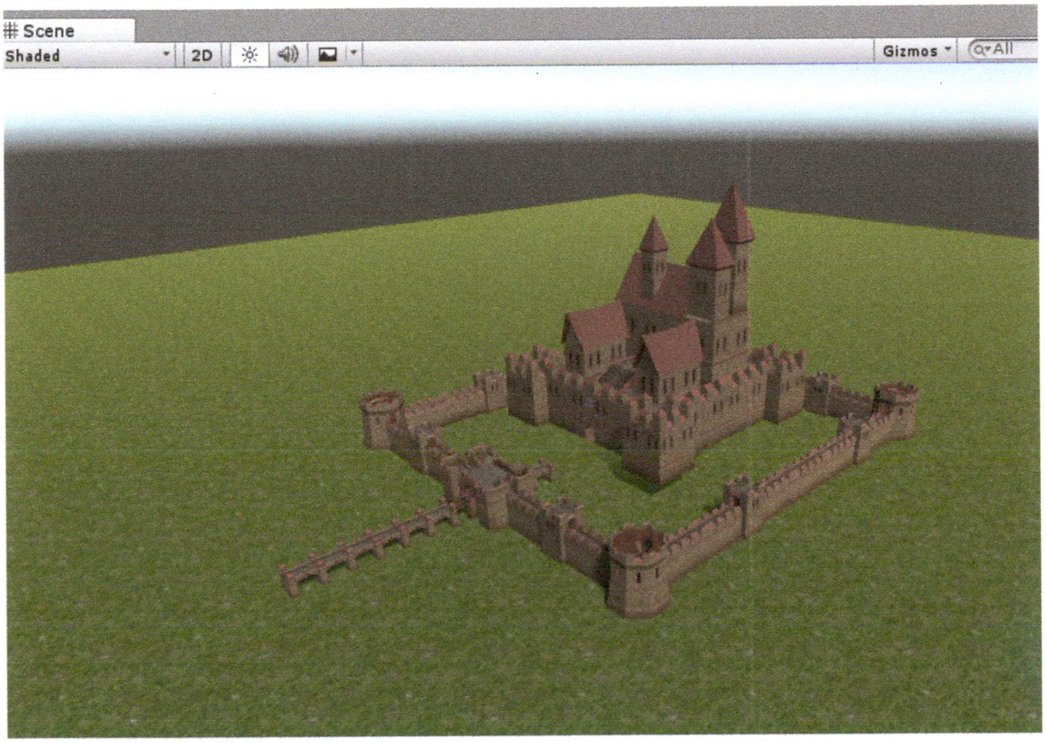

IMAGE 10.15

Unity has some nice terrain tools. Click on the terrain to select it. Over in the Inspector, select the second from the left tool icon, "Paint Height." This tool will raise the terrain to a specified height. Change the Height in the Settings area to 4.0. Make the Brush size 34 and the Opacity 4. Next, use the mouse as a paint brush, clicking and dragging the brush under the Castle Keep, raising the terrain to the Keep's bottom edge. To change the view in the viewport, the mouse wheel is zoom-in/zoom-out, and right-mouse click is rotate the scene up, down, left and right. The WASD and arrow keys move in the arrow directions. Continue raising the terrain all around the castle, closing any gaps between the mesh and the terrain.

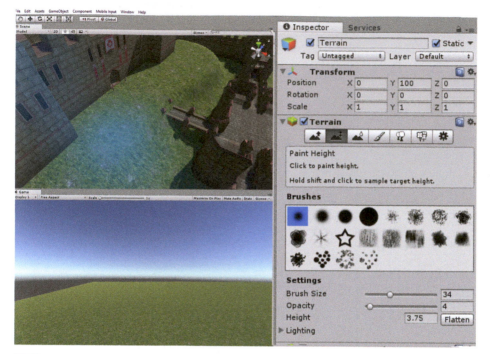

IMAGE 10.16

In the four corners where the Corner Turrets are, raise the terrain using a Height setting of 1.25, a Brush size of 13 and an Opacity of 4. This worked as we wanted, but there are some rough transitions between the two levels we just created. Switch to the third from the left tool icon, the "Smooth Height" tool. Set the Brush size to 78 and the Opacity to 20. Carefully drag a few strokes over the terrain between and onto the two different heights we made and notice the terrain smoothing out to a more natural flowing surface. Go easy and watch so that you don't overdo it. Work your way around the Keep base to the Corner Turrets.

IMAGE 10.17

Next, we will raise the terrain around the castle group the start making the moat and to bring the ground level up to the first fixed bridge span. Use a Height setting for the Paint Height tool of 2.25 to paint the terrain around the Castle Group, leaving a margin for the moat as shown.

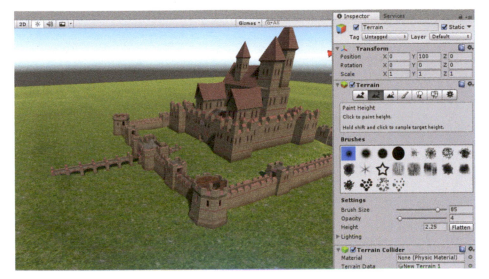

Let's bring the water into play. In the Hierarchy panel, select the "WaterProDaytime" object in the list. The water object is in the scene already, one meter below the terrain. Over in the Inspector, change the Transform "Y" Position value to 100. The water should appear. If it is barely visible, use the "Raise/Lower" terrain tool (the first icon on the left) to deepen the moat. Use a small Brush size (10–30) and a low Opacity number (2–4). Hold the Shift-key down to lower the terrain. Left-mouse clicking will raise the terrain. Lower the moat terrain area to expose the water more if needed, but don't go too deep.

Use the Paint Height tool to create a shoreline around the outer wall. Set the Height for the tool to 1.0. If you click and drag in shore strokes, the height will vary from 0 to 1, creating a more natural shoreline.

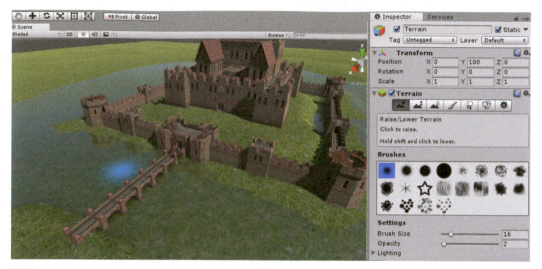

IMAGE 10.20

Our scene could use some roads or worn paths. With the terrain object still selected, switch to the Paint Texture tool and select the "GrassRockyAlbedo" texture. Set the Brush size to 4, the Opacity to 64 and the Target Strength to around 0.86 (all the setting numbers I am using are rough, just get close to them). When you paint with the mouse, a warn path will appear, replacing the grass texture. Make some paths around the castle where you think they would likely be. Again, don't overdo it.

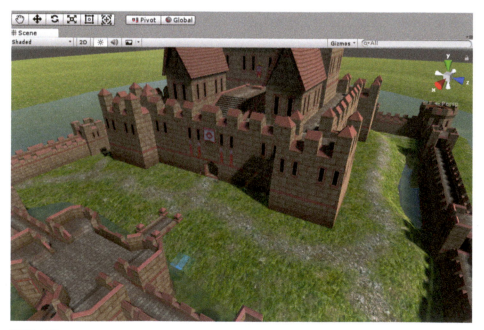

IMAGE 10.21

Lastly, create some hills around the center area, setting the castle in a small valley. Use the Raise/Lower tool with large brush sizes, but keep the Opacity low to control the tool better. Experiment with different settings. You'll learn quickly how fast things can grow out of control.

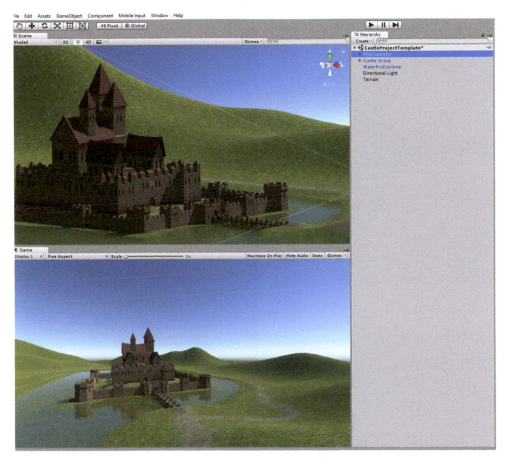

IMAGE 10.22

After creating the terrain hills, you are ready to play in this environment. The viewport below the Scene window is the Game Window. In the upper right corner of the Game window is a button, "Maximize on Play." Click this on so that you get a full-screen image. To start the game, select the Play arrow icon at the top of the UI, or hold down the Ctrl-key plus the P-key (CTRL+P). This will start the game and can be used to stop the game too. Go ahead… play!

IMAGE 10.23

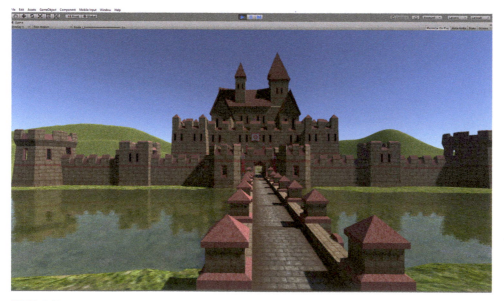

IMAGE 10.24

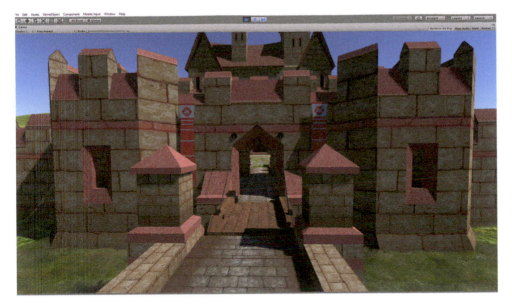

IMAGE 10.25

IMAGE 10.26

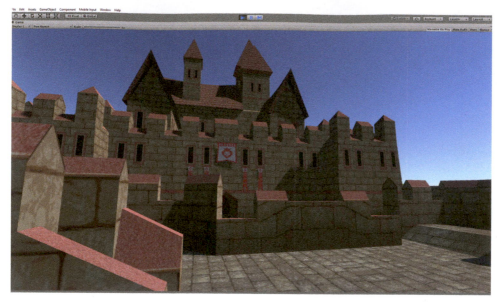

IMAGE 10.27

Hopefully, you have found the end result of seeing your models in a game environment to be satisfying and rewarding. It was a lot of effort to creat this environment. I hope you have an itch to get back to modeling… creating new models for the scene, modifying these modules, making entirely new scenes. The more you model, the more experience and skill you will acquire. When you hit a roadblock, that's your cue to start researching wherever you can to get help and solutions.

In many urban areas, there are user groups (search the Autodesk community) of people passionate about improving their skills and exploring the program's capabilities. Remember, this book was designed to be an introduction to the basics of 3D modeling. We used geometric shapes throughout. Your next goal should be to move into organic modeling: characters, rigging and animation.

IMAGE 10.28

Appendix

Companion Files

The companion files for this book, including the saved 3ds Max project iteration files from the chapters and additional notes can be found at: www.whooplah.com/book/3dsMaxBasics

Additional Topics

The following are some topics that we did not cover in the preceding chapters but are 3ds Max tools or procedures that you should be aware of.

Orbit/Pan

The Orbit/Pan button icon is located in the lower right-hand corner of the user interface (UI), to the left of the Maximize Viewport Toggle. The icon when pressed reveals four options in a drop-down menu.

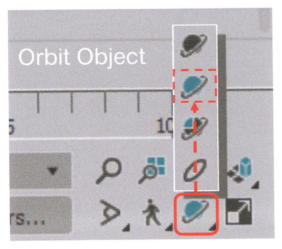

APP-01

When you use the Select and Rotate tool, you are actually rotating the selected object about its center of rotation. With the Orbit tool, you rotate the viewport around the object, sort of like the View Cube. There are four types of orbit tools options in the fly-out icon. Which one choose to use will determine the manner of viewport rotation. Using the Orbit option, the scene will utilize the center view as the axis of rotation. When using this option, it is common for an object to rotate off the screen. It is not always the easiest to get those items back on the screen! The second option, the Orbit Selected is the one I would recommend using most often. With it, the center of a selected object will be the point of axis rotation. The viewport rotates around the selected object, much easier to control.

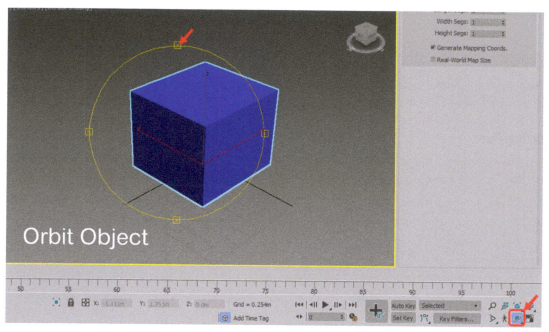

APP-02

Multi/Sub Maps

Sometimes an object in a game uses multiple maps that are applied as textures. Instead of importing those multiple maps into the game engine separately, it is possible to combine them into one texture map called a Multi/Sub Map. To create a Multi/Sub map, create a new texture in the Material Editor. Instead of choosing "Standard," select "Multi/Sub-object." The Material Editor will change to reflect the new map type.

APP-03

In the Multi/Sub-Object Basic Parameters section, treat each row as a separate texture. Each row has a unique ID number. To control the application of a texture map so only a particular collection of polygons receive the image, you need to assign an ID number to each polygon. To do that, select an Editable Poly in Polygon Sub-object level mode. Select the polygons you want to give an ID number. Scroll down to the "Polygon: Material IDs" section, and change the value of the Set ID: value box to a unique number (1–10) for the scene. If you name it "ID: 1," material ID number 1 in the Material Editor will be applied to polygons with this ID. Repeating the process, you can use multiple textures on an object in one texture map.

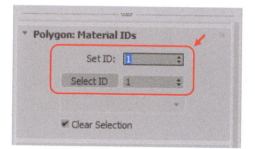

APP-04

Loft

When you create a cylinder, in reality, you are extruding a circle along a straight line. Lofting is extruding one 2D object along another 2D object as a path, resulting in a 3D object.

For example, create a 1-meter circle (2D) and a straight line as shown.

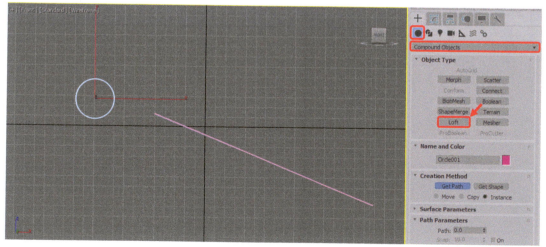

APP-05

Select the circle. In Geometry, change "Standard" to "Compound Objects." Next select "Loft." In the Creation Method, select the "Get Path" button. When you select the line as the Path, the circle will extrude to create a cylinder. The two 2D shapes are still present, and if modified, the modifications will be reflected in the cylinder. Try lofting other 2D shapes onto different 2D shapes to see the results.

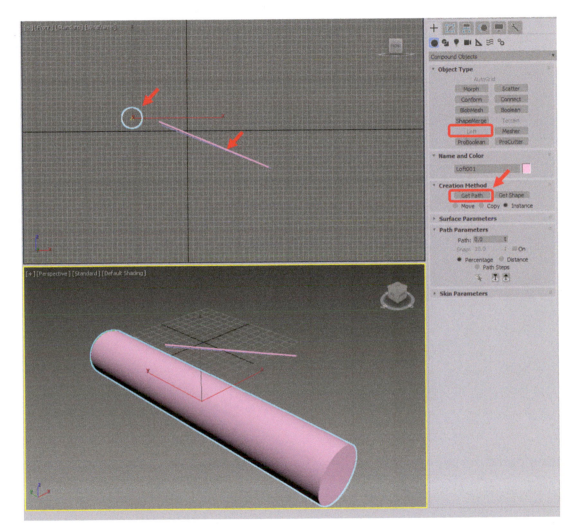

APP-06

Reset XForm Utility

Sometimes when you add rotations to an object or scale it, the object will take on new centers of rotation and pivot points. When you export the object to a video game engine, the object does not behave as expected due to those transforms. To ensure that the object will behave as expected (true to the pivot points established on creation), you can apply the Reset XForm that forces the transforms to proper positions by pushing the rotation and scale transform to the modifier stack as the XForm modifier and aligns the objects pivot points with the World Coordinate System. The tool can be accessed from two locations, in the Modifier List of the Command Panel and in the Utilities tab of the Command Panel as a separate button. Later in your development, when working with the Skin modifier on characters, you will want to revisit the Reset XForm tool before exporting those meshes to a game engine.

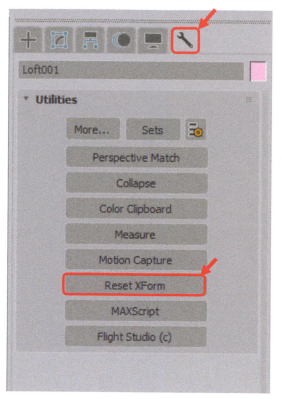

APP-07

Boolean Operation

A Boolean object is the result of combining two or more objects through a logical operation between the objects geometry. The objects used to create the Boolean object are called "operands." As an example, create a sphere and a box, positioned so one is intersecting the other. In the Compound Object heading in Geometry, select Boolean. Select the Box. Scroll down the Command Panel to the "Add Operands" button, and select it. Next, click on the sphere and then the Subtract button in the panel. Where the sphere shape is intersecting the box shape, that area will be subtracted from the box. There are five other operation options you can try to see the results.

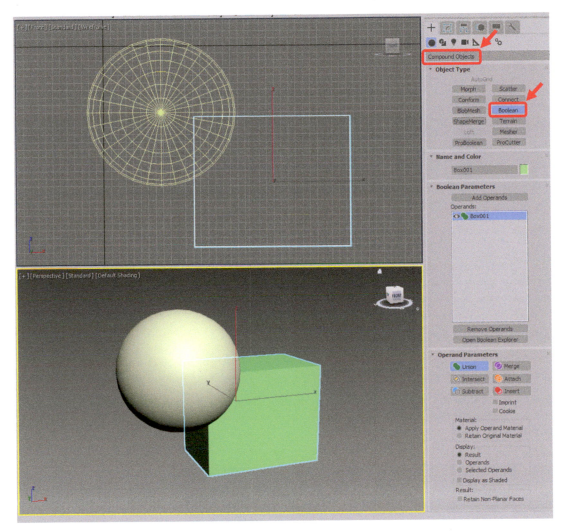

APP-08

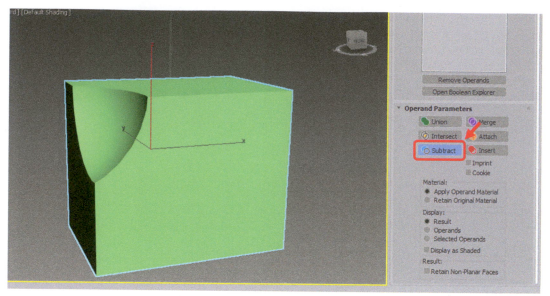

APP-09

The Boolean tool can be really useful in modeling. However, when it performs its operations, it often creates polygons that are now optimal for use in game engines. For that reason, I would recommend minimal usage. Sometimes the harder proceedure is better than the easier one.

Turbo Smooth and Mesh Smooth

The Turbo Smooth modifier can be used to smoothen the geometry of an object. It subdivides existing geometry, interpolating angles, and edges, and the result is rounder corners and edges.

In the image below, the box on the left has 108 polygons. The one on the right was identical to the one on the left and has a Turbo Smooth modifier added to it. Its Polygon count is 438, four times the original due to the subdivisions.

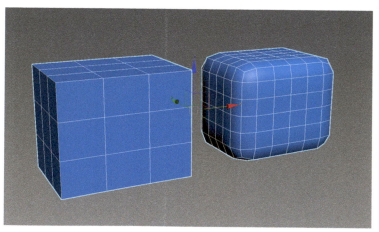

APP-10

This can be a useful tool for smoothing an object for better visual appearance. However, the additional polygons from subdivisions can kill the mesh for use in a video game. The goal is low-poly. Beginners, in my opinion, should be restricted to not using Turbo or Mesh Smooth until they have good mastery of the modeling skills. Notice that we did not use it in any of our models. We were colse to our polygon limit on most models. Applying a Turbo Smooth would have put us way over budget. Too often, beginners rely on Turbo Smooth to make their models look better. Typically, it will probably over-round some parts, acting negatively on the appearance. Modeling the objects correctly will minimize the need for turbosmooth.

Space Bar Lock Hotkey

With an object selected, if you click on the Space Bar of the keyboard, 3ds Max will lock on whatever object is selected, not allowing you to select another object until the Space Bar is depressed again. Beginners often accidentally hit the Space Bar and think that the program has crashed. When the Space Bar lock is activated, a lock icon on the lower navigation bar turns yellow as an indicator. The icon can be selected directly in the UI with the mouse.

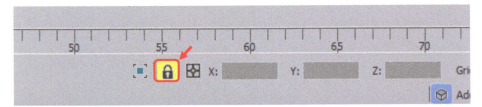

APP-11

Follow a Path

In 3ds Max, it is possible to assign an object to travel along a path. It does this by restricting the object's movement along the path only. An example of this would be to make a camera follow a path (a spline). If the path were to go around and through our 3ds Max castle scene, the camera following the path would do a "fly-thru" of the scene. To do this, in the castle scene from Chapter 9, use the line tool to create a path that you want the camera to follow. Make it swoop, circle and rise as it explores the geometry.

Next, create a target camera anywhere in the scene. Change the Viewport setting from Perspective to Camera 001 to "see" through the camera. Select the camera. On the top toolbar, in the "Animation" tab, select "Constraints." From the drop-down menu, select "Path Constraint."

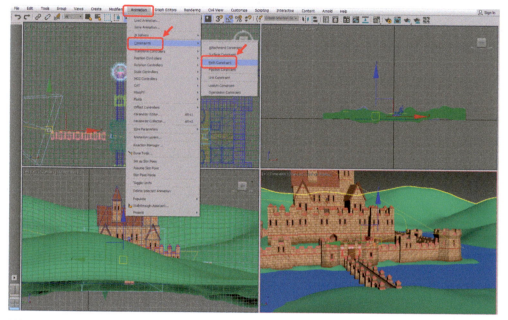

APP-12

Next, select the line segment, the path. The camera will jump to the path. It will still be pointing at the camera target. Select the target, and repeat the path constraint assigning, selecting the same path. To make the Camera target be in front of the camera and not in the same location, enter 10 in the value for the "% Along Path." The target will jump out in front of the camera. Click on the Play button to start the camera animation fly-thru. The camera stays facing the target. Try using the Free Camera and animating (Auto-Key on) its rotation as it moves along the path to aim at the castle features as it flies by them. More adjusting, but a better animation.

Index